GRACE *the* TABLE

&

STORIES & RECIPES
FROM MY SOUTHERN REVIVAL

Alexander Smalls

with *Hettie Jones*

Harlem Moon
Broadway Books
New York

Published by Harlem Moon, an imprint of Broadway Books, a division of
Random House, Inc.

A previous edition of this book was originally published in 1977 by Harper-
Collins.

PRINTED IN THE UNITED STATES OF AMERICA

HARLEM MOON, BROADWAY BOOKS, and the HARLEM MOON logo, depicting a
moon and a woman, are trademarks of Random House, Inc. The figure
in the Harlem Moon logo is inspired by a graphic design by Aaron Douglas
(1899–1979).

Visit our website at www.harlemmoon.com

First Harlem Moon trade paperback edition published 2004

Book design by Laura Lindgren

Cataloging-in-Publication Data is on file with the Library of Congress

ISBN 0-7679-1847-9

10 9 8 7 6 5 4 3 2 1

To my parents, Alexander and Johnnie Mae Smalls, who gave me the world in a bowl—a great adventure whipped with twists and turns, spiced with love, slow-cooked and overflowing, infused with their ever-growing wisdom.

Thank you for a life of Sundays and an example to follow. And thanks for saving me a place at the table.

I'm loving you too.

CONTENTS

FOREWORD

by Wynton Marsalis

"My mama makes the best fried chicken in the whole world."

"You mean she uses all the grease in the whole world. It take five or ten minutes of chewing to find some chicken underneath all that junk."

"My daddy's barbecue ribs so good, the ghost of the pig has been known to come back and thank him for cookin' it."

"My great-aunt's pot roast."

"My gramma's macaroni and cheese."

"My uncle's specially seasoned black-eye peas."

And so it goes. Around and around, year after year—and sometimes even well into adulthood—each participant struggling to verbally re-create the excitement and moment of palate-rubbing truth when some family member's virtuosic performance of note in the kitchen is once again enjoyed.

Every now and then, when it is undeniable, you might hear, "Yeah, I got to give it up. Your mama makes a good gumbo. But, just good, that's all!"

All comments, even the insults, in recognition of the soulful, the down-home, and the sophisticated culinary efforts of those you love (or should love). In recognition of the fact that eater, preparer, and eaten are locked in a dance that is, was, and will always be.

This is the world that produced Alexander Smalls. It is a world that he loves. The Friday fish fried, plastic-covered velveteen furniture in the front room with the picture of Jesus having, yes sir no ma'am sentence sayin', spit-polished shoe-shining, Saturday car-washed, Sunday hat-wearin' sisters of the sho-nuff down-home Mahalia Jackson playing most high and soulful south. Thick in the south, as we say. The south of the field-holler work ethic and the down-home discipline enforced understanding of silence. The cross-the-tracks sensitivity to human frailty (because hard times often make the most stout among us bend even if ever so slightly). This is the world Alexander knows well. It *is* him. And experience is a thing that just cannot be faked. Jazz alto saxophonist Charlie Parker used to say, "If you don't live it, it won't come out of your horn." And it surely won't come out of your pots.

Alexander understands that the culinary art is more than just a reflection of one's way of living. For him, it is ultimately a tool to heal and elevate the spirit. In this way he is like the great Louis Armstrong, who strove to make the very best of what was available to him better, so that it would be suitable for you. That's love. Mr. Armstrong always said, "They know I'm there in the cause of happiness," and that is Mr. Smalls's credo. He speaks of a "labor of love" in the kitchen because he wants to evoke the warmth and pageantry of the family dinner. "I wanted Sunday every day, a life of Sundays." He also says things like "I would never make that dish feeling the same way again." He is caught in the sweet embrace of life and he wants us to enjoy it, too!

Reading this cookbook reminds me of sittin' up late at night listening to jazz musicians tell stories. They might talk about Sidney Bechet and say, "Sidney don't care what tune you call, he'll play anything and thing is, he don't ever play a song the same way twice" or "The world just wasn't big enough to hold all his feeling" or "Yeah, and he was smart, too. Umm, hmm, he had a head on him."

Right into the recipes struts Uncle Joe, country-styled connoisseur of opera, who bellows all parts from soprano to bass as records play and the pots simmer. He passes that love of singing, as well as an improvisational cooking style, to Alexander. "The idea belongs to everybody, son, but the dish belongs to you. Do your *own* thing with it." We also get to meet Aunt Daisy, who changes men as often as bedsheets. One just isn't enough to handle all of her feeling. She gives you large steaming portions of food just like she would give heaping brown portions of that good hot love to her man of the moment. And, so as not to be bored, she loves making those unusual dishes like coon and venison. You got to watch that coon!

Alexander does not judge people, he understands them. His observations are clear and consistently optimistic. On a childhood trip to the supermarket with his father, instead of running up and down the aisles in search of the famous post-shopping boodie-whipping, he learns how much food there is to love! This love of food and the many different ways it can be prepared give his recipes a comprehensive soulfulness. He is always learning and searching for connections. He doesn't run from the unusual or the unfamiliar.

When someone is immersed and well versed in a tradition, they have a tendency to become proprietary, stiff, and proud, to become an "expert" and cling to a right way and a wrong way to best articulate the substance of that tradition. Alexander never falls victim to this self-serving position. He seeks the poetic truth of the southern low-country cuisine because he realizes the limitations of the literal when it meets the endless possibilities of the poetic. That is why he calls his cooking southern revival—it regenerates that down-home energy by infusing the essences of other down-homes from elsewhere. For example, of a Parmesan dish, he says, "In Italy, because of the purity of the dish, eating it felt extraordinary. It was like bringing two worlds together, as if I'd finally gotten to what the dish was all about, the essence of it." In this way he is most like Duke Ellington—a citizen of the world.

Alexander finds the familiar in Chinese, Italian, and French cuisine, among others, because he seeks and recognizes the things that reflect a combination of love and intelligence. He realizes that all people everywhere are drawn to that which makes us feel at home or, if not at home, loved. And eating, the world's second most favorite activity and most necessary one, is our most basic ritual. It takes us right back home to childhood and the family table for hot breakfast on cold mornings, daily dinner and discourse, and late-night snacks, snuck or otherwise.

His life as an aspirant opera singer gives him a deeper appreciation of the struggle that gives the blues its resonance. The same blues that gives the southern cuisine its bite and soul. Many erroneously call this food *soul* food to imply race. He teaches us that it is correctly named but widely misunderstood. It is food for the *human* soul, because the purpose of all cuisine is to speak to the soul through the taste buds. And a taste bud doesn't know whether it's Italian, or French, or Ebo for that matter.

As a musician, his travels allow him to see more clearly the basic connections all people share. For instance, he visits a friend's home in Italy and all of a sudden people from the neighborhood start "dropping by" to see what's happening. Just like the country folk in Spartanburg, South Carolina, would do. He says, "I had traveled thousands of miles to find the familiar." And with music and food on your side, you are never a stranger for long—no matter how far from home.

One summer when my band was on tour in Turkey, we went to the Zildjian cymbal factory outside of Istanbul. While our drummer, Herlin Riley, tested cymbals, several of us wandered out into the surrounding neighborhood.

Some kids on the street were saying I was Michael Jackson because he was the only Black American they knew about. We began to play tic-tac-toe with them. A young girl about thirteen years old and her mother were watching us from the third- or fourth-floor balcony of a typical city housing building. After several exasperating attempts to speak with us in English, the girl disappeared. Suddenly she reappeared on the dusty street with what had to be the best dishes, teapot, and porcelain cups in her house. She poured each of us a cup of freshly brewed Turkish coffee as if it were the most precious thing on earth, calmly waited for us to drink it, then collected the cups and went back upstairs amid a chorus of thank-yous. It was such an act of hospitality, of grace and style, a deeply moving experience. To be honest, I didn't even like Turkish coffee. But from that moment on, we all became instant fans. Plus had a great story to tell.

Alexander's recipes, as well as his many enlightening and entertaining stories, will put us all in the head and stomach that we want to be in. He is, as he wants to be, "an ambassador of style and grace, food and social comfort." With this book we all have the chance to join him.

ACKNOWLEDGMENTS

There are not enough words of thanks to wrap and keep this bounty of friends and family that grace me. The "Great Givers" I call them. Loved ones who feed generously my soul and spirit. Those who—at the times when my feet sought to leave the ground taking flight, chasing rainbows, riding high—sent me on my way, never thinking to hold me back or pull me down. Rather, they tied a golden string securely to my heart, tugging it ever so gently as I soared. I was never alone. And so to all of you, big . . . bad . . . and wonderful as you are to me, I love and keep you near me always.

Mom and Dad, you're dedicated. To my sisters Cynthia, Delores, and Elonda, you never knew I was keeping score. To Uncle Joe, Aunt Laura, Aunt Daisy, Grandmas and Grandpas, and J.J., I'm keeping you alive, okay? To Jeanie and David, my second parents who taught me how to better love the first ones, I'll be there for you! To Uncle Roosevelt and Aunt Roxie, Ain't life grand. To Delois, ride on, sister child. Lynn H., You always come through. Thelma G. and Vicky, Peggy B. and Bea, Kevin and Gwendolyn, David and Marc, Sharon, Louis, Jessica, Garth, Jeffrey, Rolondo, Pierre, Dita, Eric, Pat, Joe, Barbara, Jerry and Richard and Laura . . . I ain't finished yet. To Jewel, Tess, Toni, Craig, Wendy, Lisa, Rony, Mathieu, Peter, and Maria. John, Nelson, Angie, Michelin, Roderick and Opal, Mariel, Leslie, Ann, Sandy, Steve T. and Elizabeth, George, Lin, and Juliette . . . You still holding on, right?

To Willis and Laura, I'm so glad you're here with me. To Donna and Lorna, Just us chickens, girls! Hey, Dennis D., Nearly perfect as a buddy-roll. Denise and Michael D., grace in longevity lives. Ms. Freddie, lost love, Bougie Boy, Who woulda thunk it? Joan Lader, keeper of my music box. Artie Pacheco, one of my best and brightest encounters. Phylicia Rashad, We are chosen. Gaynel and Clyde, Somewhere out there. Lynn Whitfield, Gave it to me. Jenette Kahn, Something like glittering joy. Laura Torbet, a tried-and-true lifeguard. To Michael Small, the best food magician and kitchen partner I've known. David Biehl, I couldn't have baked it without you. Cicely Tyson, Bless this house. To Judy Smith, my wave of the future. To Kathleen Battle, a trust for life to keep.

To Peternelle van Arsdale, who took my story high above the mountaintops and page by page sought to spread the word. To Victoria Sanders, my literary agent, buddy, and now lioness that clears the way. Her will, conviction, and relentless pursuit that I should tell a story, sing a song, or stir a pot was my good fortune. All the love, coddling, prodding, support, and gentle drive came from her divinely and it was all good, lovingly good. To Hettie Jones, who held my stories upright in her arms and arranged them with love and kindness on clean white linen paper. Hettie, who coached, challenged, pulled, and sorted through pages of my life's impressions, sifting and combing, turning over thoughts left hanging from times gone by. A writer's writer, she created the formula for my tales, and the freedom she gave me exhausted many a fine pen. Love you, Hettie.

To Wynton Marsalis, our beloved brother of music, history, and hope. An earnest angel of love, goodness, and continual greatness. Blow your horn, boy. We need it—we need it now! Thank you for shared dreams, words, and music of wisdom . . . the push and pat of encouragement you've given so generously. Thanks for your friendship and the trail you've blazed. I'm right behind you, don't forget.

And finally I acknowledge life's fortunes, large and small. The right of dreams, thoroughfare of fancy in pursuit of passion and fulfillment. We are all attendees at the feast of life. And while food lay piled high in abundance and variety, we are left to assure that our seat will be undoubtedly secured. Now let's grace the table.

RECIPES

II OTHER CITIES, MANY TABLES

INTRODUCTION

$\mathcal{G}$rowing, buying, preparing, serving, and eating food—the whole tasty subject—has captured and framed so many of my memories that in a curious way it has not only sustained me but given me life. Good or bad, everything got better after a labor of love in the kitchen.

Nevertheless, after the success of Cafe Beulah, when a cookbook was suggested, my first reaction was *"Not me!"*—although I love cookbooks, own lots of them, and I'm the first to run out and buy the latest. But adding another to the pile seemed redundant, and anyway I felt inhibited by the form, not to mention that there are more ways to make potato salad than there are ways to eat it.

Add to this that some of the best cooks I've known never measured an ingredient, let alone owned a cookbook. You took a little of this and a little of that and as much of yet another thing, and then you cooked it, baked it, or chilled it until it was ready. And it was your business to know when it was ready.

So instead of just a set of instructions, although you'll find those, too, this book is a journey. It begins in Spartanburg, South Carolina—we called it Sparkle City, U.S.A.—where my grandfather settled with his wife and children after leaving Beaufort, South Carolina, where he'd landed after having left Charleston, his birthplace. With them came Low Country cooking, a blended cuisine from South Carolina's southernmost coast. Anyone who had ever lived and cooked there—African, French, English, Native American—contributed to it. The cities of Charleston and Beaufort, antebellum, were wide open and high living. The many stories my grandfather told, and his cooking, connected me with these ancestors. Other, newer connections attracted me, too: my aunt, in my eyes a disciple of the old kitchen, cooked fish heads and possum and things I thought of as medieval and weird; but she, like my uncle, worked as a chef in restaurants and private homes in and outside of the South and brought back to Spartanburg new ideas that I was always eager to try.

My immediate family's interest in and involvement with food was daily and continuous. We ate breakfast together; we'd get up from one meal talking about the next. Cooking and eating framed the daily drama of our lives, three times a day. Food was wealth to us, the kitchen was Fort Knox, and I felt rich just opening the refrigerator. Looking in at all those colorfully wrapped packages of meat, eggs, and vegetables was like staring at gold bullion. Food was a celebration, too, as well as a panacea for all that was wrong with the world, or the moment. A pan of hot buttermilk biscuits with fresh butter and sorghum had unknown strengths, and power over the most unruly gatherings.

I was known as a boy who loved to eat. My father, who was in the grocery business, did all our shopping, and I managed to get everything I liked by shopping with him. Food preparation interested me, too—my mother knew she could always count on me to help her in the kitchen. And with her encouragement and permission, I went solo at age five. My family applauded, my mother gave my creation her seal of approval— and I was hooked.

My passion for food and cooking was matched by my ardor for music. My uncle and his wife, with no children of their own, took charge of my talent. They bought me a piano, gave me lessons, introduced me to Caruso and Tebaldi. It was my journey into music, and eventually into the world of opera and entertainment, that took me from my familiar cuisine to other places, other tastes. The journey that began in South Carolina took me north to Philadelphia and New York, all through the States, to Canada, and eventually to Europe.

Along the way, wherever I found myself singing and living, I continued to cook, not only for myself and my friends but eventually for paying customers through my company, Small Miracle. I catered intimate dinners and large parties, experimenting with new ingredients when they turned up, exploring sources from small specialty markets to piazzas full of fresh produce, having successes—and surprises!—and always trying to create a southern presence, a southern edge. The cuisine of the American South, with its emphasis on greens and legumes, is, I feel, preeminent among our national accomplishments.

Singing opera wasn't easy, and neither was opening a restaurant; but I felt compelled to do both, and both have given me pleasure. Becoming an opera singer—a black male opera singer, a rarity—was a mission, and so has been my life as a self-described "social minister." Every minister needs a church: I needed one where I could influence the direction of southern food; create a larger, positive social presence for black people; and provide a place where people of all persuasions might commune. I have always felt that two things the races never do together are eat and pray. Now, in my restaurant, watching the colorful landscape of patrons and friends of all ages and hues come and go, I feel fulfilled. I think they were all just waiting for Cafe Beulah.

In Spartanburg, our extended family owned connecting lots, and the path that began at my grandfather's back door led straight to mine. It was so well worn that grass wouldn't grow on it and rainwater drained down it. Everything began for me there. It's almost as if that dirt path kept going and ended up in front of Cafe Beulah.

Recipes, it seems to me, are created in process, cuisines over time. Everything has a context. It was my hope to share with the reader more than just a hundred ways to cook white rice, or one more version of fried chicken delight. What you'll find in this book are stories and photographs to make you think about good times, laughter and celebration, family, friends, and food. And after you're sufficiently excited, there are recipes and suggestions to help you re-create and present this bounty as your own.

PART 1

Sparkle City, U.S.A.

1 SUNDAY DINNER ON THE SIDE PORCH

*I*n Sparkle City, Sunday seemed a just reward for my week of trials and tribulations—"Bring your father his bedroom slippers," "Get me my sewing basket," "Take out the trash." Sunday freed me from all that, and besides Sunday school and church and dressing up, it offered the best eating to be had all week.

I lived for Sunday dinner. I'd start thinking about Sunday on Wednesday. Southern fried chicken, fried okra, creamed corn, powdered buttermilk biscuits, a mountain of potato salad with sweet pickles. The smell of Mom's caramelized brown onion gravy dripping off the largest roast loin of beef ever, the bowl of slow-cooked green pole beans with ham hocks that steamed my father's glasses when it was set before him. And since Dad was a Geechee in the truest sense, no meal could be served without fluffy Carolina long grain rice. (I'd seen him leave the table, refusing to come back, until my mother, who was trying to break the habit, made him some.) Mom also made the best macaroni and cheese in town and, knowing it was a favorite of mine, she would often place this heavenly casserole in front of my plate like a trophy. I was her favorite—an unspoken but all-too-well-known fact—so all my beloved dishes were generously considered and prepared. There was no order or balance to Sunday dinner, healthwise or otherwise, except plenty of everything and everything good, including large glasses of lemonade or the usual "sweeter than sweet" iced tea, spiked with the mint I'd gather from our garden.

Cynthia, me, and Delores.
Nobody outdressed the Smalls family
in Spartanburg—nobody.

I was a curious, energetic boy, so busy being busy that I sometimes had no idea what I was being busy about, but I did know that food excited me like nothing else. I was Mom's chief helper in the kitchen, since my older sisters, Cynthia and Delores, were never as willing. To me food was magic, and cooking was creative as well as satisfying to a kid who always needed a lot to do. Early Sunday morning I'd head for the kitchen in my cowboy pajamas and slippers. Was there okra to chop? How many ears of corn to shuck? Mom would send me out on the side porch with a brown paper bag full of corn, old copies of the Spartanburg *Herald Journal* to shuck it on, and a toothbrush to scrape out the silk.

On Sunday all the life of our house moved to that side porch, a big, screened-in area with cushioned chairs, gliders, reclining seats, and a dark green bamboo shade that came down when we dined, because Mom insisted on privacy. Two doors, one from the kitchen and one from the living room, opened onto it. Every Sunday morning, while religious music played on the television, or a tape of Mahalia Jackson on the stereo, my father would come out on the porch to shine and spit-polish all his many pairs of shoes—he was always immaculate, one of the best-dressed men in our community. He also had an amazing tenor voice, often heard solo in our church choir. As I sat there shucking corn, he would sing church hymns, or old songs that seemed too personal to understand. And I'd hum along. Father-son relationships are often difficult, and ours was no exception. But on Sunday, on that side porch, we were bound together in our grace.

Mom would venture out on occasion to check my handiwork or speed me along. Sometimes she came out to iron a shirt or blouse for one of us, or sew a button or a hem. She loved that side porch, needed it. Years later, when they remodeled the house and enclosed it, she had another porch built outside.

Sunday dinner had been started on Saturday night. In fact, all day Saturday had been devoted to getting ready for Sunday—the car washed, the house cleaned, "Boy, go out and cut the grass" followed by "Son, I need you to weed the flower beds." My mother and I would begin cooking about eight in the evening if there were pies or cakes or yeast rolls to be made.

At six years old I was quite fond of icebox lemon meringue pie, and (until I experienced the revenge of the lemon, which sent me running to the bathroom) I would always make two—one for the family and one for myself. How I loved making graham cracker crust, molding soft butter and crumbs together with cinnamon and nutmeg and often chopped coconut. The condensed milk filling, whipped with juice from fat Florida lemons, spiked with crushed mint and a drop of vanilla, brought me to my knees. What I disliked, though, was grating lemon peel. I still do, even now finding that my knuckles are often caught too close to the grater. I would assemble those pies of mine, separate egg whites to whip up a stiff meringue with lots of sugar holding it firm, and then, with the meringue spooned on, would run the pies under the broiler. What a wonder to me, the sight of that golden fluff! Now as then I am hard-pressed to eat such a treat in moderation.

By Sunday morning, breakfast and dinner were both happening at once—roast roasting, bacon frying, grits bubbling, potatoes boiling—

so the kitchen was already a profusion of smells when I brought in the shucked corn. Mom would rinse it and begin to strip it. I find it amazing now that with only three good knives she could do anything. She cut the kernels off the cob with an upward motion and then scraped down to get out the juice and the remaining pulp. After she'd done the first two or three ears, we'd take the rest to a pot on the kitchen table, and I'd do them. My mother trusted me with that knife—a butcher knife with a 5-inch blade—when I was only six.

After I finished the corn, I might be given pole beans to snap, or I would be handed a paring knife to cut up okra. I'd cut the ends off, slice the rest into ⅓-inch rounds, put these into a mixture of one part cornmeal and one part flour in a brown paper sack, and then run around the kitchen shaking it. While Mom prepared macaroni and cheese or a hen to be baked, or fried chicken, I told her stories about school, or we talked about the flow of Sunday dinner and about going to church. I was learning not only about food, of course, but also about caring and relationships.

Cooking with Mom was always interrupted by nine A.M. in order to prepare for church. My father, assistant superintendent of the Sunday school, would drive us there, leaving Mom to finish dinner and join us at eleven for the main service. It was understood that we would go to Sunday school every Sunday until we graduated from high school. That was a rule. One could occasionally be excused from the three-hour-or-so church service, but Sunday school was nonnegotiable—and besides, I loved it. It was show-and-tell time, and you wore your finest clothes, shoes, and manners. Everybody was dressed up, including my school buddies, Ronnie Pitts, Moses Murphy, and big bad Leroy Jenkins, the bully. Girls like Diane Logan and Edwina Ferguson clutched miniature pocketbooks and wore extra ribbons, bows, and fancy clips in their hair, ruffled slips, crinolines, bracelets, and white cotton gloves. As a child with an appetite for words that invariably shaped a point of view, I was often called upon in class to express my opinions on citizenship and good leadership for my peers. I also would regularly read Scripture and nursery rhymes, or sing a short song to the delight of the teacher.

Church service, however, was not a party like Sunday school. It was long, tiring, and stiff. After the great hymns that I loved were sung and the welcoming of visitors over (it was always exciting to see new faces), and after the candy Mom had bribed me with was gone, I had had it. The next hour or so was rated "adult" in my book and not meant for children. So while the Reverend C. M. Johnson called upon the saints and waged war against evil and human frailties, I slept quietly with my head in my mother's lap, dreaming of Sunday dinner. Mom would wake me for the last hymn and the benediction. With her soft embroidered cotton handkerchief she'd clean the sleep from my eyes, run her fingers through my hair, and pinch my cheeks. Then, holding hands, we'd plow through the ritual of "How do you do?" "Nice to see you," "Boy, that child has grown something terrible," and "He looks just like you, child" until we'd made it to the curb.

I always felt a bonus was needed after all those hours, and my father must have agreed, because when the ordeal was over we'd usually be taken to Miss Lily's store for a treat. A very white-looking black woman with more freckles than she needed all over her face, Miss Lily never smiled and we feared that she disliked children intensely. Nonethe-

*My kindergarten class photo: I'm second
from the right in the second row from the top.*

less she stocked a few of my favorites, including her famous praline candy squares. For a nickel I bought this homemade delicacy—not found anywhere else in town—and savored it slowly on the ride home. Sometimes, if my sisters and I were allowed to walk home by ourselves, we might venture up to Oliver's pharmacy for ice cream malts, or down to Mrs. Abercrombie's South Liberty Street Cafe for big cones of soft vanilla ice cream. Funny how this never affected my appetite for dinner.

On birthday Sundays, or when relatives visited, we'd have homemade ice cream. If we crossed Main Street and headed for Highland Homes while driving home from church, I knew there was a good chance we were going to the icehouse—a wonderful place, a long warehouse with a loading dock you'd drive up to. After my father paid the cashier, he'd find one of the icemen working the dock, who would open a door to enormous blocks of ice stacked on top of each other. The iceman brought one out with iron tongs and placed it in a large ice crusher, which—thanks to my father's generous tip—I was always allowed to start up.

The custard for the ice cream would have been made in the morning, before church, and when we got home it went into the old-fashioned wooden churn with salt and ice. It was my job to churn. I hated chocolate, liked vanilla and strawberry. My mother would use fresh fruit, often featuring South Carolina peaches.

At mealtime the kitchen table with all its extensions would be moved out to the side porch. My father was always first at the table, and it was understood that he was not to be kept waiting for the food or the rest of us. All my favorite foods lay stretched across the table like a patchwork quilt. By this time it was well after two, and apart from my treat after Sunday school, I hadn't eaten since breakfast at eight-thirty. Anticipation and control fought a hard battle as I locked my eyelids closed while my father's grace for our meal ran way into overtime. He'd thank a long stream of people and spirits, and if it was a holiday or the sermon at church had been particularly moving, he was inspired to ramble. I often wondered why he went on so long, and sometimes, as he was getting his second wind and praising some saints twice, I would open my eyes to see Mom making faces or snickering to herself—until that final "all we receive for the nurturing of our body and soul . . . in Christ's name, Amen." *Amen!* I'd think as the smell of sweet butter hit my biscuit en route to my mouth, while Mom looked over at Dad to ask, "Well, Alex, did you leave anybody out?" And Dad would grunt and we'd giggle, for it was clear that he was as hungry as the rest of us by the way he grabbed the rice bowl and gravy boat.

Not missing a beat, though, we'd pile our plates high. It wasn't easy getting all that food onto one plate; you had to be creative, and I was very creative. And though I always had good manners (I was a Smalls and that was expected), when I was a boy I took great delight in mixing all my food together on my plate before eating it. I also enjoyed food better if I ate it with a spoon instead of a fork, and still very much do. This was odd not only to my family but to the neighbors, who, seeing me eat or hearing about it, found a need to voice their opinion on the subject. I have since shed the habit of mixing up my food, but I think it somewhat explains my lingering love of casseroles and one-dish dinners.

After several pounds of food were consumed, the table cleared, and my sisters busy washing up (every now and then, if I got too smart-mouthed, I'd have to help), Mom, Dad, and I retired to lounge chairs, where they attempted to read until sleep took them over. I often followed, dreaming of Sunday evening supper: a roast beef and potato salad sandwich combo, or creamed corn on Wonder bread with mayo, sliced tomatoes, and a light sprinkling of sugar.

But sometimes, instead of sleeping, I'd set the wishbone I was always given on the kitchen windowsill to dry, and then I'd go into the living room to play the piano (my aunt Laura was giving me lessons). Except when company came or on Sunday, no one was allowed to sit in the living room. So I knew that today I could be there and not be bothered by Cynthia and Delores, surrounded by vases of fresh-cut roses from Mom's garden, or gardenias from the bushes that grew in the front yard. Before dinner I'd have changed from my Sunday-go-to-meeting clothes, the crisp white shirt and string tie, the collarless blazer and Bermuda shorts my mother had made for me. I'd sit at the piano, relaxed, full, and satisfied. I'd play traditional songs and hymns initially, and then I'd improvise, making up songs, singing along. I wanted Sunday every day, a life of Sundays.

To this day the idea of Sunday dinner at home conjures up smells of divine fulfillment. Young chickens sizzling in black cast-iron pans of shortening, sounding a kind of urgency as they crack and pop against that old beat-up metal lid placed slightly ajar. Mom's gravy spittin' at you while it takes its good time turning brown and thick before your eyes. These palate pleasers, along with creamed corn, macaroni and cheese, and roast loin of beef, say more about Sunday than I ever could.

ROAST LOIN OF BEEF

I 2 SERVINGS

¼ cup cracked black pepper
¼ cup garlic, minced
1 tablespoon salt
2 tablespoons olive oil
1 5- to 6-pound beef tenderloin, trimmed
2 tablespoons vegetable oil

In a small bowl, mix together black pepper, garlic, salt, and olive oil. Rub all sides of the beef with this mixture and let marinate 2 hours. Heat vegetable oil in a large skillet. Brown beef on high, turning to brown all sides evenly. Put in roasting pan and place in oven. Cook in preheated 400-degree oven 35 to 40 minutes for medium rare. Take out of oven and let rest 10 minutes before slicing.

SOUTHERN FRIED CHICKEN

෨

2 cups all-purpose flour
1½ teaspoons cayenne pepper
½ teaspoon garlic powder
1 teaspoon salt
black pepper to taste
1 3-pound broiler-fryer, cut up
1 teaspoon celery seed
1 cup buttermilk
1 quart vegetable oil for frying

In a bowl, combine flour with ½ teaspoon cayenne pepper, ½ teaspoon garlic powder, ½ teaspoon salt, and black pepper to taste.

Wash chicken and pat dry. In another bowl, mix chicken with the celery seed, the remaining cayenne and salt, and the buttermilk. Let sit 2 hours or overnight. Heat oil in a deep skillet to 325 degrees. Dip chicken pieces in flour, dusting off excess. Fry 25 minutes or until browned, turning once. Drain on paper towels.

CARAMELIZED BROWN ONION GRAVY

4 SERVINGS

❧

½ stick (4 tablespoons) butter
  (or ¼ cup olive oil)
2 medium onions, minced
2 tablespoons flour
1 cup milk (or substitute 1
  additional cup of stock)
1 cup chicken stock
2 teaspoons fresh thyme, chopped
  fine
salt and pepper to taste

Melt butter in a medium saucepan. Add onions and sauté until brown and caramel-colored, about 20 minutes on medium heat. Whisk in flour and cook 3 minutes. Add milk and chicken stock and bring to a light simmer. Add thyme and salt and pepper. Cook on medium heat for 3 minutes.

MACARONI AND CHEESE

4 SERVINGS

&

½ pound macaroni
1 cup heavy cream
pinch cayenne
salt and pepper to taste
¾ pound sharp cheddar cheese, grated
1 tablespoon butter, softened (or
  1 tablespoon olive oil), for the
  casserole

Boil macaroni until half-cooked. Drain. In medium saucepan heat heavy cream with cayenne and salt and pepper. Add macaroni and ½ pound cheese and cook on medium heat until cheese melts. Pour into a buttered casserole and top with the remaining ¼ pound of cheese. Bake in preheated 350-degree oven 15 minutes, until cheese melts.

CREAMED CORN

❧

½ small onion, grated

*2 tablespoons butter (or 2 tablespoons
    olive oil)*

4 ears fresh corn kernels, cut off cob

pinch dried thyme

pinch dried basil

pinch freshly ground black pepper

½ teaspoon salt

*½ cup heavy cream (or ¼ cup heavy
    cream)*

¼ cup parsley chopped fine, for garnish

Sweat onion in butter without letting it brown. Add corn and cook 4 minutes. Add spices, salt, and cream and bring to a boil. Turn down fire and simmer for 10 minutes. In the bowl of a food processor, puree half of the mixture. Combine the puree with the other half of the corn mixture. Put into serving bowl and garnish with chopped parsley.

2 GRANDPA ED SMALLS, CITY FARMER

*G*randpa was a quiet mountain, slow to anger but quick to action, with the power to solve all problems, especially mine. His smile was enormous, his laughter long, his promises always kept, and his strength generously shared. He was my best friend.

Born Edwin Smalls in Charleston, South Carolina, around 1897, he was one of the fourteen children of Ned Smalls and Liza Bowman Smalls, former slaves and country farmers. They were poor people with few worldly goods: two horses and a covered wagon, some farm tools, a few cherishables, a Sunday outfit for each family member. When Grandpa was a boy, Ned and Liza moved the family to Burton, a farmland area some fifty miles away in Beaufort, the older children walking alongside or behind the wagon the whole distance. Grandpa often recalled that journey, telling the story the same way each time, with gestures, head bobs, knee slaps, and bursts of laughter that always made it real.

He liked to talk about the week before the move. Apart from her usual chores and child rearing duties, Great-Grandma Liza Bowman had cooked all week. Not knowing how long the trip would take, or exactly what awaited them in Burton, she made tons of hoecake biscuits, pan after pan of cornbread, fried rice cakes, pickled vegetables (tomatoes, okra, beets, string beans, squash), and jar after jar of cooked beans. She prepared cured and smoked bacon, slabs of salt pork, hams and jerk beef; she packed sacks of cornmeal, flour, grits, dried beans, and rice; she wrapped dried apples, peaches, pears, and herbs tightly in brown paper bags. Every time Grandpa told this story, the significance of food and its preparation was brought home to me. Food was not only sustaining, it was also the way Liza Bowman cared for her family. This was love. I could see it in Grandpa's face as he held every word and caressed each phrase.

As a teenager, Ed Smalls was hired out to a wealthy northern white widow who owned a nearby farm and sent his wages directly to his family. It was always said that he became involved with his lonely mistress in an intimate relationship so smothering that his only way out was to run away. He had set his sights on Lizzie Johnson of nearby Green Pond, whom he had met at a dance. They were both around seventeen when Ed walked through the night to her house and they eloped.

My father was the youngest of their four children, and on his twelfth birthday they moved from Beaufort to Spartanburg. From then on our family called the Charleston-Beaufort area "the old country"—which was as close as we could come to a country of origin. In the nineteenth century Charleston was America's major slave port, and its great antebellum wealth, particularly its rice crop, depended on the farming expertise of the Africans brought there. Grandpa's stories and cooking connected me to these invisible ancestors, people whose cuisine formed the basis for Low Country cooking.

The Phoenix Furniture Company employed Grandpa for twenty and then another twenty years (I have both his commemorative watches). Fixing, delivering—he'd do anything that needed to be done; he was also foreman over all the other shop workers. He believed that if you stopped working, you'd die: simple as that. He'd say, "Look at Mr. Lipton; he's dead. I told him if he could only retire and sit up on that porch, he'd rock himself into the grave." He also loved showing me off, which meant that often I went to work with him. I would climb into the big green Phoenix Furniture truck and spend hours fetching Grandpa his tools, holding a screwdriver, or talking for what seemed like forever to women like Mrs. Means, who worked for Lawyer Smith's family in Converse Heights and would feed me cake and Kool-Aid, and Mrs. Paterson, who I thought sometimes broke her washing machine just so she could call Grandpa every month or so.

Though he had become an electrician and a mechanic, Grandpa never lost his farming skills. A lot of what we ate came from his acre garden, where he grew okra, corn, potatoes, lettuce, turnips, collards, peas—everything but watermelon (somehow his watermelon never came out right)—in a well-manicured, middle-class neighborhood of professionals, small-business owners, and people who worked two jobs for the privilege of living there.

Every spring, to plow his miniature backyard farm, Grandpa brought in a mule. On the appointed Saturday morning, sometime before eight, I'd hear the creaky sound of the old wagon and horseshoes clopping up High Street past my house to Connelly Street, where Grandpa lived. His property adjoined ours, so to reach it I didn't even have to go out into the street but simply took the path that led from his back door all the way down past his garden and to our back door. By the time Grandpa, his friend Mr. Johnson, and that mule—Old Sally, the funniest horse I'd ever seen—reached the garden, my friends and I had gathered on the path to watch. Grandpa and Mr. Johnson unloaded a large plow from the wagon, harnessed Old Sally to it, and as she stood patiently, almost a still life, they walked all over the field orchestrating every inch of ground. Finally Old Sally began her workout, her tail in constant motion, swaying, cutting the breeze, chasing the flies. It was like ballet—field ballet. Grandpa, in his flannel shirt, khaki work pants, and work boots, walked behind Old Sally holding the plow tight and steady. Row after row of turned dirt appeared. In no time, that old mule had not only readied the field but fertilized it, too. Years later Grandpa replaced Old Sally with a heavy-duty gas plow, retracing her steps behind "Mighty Mike the Rototiller." He plowed that field until the year he died, at ninety-three, never having missed a planting season.

Grandpa was a great cook, but breakfast with him was what I loved most. Around six in the morning, still half-asleep, I would walk up the path between our houses, past the garden, just to eat with him. The back door was always open and the smell of fresh coffee intoxicating. There'd be a full pan of biscuits rising in the oven, and popping on the back burner would be slabs of fresh hogshead bacon or sausage, made from Grandpa's own livestock, raised and butchered in the countryside, where

Grandpa Smalls and my cousin Patricia.
Grandpa was always there for us,
and Patricia knew that better than anyone.

he leased grazing land. The sausage was hot and spicy with plenty of sage, hot peppers, and a touch of celery seed. I remember Grandpa sitting at the kitchen table with a small tin washtub, combining his secret ingredients with Bertha, the name I had given one of his biggest hogs.

Grandpa, who felt breakfast should be a banquet, seemed to cook everything in the refrigerator just for the two of us. He made catfish, onions and scrambled eggs, redeye vinegar gravy with the sage sausage, skillet rice with fresh parsley and churned butter (I loved how the rice would stick to the pan just long enough to cluster and brown). Sometimes we'd have a big pot of hominy grits (Jim Dandy grits) with lots of lumps—so great!—and maybe gravy from the previous night's veal or beef stew. But no matter the menu, Grandpa's breakfast was not complete without biscuits and sorghum or molasses. After we'd eaten everything, he'd mop his plate clean with a piece of bread and then put a large pat of butter on the plate and cover it with dark syrup. Then with a fork he'd spread the butter into the syrup, creating a creamy mixture, and then he and I would polish off that pan of biscuits in no time. Wow!

We'd sit talking about the past—his mother, Liza, and his father, Ned, who had his master's brand burned into his flesh. Grandpa made sure I knew this and everything else he could remember. And then we'd talk about the future—my dreams and his dreams for me. I loved his smile, and I'd do anything to see it as often as I could. The kitchen table always afforded me that, because we both loved to eat, and that says it all. The best food, the best company, the best time.

———— ❦ ————

I could eat anything with Grandpa, and all would be right with the world. He would take the most interesting ingredients, combine them, stew or fry them, and serve them with a pot of rice or rice cakes—and fulfill all my expectations. Mostly, being with him made everything taste special. This was Grandpa's idea of breakfast, whether at six A.M. or ten P.M. He had a hearty sense of morning chow. You might want to get the coffeepot going right about now....

———— ❦ ————

CATFISH, ONIONS, AND SCRAMBLED EGGS

4 SERVINGS

❦

2 catfish fillets (8 to 9 ounces each)
salt and pepper to taste
¼ cup bacon fat (or ¼ cup vegetable oil)
1 large onion, chopped into medium dice
pinch nutmeg
pinch cayenne
¼ cup chopped parsley
6 eggs, beaten

Season catfish with salt and pepper. In a nonstick skillet, heat bacon fat to hot but not smoking. Sauté catfish fillets and onion on medium-high heat. Cook catfish 5 minutes on each side until nicely golden brown. Drain on paper towels and set aside.

Pour off all but 1 tablespoon of bacon fat. Add rest of ingredients to skillet with onions and cook, scrambling eggs. Break catfish into pieces and toss with scrambled eggs. Serve on warm platter.

HOT AND SPICY SAGE SAUSAGE
WITH REDEYE VINEGAR GRAVY

❧

2½ pounds lean pork

½ pound pork fat

1 teaspoon salt

2 teaspoons red pepper flakes

1 teaspoon freshly ground black pepper

1 tablespoon rubbed sage

2 teaspoons celery seed

GRAVY

pan drippings from sausage

2 tablespoons flour

2 cups chicken stock

¼ cup strong coffee

3 tablespoons white vinegar

salt and freshly ground pepper to taste

Using the coarse grind attachment of a food grinder, grind the pork and the pork fat. Grind remaining ingredients in a spice mill or blender. Add spice mixture to pork mixture and combine well. In a frying pan, fry a little piece of the sausage to taste for seasoning. Correct if necessary. Put the meat mixture back through the meat grinder, using the fine attachment. Shape into patties and fry. Drain on paper towels.

GRAVY
Drain off all but ½ cup of fat. Stir in flour until smooth and cook 3 minutes. Add chicken stock, coffee, and vinegar, bring to a boil, and simmer 5 minutes until sauce is thickened. Season with salt and pepper if needed.

FRIED RICE CAKES

4 SERVINGS

❧

2 cups cooked rice
¼ cup parsley, chopped
¼ cup plain bread crumbs
pinch cayenne
2 beaten eggs
salt and freshly ground pepper to taste
½ cup bacon fat for frying (or ½ cup
vegetable oil)

In a medium-size bowl, mix all ingredients except bacon fat. In a large skillet, heat bacon fat until hot but not smoking. Divide rice mixture into four parts. Using hands, shape into four patties. Fry until golden brown on each side. Drain on paper towels. May be served with gravy, tartar sauce, or chutney.

HOECAKES (OVERSIZED BISCUITS)

8 SERVINGS (8 BISCUITS)

ॐ

2½ cups flour
4 teaspoons baking powder
1 teaspoon baking soda
½ teaspoon salt
8 tablespoons vegetable shortening
¾ cup buttermilk

Reserve ½ cup flour for dusting surface. Sift together remaining flour with other dry ingredients. With a pastry cutter, blend in the shortening until mixture resembles a coarse meal. Make a well in the center of the flour mixture, pour in buttermilk, and mix with hands until dry ingredients are thoroughly mixed and dough forms a ball. Knead on a floured surface 4 to 6 minutes and roll out to ½-inch thickness. Cut with a 4-inch biscuit cutter. Place biscuits close together on a baking sheet and bake in a preheated 400-degree oven for 12 to 15 minutes until golden brown and puffy.

3 MY FIRST MEAL

My mother, Johnnie Mae Shaw Smalls, was a goddess in a print apron, wielding oversize spoons, bowls, pots, and cast-iron skillets in a ritual I never failed to notice. When I offered to help she'd pile pillows on a chair and sit me on it, wrapped head to toe in towels. She was a natural to watch and a great teacher, introducing me first to the dishes that were truly my favorites: okra, macaroni and cheese, caramel cake. I went from licking the beaters and bowls to slicing, stirring, pulling, and beating while she sang or hummed, her bedroom slippers—her cooking shoes—playing the floor and keeping the rhythm. It was during these times that she spoke of her parents who had died before I was born, her ideas about manhood, her dreams for me.

My mother was captivating, as beautiful as any mother could be. When she'd drop me off at school or stop by my Sunday school class to give me change for the collection plate, my friends often thought she was my sister. She set styles and trends, and as one of the premiere dressmakers of Spartanburg, was looked to for a sign as to when furs should be taken out of storage, or when straw hats were to replace felt or wool (her hats were legendary). She also made most of our clothes. I adored her and would sit for hours at the end of her sewing table. I think I started cooking as a way of spending even more time with her.

As a child I thought my mother was the strongest person on the planet. To me she embodied *woman,* and a woman was an interesting mix

*Mom (16 years old) took this
keepsake photo for Dad on his way to war.*

of femininity and masculinity. Women rolled up their sleeves, got down to business, and dealt with whatever had to be done. Yet Johnnie Mae seemed to live by a creed of modesty and understatement. Always an outsider in my father's clannish family, she kept her distance—and showed her respect—by calling her in-laws Mr. and Mrs. Smalls. In church, I loved sitting by her because her soft voice was so sweet and fragile, but I never saw vulnerability in her at any other time. She never praised herself or her children. We were just people with exceptional expectations for ourselves. When later in life I began to be noticed, I could never figure out if Mom was pleased or embarrassed that I was calling so much attention to myself. Once, years later, when we were talking on the phone in the early morning as we often do, she told me how proud she was of all I had accomplished. It never had to be said again.

Being talented in the kitchen was a given for Johnnie Mae. I particularly loved her one-dish meals like chunky soups, stews, and casseroles.

There was something special about putting a hundred and one ingredients together and cooking them for hours. This would occur generally toward the end of the week, a Thursday or a Saturday. I can remember the smell of veal stew simmering; I can even recall how it sounded slowly low boiling, gurgling playfully as if to tease you.

My mother used thick veal shanks, first washing them in warm salted water. Then she'd pat them dry and season them with salt, pepper, and celery seed, then dredge them in flour and lightly fry them in a saucepan with vegetable oil. When golden brown, the meat was transferred to a large pot filled with water, covered, and placed on a back burner to boil. Next, in another saucepan with oil, Mom would sauté chopped onions, celery, carrots, and parsley until their color disappeared. To this she would add thyme, sage, salt, pepper, and a little Worcestershire sauce, and pour the mixture into the pot of boiling veal. By now the air was thick with aroma and temptation, the next hour or so pure torture to the senses. But there was more to do. While the stew turned in its pot we made cracklin' cornbread, Carolina rice, and cold cabbage slaw with lots of sweet pickle relish and sweet red peppers. In season we also had fresh garden tomato slices and chilled cucumber wedges.

The last step in preparing the stew was making the sauce (thickening, Mom called it). She heated the flour, drippings, and oil left in the saucepan and added veal stock and more flour to make a roux. This was seasoned and cooked till brown and smooth. Then it was poured into the pot of veal and the flame was turned up to a rapid boil for the next few minutes. This climax sent me scurrying around the kitchen table with plates and silverware.

My mother could always count on me as her in-house prep cook and kitchen partner, but like all advancing chefs I grew tired of the prep station and cold foods. I wanted gas; I wanted to raise the temperature of my grandmother's cast-iron skillet—I wanted to *cook*.

Friday was fish night at our house, and because I didn't like fish, especially the kind with bones, my mother would usually make me a special dinner of franks and beans. One night she forgot, and I didn't take the news too well. Ranting and raving, pushing and panting, I worked myself into a state as only a five-year-old can do. At the conclusion of this performance Johnnie Mae, luckily in good humor, suggested: "Then make it yourself."

Thrilled I was. Pure ecstasy reigned. This was my moment. Through tear-soaked eyes, past my laughing sisters and staring father, I made my way to the kitchen, straight for the trophy I coveted: my grandmother's cast-iron frying pan. It was all I could do to lift it, but I managed to coax my sister Cynthia into putting that black pan on the griddle iron. Full of excitement, I raced around the kitchen gathering up choice ingredients. I wanted to put everything imaginable into this great pan of heritage. My mind pumped out orders: celery, bell peppers, Spanish onions rolling around the kitchen floor. I fetched all for my masterpiece, my solo flight, my dance in my mother's shoes. The recipe was the easy part:

> All the celery I wanted, chopped
> All the bell pepper I wanted, chopped
> All the onions I wanted, chopped
> Lots of butter (lots)
> Lots of black pepper
> Ketchup
> Beans
> Franks

After chopping all my vegetables and heaving a large piece of butter into the grand pan, I grabbed a chair, pulled it to the stove, and turned on the fire. How the flame roared! "Not too high" came a right-on-time reminder from my mother, from somewhere in the house. (It has always amazed me how mothers know just what to say even if they're not there.) From my pedestal I grabbed fistfuls of chopped vegetables and flung them toward the skillet with the advance of Michael Jordan—*whish,* into the pan. What a sound—sizzling, popping, crackling! I was cooking—my first dish was unfolding before my eyes!

The smells and smoke brought Cynthia back to the kitchen, where she promptly adjusted the burner and, with some prodding, opened a can of Van Camp beans. In they went, followed by ketchup, lots of pepper, and more butter. By now I was ready for the ultimate ingredient, hot dogs. I loved hot dogs (I still do). Cutting them into small rounds, my only consideration being how many I could get away with eating, I put them one piece at a time into the magnificent, bubbling panful of goodness. After letting them cook until I felt they were done, I turned the fire off and stood there on my chair, staring down into this display. My emotions were running high; the anticipation was overwhelming.

What had seemed to be moments had extended well into the dinner hour and drawn the curious and the restless, my father inquiring only whether I was going to eat it all and my sisters trying to steal bits of the franks. And then Mom could be heard in the distance, bedroom slippers tapping out her arrival. I braced myself for her inspection. Her approval or disapproval could be expressed in the briefest of words or gestures—it was a special way that she owned. She grabbed the spoon I was clutching and lifted out a taste. Butter oozing gravy fell from the spoon to her cupped free hand. My sisters giggled and posed, my father stood silently in the doorway, and I remained motionless on my chair, protecting the remains with my eyes on Mom.

"Needs some salt," she said, winking at me with a smile of approval.

Wow. Mom helped me fix my plate and then put the rest away for tomorrow. It was my greatest triumph. My first feast. I savored every bite, wishing never to finish, feeling proud about what I'd done—and knowing that no matter what happened in my life, I would never make that dish feeling the same way again.

Never, ever do I want to lose my appetite for pecan caramel cake! I would look forward to this trophy dessert on special occasions or when Mom sought to dress up simple fare, such as a dinner of veal shanks, cabbage slaw, and Carolina rice. This was love.

VEAL STEW (SHANK)

4 SERVINGS

2 pounds veal shank, cut into pieces
salt and pepper to taste
¾ cup flour
3 tablespoons vegetable oil
2 carrots, peeled and cut into pieces
1 rib celery, minced
4 bay leaves
1 bunch thyme
8 cloves garlic, minced
2 large onions, peeled and chopped
3 cups red wine
4 cups chicken or veal stock

Season veal shanks with salt and pepper. Lightly dust with some of the flour. Heat oil to hot but not smoking in a large stockpot or Dutch oven. Brown pieces of veal shank on all sides. Add carrots, celery, and herbs and cook for 10 minutes. Add garlic and onions and sauté another 10 minutes. Sprinkle in 3 tablespoons of flour and stir to coat the mixture. Deglaze with red wine and simmer 10 minutes. Add chicken or veal stock and bring to boil, stirring often. Reduce heat to low, cover, and simmer for 2 hours. Remove veal shanks from pan and cook the liquid 1 hour more. Put shanks back into pot; let simmer 10 minutes. Serve with rice or pasta.

CAROLINA RICE

❧

4 strips bacon, chopped
1½ cups Carolina rice
3 cups veal stock
salt and pepper

In a 4-quart saucepan, brown bacon. Drain off all but 1½ tablespoons bacon fat. Add rice and stir to coat with bacon fat. Add veal stock and salt and pepper. Bring to boil. Cover, reduce heat to low, and cook for 20 minutes. Fluff rice with fork and serve.

COLD CABBAGE SLAW

6 SERVINGS

❧

1 large green cabbage
1 large sweet red pepper
1 small onion
1 cup sweet pickle relish
¼ cup pickle juice
1 teaspoon celery seed
1 rib celery, minced
½ cup mayonnaise
  (preferably homemade)
salt and pepper to taste

Use a large mixing bowl. Halve cabbage and core. Cut into strips and small dice. Seed red pepper, cut into strips, and dice. Mince onion. Toss cabbage, red pepper, and onion with rest of ingredients. Chill ½ hour before serving.

CARAMEL CAKE

8 SERVINGS

CAKE

1 stick unsalted butter (¼ pound)

½ cup white sugar

½ cup brown sugar

2 eggs

1 teaspoon vanilla

2 cups all-purpose flour

½ teaspoon salt

2 teaspoons baking powder

1 teaspoon cinnamon

¾ cup milk

¼ cup chopped pecans

CAKE

In a bowl of a mixer, using paddle, cream butter and sugars until light and fluffy. Add eggs one at a time. Add vanilla. Sift together flour, salt, baking powder, and cinnamon. With machine running, add flour mixture and milk alternately in thirds, scraping down sides of bowl each time. Fold in pecans. Pour mixture into two greased 8-inch round pans. Bake in center of preheated 375-degree oven 20 to 25 minutes. Cool in pans for 15 minutes; then turn out onto cooling rack and let come to room temperature before frosting.

FROSTING

¼ pound (1 stick) butter or margarine

1 cup brown sugar, packed

¼ cup evaporated milk

1 teaspoon vanilla extract

2½ to 3 cups sifted confectioners' sugar

FROSTING

In a medium saucepan, melt the butter and stir in the brown sugar. Cook and stir over medium-high heat until bubbling. Remove from heat, add the milk and vanilla extract, and whip vigorously until smooth. Add the confectioners' sugar ½ cup at a time until mixture reaches desired spreading consistency. Frost the cooled cake immediately before icing hardens.

4   PAGLIACCI AND POTATO SALAD WITH PEAS

*R*ebel, renegade, and thorn in Grandpa's side, Uncle Joe, my father's older brother, was simply my hero. Family lore has it that Grandpa departed for battle overseas during World War I and returned home some years later to find that Lizzie, his wife, had given birth to a child now less than a year old. "This is your son Joseph" was all she said. Grandpa took the baby to the front porch and held him in his arms for practically the entire day. He rocked and cried and laughed with Joseph until Grandma, who for hour after hour had been cooking everything she could find to cook, summoned her strength to leave the safety of the kitchen and fetched Joseph to put him to bed. The neighbors counted the months of Grandma's pregnancy while Grandpa counted his blessings and sought to make a place in his heart and home for Joseph. No more was ever said of Lizzie's indiscretion.

Uncle Joe was foreign to my little Carolina world, bigger than life and seeming to paint my black-and-white surroundings into full and exaggerated color. Nothing with him was ever simple or understated. He favored fine spirits and wines, but after the fourth or fifth glass his discriminating palate had no trouble adjusting to Thunderbird. He pushed every situation to the limit. Grandpa could often be heard saying to him, "You always go too far. You never know when to quit, son."

It was not surprising, then, that after I was born, Joseph and his wife, Laura, who had no children of their own, moved to Spartanburg to plan my education and the course of my life. They bought a house that adjoined both Grandpa's property and ours. If I timed it right, I could eat dinner at all three places; this was challenging but deliciously rewarding on Sundays, when everybody cooked favorites, banquet-style.

Aunt Laura kept an immaculate house filled with antiques. The smell of good food permeated the rooms—something was always cooking. Uncle Joe's culinary feats were extraordinary, rivaled only by his unpredictable social antics, which on occasion resulted in his being asked to leave a restaurant or public gathering, tossed out of church, or thrown into the slammer overnight. There was no shortage of creativity in this self-taught and overwhelmingly entertaining man. He spoke perfect English and was a stickler for grammar—an entire conversation with him might be spent conjugating verbs. He had taught himself to play the piano after marrying Aunt Laura, who was an accomplished pianist, and often the two would play duets.

Having been classified as a disabled veteran, Uncle Joe worked only occasionally as a chef for special events, which meant that he had lots of time to fulfill what he believed to be his calling, which was the "greening" of my manhood. A typical day with Aunt Laura and Uncle Joe might start by my arriving at their house for my second breakfast around

Uncle Joe, relaxing with Life *magazine:*
I know he fancied himself on those pages.

nine. Aunt Laura always had a large glass of buttermilk, no matter what, and on occasion would eat burned toast, which she declared her favorite. She was her husband's sidekick, hostess to his host. They were like Burns and Allen. Uncle Joe would preside, with her very sweetly woven into the scenario, to position his jokes, to make sure that everyone knew that the focus was on him. A fragile beauty with porcelain skin and thick, dark hair that draped her shoulders, she always knew what to say and how to clean up anything that needed to be cleaned up. She was the one who took the heat if something didn't go quite right, the one who always reached for the flawed pastry, saying, "Oh, Joe, leave that piece for me, you know I like mine just a little thrown around!"

We would sit around the table discussing my future and the need to have well-laid plans to succeed in this rarely cooperative world. Depending on his mood, Uncle Joe would cook crepes, French toast with fresh fruit, or an egg casserole with cheese, bacon, and a crust of milk-soaked bread spiced with nutmeg. He had learned this egg dish in his travels to the Caribbean. He'd been all over the world during World War II, had worked on cruise ships as a chef, and as a chef and butler had traveled with and worked in some of the wealthiest households throughout the South and the East Coast. He also told stories about New York, and his eyes would sparkle when he spoke of clubs and concerts and nights on the town with Aunt Laura, dressed to kill, dancing till dawn among singers, musicians, boxers, baseball players, and famous gangsters. Aunt Laura seemed to hang on his every word and inflection. He had told these tales a thousand times—even I knew them by heart—but she always looked at him so lovingly, as if it were the first time all over again.

Then we followed Uncle Joe into the living room, where he put Tebaldi's *La Traviata* or Caruso's *I Pagliacci* on the stereo, settled deep into his chair near Aunt Laura's Story and Clark piano, and began the music lesson. We would sit for hours taking an opera apart, every singer and every nuance, until I knew the libretto as well as my own name. Uncle Joe could sing all the parts and did, as it suited him. I was often required to join him in duets and most assuredly in every chorus.

Sometimes I'd stay for dinner. Uncle Joe was a very different cook from my mother or most people I knew. Watching him fascinated me.

There were exceptional cooks in my family, but he was a magician. His deep love for cooking was the difference. There was a driven passion in his way of combining foods and cooking techniques that developed from conception (meal planning, shopping list) to execution (cooking, procedure, performance) to presentation (the finished product on the table). There were no rules as far as he was concerned, except that the food had to look good and taste great. Every kind of ingredient had the possibility of marriage in a dish, pot, or pan. He gave me license to be inventive and creative in the kitchen. Cooking could be imagination working at its best. He never made a dish the same way twice, not even with the same ingredients. Every dish was unique, every time he made it. "Recipes are for reference, not for cooking," he would say. "The idea belongs to everybody, but the dish belongs to you."

Uncle Joe took traditional southern recipes and stretched them to the point of reinvention. Potato salad became "potato salad with fresh green peas, roasted sweet red peppers, and leeks." His chicken and dumplings were the drunkest in town after absorbing half a bottle of sherry as well as quail eggs, chopped gizzards, chicken livers, and an abundance of fresh herbs and cracked black pepper. The dumplings themselves were often filled with minced shallots and celery seed.

The other half of the bottle of sherry went to ensure Uncle Joe's digestive comfort. If the sherry was kind, or if in the process of cooking the bird consumed more than Uncle did, he would still be amused and sober enough to go on with the evening after dinner. This was the reading hour, and one by one he, Aunt Laura, and I would read from Shakespeare, John Donne, T. S. Eliot, or Edgar Allan Poe. My signal that the evening was over came when Aunt Laura began one of many poems she read by Langston Hughes. My head filled with fantasy, I would fly down the path toward home.

Often Uncle Joe would phone me early Saturday morning. The familiar tap of Mom's bedroom slippers would arrive outside my room. "Joe's on the phone for you," she'd bellow, "but don't get any ideas about leaving this house without mowing the lawn, snapping those green beans in there, and laying down the fertilizer around my rosebushes." (What a way to start the morning.) "Joe knows you have your chores on Saturday; he's always finding something else for you to do; you're my child, not his."

By this time she was down the hall and I was free to hear the great news that he was planning a dinner party that night and would need my help. I jumped at the chance. I loved parties. I raced through all my chores, then hurried up the path to Uncle's. With Aunt Laura I polished silver platters and bowls, tableware and ladles, and carefully wiped spots off imported crystal. Then Uncle and I jumped into his big old Oldsmobile Delta 88 and sailed over to Winn-Dixie, where we loaded up on crabmeat, chicken, steaks, livers, bags of produce, cake flour, herbs, and spices— enough brown paper bags to cover every inch of the car's trunk space.

In the kitchen, Uncle Joe was a one-man band. Aunt Laura's job was to make sure everything he needed was on hand and then stand back, not hovering but not too far away, in case she was needed. Joe enjoyed giving me little tasks to perform: peeling potatoes, chopping vegetables, and stirring anything. Celery ribs were to be filled with two

Aunt Laura was a great beauty—
pretty as a picture.

kinds of cheese paste—smoked oyster and cream cheese (very adult-tasting), and pimento cheddar (my favorite). I would mix mounds of finely grated cheddar with pimentos that he had roasted the day before, salt, pepper, a hint of cayenne, and spoonfuls of Duke's mayonnaise. Sometimes I'd add a little sour cream if we had some. Then, putting the mixture into a cloth pastry bag or cheesecloth folded with a small hole in the tip, I'd fill each celery rib. Aunt Laura helped me put them on a tray and wrapped them tightly with plastic wrap to keep them fresh.

By this time Uncle Joe was well into orbit and had every burner going in a symphony of sight and sound. Vegetables were browning, stocks simmering, chickens frying, steak pieces marinating. While he cooked he always sang in a big, unwieldy voice that often wobbled and broke. He could easily go from a Verdi aria to a church hymn, or to a sassy hip-twitching ballad of love and intrigue. These sultry tunes brought a mischievous smile to his face, and his eyes rolled in his head as he seemed to forget we were there. He made me want to cook. I wanted to feel what he felt, that sense of power that was so intoxicating.

I had just enough time to dash home, bathe, and get dressed in my favorite black suit with a white shirt and string tie like Wyatt Earp's. Then I raced back up through Grandpa's garden to Uncle's house, where the guests were just arriving. Cars lined the small street and people in suits and fine dresses strolled up the walkway. Aunt Laura, more gracious than the pope, was planted in the doorway, wearing a pale blue cocktail dress with a peach sash, strap heels, and a single strand of pearls, her hair pulled back in a French twist. Her ready laugh, her way of always taking your hand when she spoke, and the way she held her head slightly to the side suggested a sincere humility. "Welcome, Sister Johnson and Brother Tucker. How've you been?" she said.

Uncle Joe and Aunt Laura were Jehovah's Witnesses, and it was their way to call everybody brother or sister, in the spirit of family. I liked that a lot. When I first went to the Kingdom Hall with them, I thought all these people were related. They called me Brother Smalls, and I thought: Wow, these people are my family, too. It got really confusing when people older than my mother and father called me brother. I knew my parents couldn't be their parents, too. But we got all that straightened out, and now I moved easily through the group, greeting all the brothers and sisters as they came.

The modest house seemed to grow smaller as the dozen or so guests positioned themselves in the living room, helping themselves from the gleaming silver punch bowl full of fruit and juices and spiked with lots of lemons, mint, and brown sugar. Uncle said this gave the punch a kick, but I think it hid the presence of old-fashioned white lightnin' (which may explain why I wasn't allowed to drink it). While he put the finishing touches on his lavishly garnished buffet, he sent me out among the tribe to pass the celery ribs and crabmeat biscuits. I was usually the only child present, which suited me fine, since I generally preferred the company of adults to children. Because I asked more questions than most, adults found my curiosity interesting and my spirit quite old and comforting. I guess it was because I spent so much time with grownups that I learned to be like them early. My mother used to say, "My poor baby never had a childhood."

At last Uncle Joe made his much anticipated grand entrance. Now, nobody outdressed Uncle Joe, nobody. In a town like Spartanburg, you'd be considered racy for wearing red before noon or two different shades of the same color at the same time. "Provocative" was a smile that lasted too long, a glance uninvited, or a low moan unchecked. But Joe hung himself in that living room doorway like a painting of Errol Flynn. Groomed to perfection, his black suede slippers wrapped around brilliant red socks, he wore pleated gray sharkskin trousers, a velvet smoking jacket with satin collar, a white tuxedo shirt with black onyx studs, and the largest cuff links I'd ever seen dropping from his wrists. All of this was outdone by his most enticing asset—his smile, with a center gap in his otherwise perfect teeth.

At his dinners Uncle Joe sought to bring culture and vision to a town he viewed as having none. Everybody was beneath him and looked upon with polite disdain, but people marveled at his condescension, indeed would have paid just to be exposed to his indifference. He spoke as if to give grace or bless all who had gathered, addressing them as loyal subjects who'd come in the name of the Lord . . . Lord Joe. He made his way through his following, extending his hand and casting words of wisdom. But unlike Aunt Laura, he rarely embraced anyone—that would have been too familiar, simply not done.

Meanwhile, smells from the kitchen wandered in and settled around the room. Food was flying off the platters I had placed about, and Aunt Laura and I scrambled to keep people pacified. Uncle Joe loved making people wait for dinner, though it was more than clear that people wanted to eat. But he liked creating the illusion of protocol; after all, these dinners were done somewhat for his amusement and to recover his lost sense of self in a social stratum that misunderstood him. Finally he excused himself, went to the kitchen, and began bringing out the food, with the help of Aunt Laura, me, and Helen, an older woman he always hired, who would wear a uniform to add that touch of suggested wealth. Helen stood by the table lighting chafing dishes and arranging parsley stems and other weeds and prickly twigs, waiting for Uncle Joe's commands like an eager soldier. "Plates ready, napkins folded, bread hot, salad tossed," and on he'd go while she stood shaking her head. Then he'd approach the table, straighten the cloth, rearrange the basket of silverware, light the candles, and finally turn off the overhead light and light the lamp to create a more intimate mood.

"Dinner is served!" He would almost sing it, then challenge everyone to come forth and break bread. The table was jammed with trays and bowls, covered dishes and small plates of olives, pickled onions, okra, tomatoes, crudités, and sweet pickles. A small bowl of quail eggs topped with caviar and lemon wedges sat on a tray surrounded by toast points (crusts removed); a deep dish of petit venison meatballs with creole sauce was more than tempting. Uncle's famous drunk chicken (which he preferred to make with hen) was placed in the center of the table in a large chafing dish heaped with vegetables and a golden brown gravy. There were a delicious savory rice and cheese casserole, orange-flavored spinach, and warm potato salad with sweet green peas and carrots. Peppered hush puppies rounded out the breadbasket of buttermilk biscuits.

Aunt Laura and Helen directed the self-service banquet. There was very little conversation at this time. Forks and knives banged on plates, ice danced in glasses. Aunt Laura fixed a plate for Uncle Joe, and Helen and I dined alfresco on the screened-in back porch. Aunt Laura never served herself; she ate like a bird every few hours or so, and never on any plate larger than a saucer. Helen, who inhaled everything she ate at rocket speed, finished almost before sitting down and then busied herself filling glasses, getting seconds for some guests, and clearing dishes for others.

Earlier, Uncle Joe had more than taken care of the music by stacking on the recently purchased stereo console six long-playing records, most of them classical and somewhat intimidating. But by this time Aunt Laura had stopped the recorded music and was playing classics on the piano (she loved Chopin). She was my first piano teacher and had taught me to play with curved fingers, though she herself played with fingers extended straight out, to protect her long nails. You got the impression from the tapping of her nails on the keys that she was dancing. Hearing her play, I began to experience familiar butterflies: I had promised Uncle Joe that I would play a duet with her, and the time was fast approaching. Making her way through all the applause, Aunt Laura came out to get me for my moment. She could see the fear in my eyes and at once held me near. "It will be so much fun, honey," she said. "These people love you and we're so proud of you." I would do anything for Aunt Laura, so—fear or no fear—we played that duet well, in fact so well that we did it one more time. I went home that night feeling so much a part of the world, full of the best food in town and some of the best memories I would ever have.

Uncle Joe always remained in that great space and capacity in my life. He taught me that a cooking spoon was like a magic wand in a kitchen of great adventure. He gave me permission to be different, if different was what in fact I was, and courage to move beyond what was in front of me, if what was in front of me blocked my way.

There is just no way to do Uncle Joe justice in the kitchen. It's not so much his recipes that made his time-honored culinary inventions great, but the ceremony he evoked. In the following recipes, some insight into his creativity is apparent, but by no means is it the sum total. These basic, solid dishes involve the simplest technique. Now you must run with your imagination, shower the chicken and dumplings with sherry, herbs, and even seasoned chicken livers. Be bold and daring, and have a ball . . . all in the name of Uncle Joe.

PETIT VENISON MEATBALLS WITH CREOLE SAUCE

8 SERVINGS

CREOLE SAUCE
½ cup onion, minced
8 cloves garlic, minced
4 tablespoons olive oil
2 green peppers, chopped
3 ribs celery, chopped
4 bay leaves
1 tablespoon dried thyme
1 tablespoon cayenne
1 teaspoon chili powder
3 cups tomatoes (chopped or stewed)
2 cups chicken stock
¼ cup dry sherry
¼ cup chopped parsley
3 tablespoons brown sugar
1 teaspoon salt

MEATBALLS
1½ cups rye bread crumbs
1 cup milk
1¼ pounds ground venison
1 small onion, minced
½ teaspoon salt
¼ teaspoon poultry seasoning
4 tablespoons vegetable oil

SAUCE

In a large stockpot, sauté onion and garlic in olive oil until onion is translucent. Add green peppers and celery; cook 5 minutes. Add bay leaves, thyme, cayenne, and chili powder. Cook 5 minutes. Add rest of ingredients, bring to boil, reduce flame, and simmer 20 minutes.

MEATBALLS

In a large bowl, mix the bread crumbs and milk. Add meat and rest of ingredients and combine. Form mixture into balls about 1 inch in diameter.

In a large skillet, heat oil until hot but not smoking. Add meatballs in a single layer and cook until brown on all sides, about 6 minutes. Remove from skillet and drain on paper towels. Put meatballs in a baking dish and pour in creole sauce, halfway up the sides of the pan. Bake at 350 degrees for 30 minutes.

CHICKEN AND DUMPLINGS

☙

1 3-pound chicken, cut into 8 pieces
½ teaspoon salt
3½ tablespoons flour
½ cup milk
½ cup cream
additional salt and pepper to taste

DUMPLINGS
2½ cups flour
3 teaspoons baking powder
¼ teaspoon salt
2 tablespoons bacon fat (or
  2 tablespoons olive oil)
1 cup buttermilk
1 teaspoon rubbed sage
pinch cayenne

Clean chicken well. Place in a stockpot or Dutch oven and cover with water. Season with ½ teaspoon salt. Cover pot and simmer for 1½ hours.

Make dumplings (see method below).

Remove lid of stockpot or Dutch oven and reduce liquid to 4 cups. Mix 3½ tablespoons flour with milk and cream and season with salt and pepper. Add this to simmering liquid. When the liquid is slightly thickened, drop dumplings by spoonfuls on top of the stew. Cover tightly and cook slowly for 15 minutes. Spoon into bowls.

DUMPLINGS

Sift dry ingredients. Cut in fat with pastry cutter. Add buttermilk and mix. Add sage and cayenne. Set aside.

POTATO SALAD

❧

4 large Idaho potatoes
1 cup fresh (or frozen) green peas
2 leeks, washed, halved lengthwise, and
  chopped
1 tablespoon olive oil
½ cup sweet peppers, chopped
1 small onion, chopped
1 cup celery, chopped
1 cup bread and butter pickles, chopped
4 eggs, hard-cooked
1 cup mayonnaise
salt and pepper to taste

Peel potatoes and cut into large dice. Boil in salted water with fresh peas for 15 minutes and check for doneness. (If using frozen peas add them unthawed to the boiling potatoes in the remaining 3 minutes of cooking.) Drain and reserve. In a medium skillet, sauté leeks in 1 tablespoon oil for 10 minutes. Add to potatoes. Put potato-and-leek mixture in large bowl and toss with rest of ingredients. Taste for seasoning and adjust if necessary, then chill.

ORANGE SPINACH

4 SERVINGS

❦

1 tablespoon shallot, minced
2 tablespoons butter, clarified
  (or 2 tablespoons olive oil)
1 teaspoon orange zest
1½ pounds fresh spinach, cleaned
¼ cup cream
1 teaspoon salt
pinch nutmeg

Sauté shallot in clarified butter. Add orange zest and cook 1 minute. Add cleaned spinach and toss 3 minutes. Pour in cream, season with salt and nutmeg, and cook 4 minutes. Arrange in serving dish or platter.

5 WHENEVER AUNT DAISY CAME TO TOWN

*A*unt Daisy was just the kind of person you wanted to be around, someone who loved to laugh and seemed to care about everything that happened to you. She called everybody baby. "What's the matter, baby?" she'd ask. And she'd make you a sticky bun in a minute, just stick a buttered biscuit with lots of sugar or molasses into your mouth. Whenever Aunt Daisy was expected, the energy in the air heated up.

My father's older and only sister, Aunt Daisy was the apple of Grandpa's eye. She lived in New York but came home to visit, usually with a gentleman caller, boyfriend, or at times husband. These men varied in their appeal, but they all loved the ground Aunt Daisy walked on—which made it easier for Grandpa to endure them.

Grandma Lizzie, who had suffered a stroke and was bedridden for several years before passing on to glory, knew all too well the provocative and restless side of Daisy. They were much alike, which explains why the same house, town, and state may not have been big enough for them both. Many times, even while Grandma held court in her sickbed, Aunt Daisy tried to live in Spartanburg, to settle down and be an attentive mother to her two daughters, Patricia and Jeanie. But the call of the wild wouldn't leave her. The expression "Once you leave home, you'll always be gone" was well applied to Daisy Smalls Edmonson Williams Campbell. Grandpa was the only father and constant provider Patricia and Jeanie had. But those girls, like me, loved their mother, and a little bit of her every once in a while was better than nothing.

"Daisy's here!" Grandpa would shout over the phone. You were expected to know just who was calling, that this was all he had to say, and that you should be halfway up the path to his house by now. We all took off running except for Mom, who kept her usual distance. Uncle Joe was always there ahead of us. He and Aunt Daisy were pranksters from way back, they had chosen similar work as chefs, and both had enough scandal in their private lives to turn Spartanburg upside down. "Neither of them has any shame," Mom was quick to say. But whereas Uncle Joe had his very proper facade, his perfect marriage to an almost white wife (Aunt Laura had passed in her day), and an air of arrogance that more than sheltered him from his detractors, Aunt Daisy was much simpler. She was a loving woman, a devoted daughter to her father, but a naughty coquette. She loved men—any man, anybody's man. She changed husbands the way most people change clothes, and by the time she'd dressed for you, cooked for you, and danced for you, she had done you and was gone.

Grandpa's house was full of excitement. Food was everywhere! The extended kitchen table was twice its normal size. Aunt Daisy had

Brothers Joe, Alex, and Edward Smalls:
hams, showing off for the camera.

brought baskets, boxes, cartons, coolers. The trunk of her car—she always arrived in a big, shiny new car, since it was important for people who returned home to the South to look prosperous—was full of big containers, cans with peeling labels (a few with foreign markings), large sacks of dry goods, and what appeared to be fancy vinegars and oils for Uncle Joe. Rummaging, I found what I thought to be yet another vinegar bottle and ran toward the house to give it to Uncle Joe, but in my haste tripped over the first step to Grandpa's porch. The bottle flew toward the front door, but providentially into the long hand of Mr. William, Aunt Daisy's current companion, who helped me to my feet. "This is special medicine for adults, son," he said. "You best be careful; it's expensive, too." Cousin Jeanie, watching, screamed with laughter as Mr. William walked back around the house. "Fool," she said, "you almost broke his bottle of liquor"—which by this time I knew was a big part of any function when the Smalls family got together.

Aunt Daisy had commandeered the kitchen. She cooked like a sergeant in the military, everything fast and furious, her pots all racing at high flame, the oven throwing waves of heat into the room every time she checked the bread or rotated the cobbler. On the back burner an onion, veal, and pepper–based creole sauce slowly simmered with herbs and garlic, and on the kitchen table were the freshly killed, cleaned, and seasoned rabbits Grandpa loved so well. Aunt Daisy dredged them in seasoned flour, as if she were frying chicken, browned them in an iron skillet partially filled with fat, then arranged them on a brown paper sack to drain off the grease, while she made a brown gravy paste from the remaining fat and flour.

Cousin Patricia and my sister Cynthia were carefully wrapping wilted cabbage leaves around balls of spiced ground veal and rice, and sticking toothpicks through the stuffed cabbages, which to me provoked images of voodoo dolls and evil spells. Outside, my sister Delores and Jeanie sat on wooden crates near the back steps, shelling fresh peas from Grandpa's garden. The men—my father, Mr. William, Uncle Joe, Grandpa, and I (when I wasn't in the kitchen, where I preferred to be)— had gathered in the backyard near Grandpa's tool shack, where the Phoenix Furniture truck was always parked. My father had brought out a

Jeanie, Cynthia, Delores, me, and
baby sister Elonda: a lazy, hot, summer
Saturday-afternoon pose.

card table and folding chairs. A cooler of ice and beer sat nearby, and from time to time Aunt Daisy brought out tall tin cups, wrapped in paper towels, for the "adult medicine." Soon she appeared with Uncle James, Grandpa's nephew. "All my menfolk, coming to welcome Daisy home," she boasted. James, hugging and kissing her and grinning ear to ear, knew just what to say to turn the pressure up on the moment. "Girl, you're looking as good as chocolate cake on a plate, and I know you taste great!"

With that, Aunt Daisy threw her head back and did a wiggle with her hips that challenged the seams of her broadly printed low-cut shift dress. Then she removed the handkerchief she kept tucked in her bosom, patted her moist head and neck, and pushed Uncle James gently away to join the men. I can still see her standing there, following his every step with her eyes, her hands clasped and pressed against Grandma's permanently soiled apron. Even then I imagined a sadness about her—faded youth, painful joy, uncertain tomorrows. These trips home to Spartanburg always came with a price.

A moment later Aunt Daisy was dropping the peas Delores and Jeanie had shelled into a pot of boiling smoked ham hocks. A large pot of Carolina long grain rice steeped away, well seasoned with whipped butter. By now the rabbit, nearly done, simmered in brown gravy with big chunks of slightly salted country ham. Pieces of cracked black pepper floated on the surface. Aunt Daisy had cut up white potatoes and added them to the pot for texture and to absorb the salt, so she said. Never knowing who was going to show up meant cooking a lot—a whole lot.

Up the back path past Grandpa's yellow corn bushes I could see Mom and Aunt Laura making their way. Aunt Daisy, like a newly presented debutante, positioned herself at the top of the steps, arms reaching toward the heavens as she called out, "Johnnie Mae and Laura Smalls—now I know you ain't gonna not come over here and see me!" Aunt Laura, screaming, "Daisy, child, so good to see you; oh, it's been too long!" managed to get to Daisy as she left the last step, and Mom, not one for big emotions, reached them both in time to ride on the momentum already in progress.

After Grandpa graced the table and we had all graced our appetites, Uncle sent me to his house for his Latin LPs. He and Aunt Laura tangoed, then did the rhumba and the mambo to perfection. Aunt Daisy, not to be outdone, grabbed her Mr. William and did the merengue, or what she believed it to be, and the cha-cha-cha, song after song.

Throughout my childhood, Aunt Daisy's warmth, mystique, sassy sense of humor, and style remained a constant. Whenever I heard she'd arrived, I would beat it up the back path to Grandpa's house and wait around for whatever came out of the oven. She'd cook familiar food, like roast turkey and cornbread stuffing with sage sausage. But she did some things differently from my mother—rice, for example. Mom boiled rice and then steamed it in a colander. Aunt Daisy cooked rice the Caribbean way: she'd rinse off the starch two or three times, put it into a pot, add butter or a piece of fatback or a slab of bacon, and some salt, and put it on to boil. Once the rice reached the same level as the water, she turned the heat down, put a top on, and let it sweat until it was ready. And she also made things my mother never made, like coon, and chitlins, and venison. She fixed catfish, mullet, porgy—all those fish with bones. She'd make fish-head stew. As a kid, I couldn't understand why she did it, but to a chef it makes perfect sense—fish heads are great for stock. Cook them with celery, salt and pepper, carrots, parsley, and herbs like bay leaf, rosemary, and sage.

Grandpa's house was run more traditionally because he came home for lunch—in Charleston, where he was from, you had your big meal in the middle of the day. When Aunt Daisy was in Spartanburg, she started lunch about ten in the morning, and it was amazing to watch her juggle large amounts of food. She would cook two meats and one or two vegetables. When she fried okra, instead of using my mother's flour-and-cornmeal method, she just threw some oil or fatback into a pan, fried the okra, then added a little water and let it stew down. She'd stew greens, too, with a hambone, or sometimes with oxtails, which she'd boil first with salt and pepper until they were tender.

The single best thing about Aunt Daisy's greens was that she made them with cornmeal dumplings. My mother, who for some reason was stingy about dumplings, made them only when we had company. I could never get enough, so I just loved Aunt Daisy's. She used cornmeal flour, shortening or butter, salt and pepper, and probably some sage, and mixed this up with some of the broth from the greens, and an egg, and then spooned the batter into the boiling greens, so the dumplings were almost like balls.

Aunt Daisy was also the first person I knew who put tuna fish in macaroni salad. It was as if I'd died and gone to heaven. In quiet moments, when no one else was around, we'd eat macaroni salad with tuna and saltine crackers, and she'd make up stories or reminisce about my father, or about New York. And we would just laugh.

I loved Aunt Daisy's yellow cake with butter frosting and her orange spice cake with frosting and Pet ice cream (always vanilla). Unlike my mother's polite-size pieces, her servings were like wedges—you could choke on Aunt Daisy's piece of cake, and she'd be more than willing to give you another. Sometimes she slipped me a plate to take home. And I'd have to lie to my mother when she served our dinner and say I hadn't eaten.

Daisy remained predictable, her fear of intimacy and commitment unresolved. Mr. William would be replaced, like others before and after.

Aunt Daisy: just a good-time kind of girl.

In Spartanburg a proper woman stayed in with her family, waiting for her husband to decide to come home. But Aunt Daisy went *out* at night, and she knew where to go (even her hangovers were worldly). She had a good figure that might be considered fat today—when she walked, everything went *whoomp, whoomp, whoomp.* But she was well-proportioned, and her New York outfits pushed the boundaries of little Spartanburg. I remember a tight smoky gold dress, and a hot pink number with a built-in push-up bra, big ornamental costume jewelry that glowed in the light, and lots of Evening in Paris perfume. Because she was short, Daisy wore high heels, always with a silver ankle bracelet and sheer nylons with back seams and garters. It was this outfit, I'm sure, that caught the attention of Mr. Charles Campbell, next victim in waiting, with whom Aunt Daisy slipped off one dawn during a short but passionate affair. She took only the essentials (knowing too well that Grandpa would ship her remaining belongings), leaving no note, no flowers, no instructions for Mr. William as to what to do or where to go next. After a month, Grandpa packed Mr. William's bags and brought him to a friend's house and bade him well. He stayed in Spartanburg, and we would occasionally see him in passing. Mom could only shake her head, saying, "Another one of Daisy's lost children."

To look at Aunt Daisy was to look upon a woman who loved to cook and eat. Her kitchen offerings were often eagerly awaited by the Smalls clan, who downed large glasses of overly sweetened Kool-Aid in anticipation. Aunt Daisy, a bit of a prankster, once chased me around the kitchen table waving fish heads in one hand and a plucked rabbit in the other. It was fun when she cooked. Her dishes were big and full-bodied. These recipes will most certainly channel her spirit into your home. Make the yellow cake with butter frosting first. That way, while the rabbit's browning, the fish heads boiling, and the greens simmering, you've got your eye on the prize.

SEASONED RABBIT
WITH COUNTRY HAM AND POTATOES

8 SERVINGS

1 2½-pound rabbit

3 tablespoons vegetable oil

flour for dredging, seasoned with salt
   and pepper

1 large onion, diced

2 large Idaho potatoes, peeled, cut into
   large cubes

¼ cup vinegar

1½ cups veal stock

1 tablespoon fresh thyme leaves

1 tablespoon fresh tarragon

3 bay leaves

2 cups cooked country ham, diced

parsley, chopped

salt and pepper to taste

Debone rabbit and cut into strips. Reserve bones for stock or discard. Heat oil in skillet. Dredge rabbit strips in seasoned flour and brown evenly. Pour out all but 1 tablespoon oil. Add diced onion and potatoes and cook 5 minutes. Add vinegar, veal stock, herbs, and bay leaves. Bring to boil and simmer until potatoes are almost cooked. Toss with country ham. Check seasoning. Arrange on platter and garnish with chopped parsley.

FISH-HEAD STEW

4 SERVINGS

❧

½ cup diced salt pork
1 large onion, sliced
2 large potatoes, diced
juice of 4 lemons
2 pinches cayenne
4 heads porgy, gills removed,
   cleaned
1½ quarts water
salt and pepper to taste

In a Dutch oven, brown the salt pork until it is golden brown and the oils have been released. Add, in this order, onion, potatoes, lemon juice, cayenne, porgy, water, and salt and pepper. Bring to a boil, turn heat to low, and simmer 30 minutes. Remove fish heads, pick off any meat, and add to stew. Discard heads. Serve stew in heated bowls with buttered bread or biscuits.

ONION, VEAL, AND, PEPPER-BASED CREOLE SAUCE

8 SERVINGS

❧

½ cup onion, minced

8 cloves garlic, minced

4 tablespoons olive oil

2 green peppers, chopped

2 ribs celery, chopped

4 bay leaves

1 tablespoon dried thyme

1 tablespoon cayenne

1 teaspoon chili powder

3 cups canned tomatoes,
*   or 5 cups fresh tomatoes*
*   stewed for 30 minutes*

2 cups veal stock

¼ cup dry sherry

¼ cup chopped parsley

3 tablespoons brown sugar

3 teaspoons salt

In large stockpot, sauté onion and garlic in olive oil until onion is translucent. Add green peppers and celery; cook 5 minutes. Add bay leaves, thyme, cayenne, and chili powder. Cook 5 minutes. Add rest of ingredients, bring to boil, reduce flame, and simmer 20 minutes or to desired thickness.

GREENS STEWED WITH OXTAILS

8 SERVINGS

❦

1 stick (¼ pound) butter
  (or ½ cup olive oil)
1½ pounds oxtails, cut into small
  pieces
1 large onion, chopped
8 cloves garlic, minced
5 pounds collard greens, cleaned,
  sliced in strips or whole
2 quarts chicken stock
½ cup vinegar
¼ cup maple syrup or sorghum
  to taste (optional)
salt and pepper to taste

In a large stockpot, melt butter, add oxtails and onion, and brown. Add garlic and cook 4 minutes. Add collard greens and toss until coated with butter and onions. Cook 5 minutes on medium heat. Raise heat to high and add chicken stock, vinegar, and maple syrup or sorghum. Season with salt and pepper, bring to a boil, turn heat to low, and simmer 1 to 1½ hours.

YELLOW CAKE WITH BUTTER FROSTING

8 SERVINGS

❧

CAKE

2 sticks (½ pound) butter, softened

2 cups sugar

4 egg whites

1 teaspoon vanilla

3 cups cake flour

3 teaspoons baking powder

¼ teaspoon salt

1 cup milk

FROSTING

1½ cups water

3 cups sugar

¾ pound cold butter

4 egg yolks

2 teaspoons vanilla

CAKE

Cream butter and sugar until light and fluffy. Add egg whites one at a time, allowing each to absorb completely. Add vanilla. Sift together flour, baking powder, and salt. Add flour mixture and milk alternately in thirds. Pour into two greased 8-inch round cake pans. Bake in preheated 350-degree oven for 35 minutes. Remove from pans and cool on rack before icing.

FROSTING

Dissolve sugar in water. Place in small pot over high heat, bring to a boil, and let boil for 5 minutes. While sugar water is boiling, beat yolks in mixer until pale and slightly stiffened. Carefully add sugar water in steady stream while beating yolks at high speed. Continue beating until yolk mixture reaches room temperature. Cut cold butter into cubes. Add cubes to yolk mixture one at a time until each is incorporated. Continue beating at high speed until icing is of a fluffy but spreadable consistency. Add vanilla and refrigerate.

6   WHATEVER YOUR FATHER BRINGS HOME

*I*n his teens my father knighted himself Alexander Leonard Smalls—before that, he'd been known only as "L.J." When I pushed and shoved my way onto the planet without regard for convenience, and he—not the doctor—became the first to see and hold me in this world, he wanted me to carry his name. But Da compromised on Alexander Bernard because Mom was concerned that I have my own identity. (As it turned out she needn't have worried.)

To this day I call my father Da. In Spartanburg everyone knew him as Alex (pronounced *El*ec), a handsome, easygoing man, dashing in his white dinner jacket at the semiannual Masons' ball, the kind of man old ladies look for after church to pose the question of a ride home, "If you're going my way?" He was assistant superintendent of the Sunday school and the church choir's only male soloist—a heavy, meaty tenor. His good deeds were legendary. It was not uncommon for him to rise early on a Saturday and drive over to Miss Smith's or Mr. Jim's to mow the lawn. All the fellows liked Da as well. He'd drive down the street with one hand out the window and the other on the steering wheel over the horn, and he'd be waving and bobbing and blowing—it was a carnival.

When I'd ask my mother what we were having for dinner, her usual answer was, "Whatever your father brings home." Da more than brought home the bacon; he brought home the store. He worked for a chain of supermarkets headquartered in Spartanburg, and he might walk through the door of our house with a case of anything—usually something that had broken and couldn't be sold. These cases led us on culinary adventures. One of the most memorable was a case of lasagna, which we had never seen before. Since my parents were children of the Depression and never threw out anything that could be used, we had lasagna every imaginable way—lasagna with spaghetti sauce, lasagna salad, lasagna with *lima beans*. To this day I don't like lasagna.

About thirty markets were supplied by the warehouse where Alex worked, a monster of a food palace that I loved to visit, with surreal, futuristic-looking men in insulated suits running in and out of frozen-food rooms, and in the produce section what appeared to be miles of vegetables on wooden pallets growing in cement fields. Endless cases and crates stacked to the ceiling peered down at us. Loud gas-driven forklifts moved stacks of food into large trucks. To fill the orders for each store there were battery-operated carts—my favorite—that pulled three or four wagons. As a teenager I worked at this job on summer vacations or holiday breaks from school, imagining how I could cook and eat my way through the entire building, never eating the same thing twice.

In our house, food shopping was men's work, and Da and I were the best in the business. On Friday nights, when my father came home from work, he'd leave the car running and run inside to get me. At the supermarket it was as if trumpets had blown—people came from wherever they were working, saying, "Elec is here! With Little Elec!" Grocery shopping took us forever; we were gone for hours because my father enjoyed strutting me around and had to get through the entire store and every employee. The secretaries would stop what they were doing to pinch my cheeks and give me candy. And my father would allow me to choose things to put in the basket. All my friends were so limited in what they would eat—no this, no that, no vegetables—but I liked everything, for the most part, and getting through that supermarket taught me early how much food there was to value.

Da didn't cook much, since he was always on the go, out the door by seven-fifteen in the morning. In the evening he arrived expecting dinner no later than six; and by eight, in a halo of Old Spice and Vitalis, he pushed out of the driveway in his big Pontiac, headed for Hilltop

Dad, dressed to kill, as always.

House, the club that he, Grandpa, and Uncle Joe had opened on the old Union Highway. It had always been my father's dream to own a night-club—he would run the place, Uncle Joe would cook, and Grandpa would pay for it. And that was somehow how it happened. For years Hilltop House was the *in* place, the hot spot, the place to be, featuring live bands, jukebox tunes, and the best fried chicken in town (naturally, since Uncle Joe had created the recipe).

Around nine, people would start piling in through the large side door near the parking lot. Da, the concerned and considerate host, played that side door like an old fiddle. "How ya doin', fellow?" flowed like molasses from his lips. He nodded politely to all the ladies and pointed customers toward the dance floor, the restaurant area, or the lounge bar, which was quieter and warmly lit. On weekends I was allowed to hang out with Uncle Joe, who along with Helen and a gentle-man named Rosco ran the kitchen. The menu was simple, not at all up to Joe's usual fare. But my father wanted the food to be cheap, fast, and nonconfrontational: steak, hamburger, pork chop, fried chicken, and fried fish platters, with side dishes of cabbage slaw, tossed salad, french

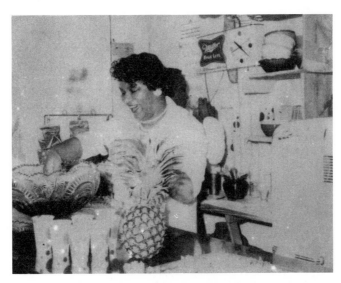

Mom at Hilltop House.
No party was complete without Mom's punch.

fries, and baked potato. Every now and then Joe tried to introduce a special, which usually resulted in a fight with Da over the waste, because no one ever ordered it but me. I was sometimes allowed to garnish the plates with sprigs of parsley; or if Uncle Joe was really feeling irreverent, we'd put cherry tomatoes, black olives, and a pickle on a toothpick standing in the center of the plate. One comment from a customer usually sent my father into the kitchen screaming about fancy girlie food.

The fact that my dad was the front man everyone loved and looked for didn't sit well with Uncle Joe, who felt *he* should be out there bathing in all the glory. Just a little Scotch and the heat of that poorly ventilated kitchen would send him out to socialize and claim the captive audience for himself. Drunk, he rarely made it back to the stove or the deep-fryer. After this happened one time too many, Uncle Joe was dismissed as chef and partner, but that was not to be the end of it. He sat for a week fuming, then, armed with a mind to tell somebody off and a fifth of Jack Daniel's to back him up (another fifth already consumed), he appeared at Hilltop House one Saturday night to settle the score. At the door Da stopped him quickly, noting his flammable breath, and after a few words responded in the only way possible—he slammed the door in Uncle's face and struck up the band. This would have finished off a lesser man, but not Joseph. Stumbling back to his car, he tripped over the very brick that would define the next twenty minutes. "Bang!" Glass was everywhere, as were people running to get away from the broken window. By the time Da and Grandpa reached the door, Joe had revved up his car and was doing figure eights all over the parking lot and front lawn. This is how the police found him some ten minutes later, the Jack Daniel's bottle empty on the front seat. Grandpa had had enough of it all, and as patriarch of the clan he closed the doors to Hilltop House. Da was cheated out of his brilliant career as a nightclub owner, but luckily he had kept his day job, so we continued to eat well.

Although he called me my mother's child, my father kissed me to sleep when I was small, taught me to drive by sitting me on his lap, cut my hair until I was old enough for the barber, and took me to ball games where we rooted for our home team, the Spartanburg Phillies. When I was eight, while riding my bicycle in front of the house I got hit by a car. Blood gushed out of my head. My father, who had been on the side porch cutting someone's hair, picked me up and wrapped my head in a towel. I'll never forget the pressure of his hand on my head as with his free hand he drove like a maniac to Bull's Clinic to get me stitched up.

There wasn't much reason for Da to be in the kitchen. If there was something Mom didn't do, Cynthia, Delores, and I usually filled in. Most memorable of my father's forays into cooking occurred when Mom was in the hospital for the birth of my younger sister Elonda. My older sisters were given preparation chores like slicing tomato and cucumber, chopping vegetables, or making a pot of rice or cornbread or biscuits. Da came home and did the rest. We'd have chops, or steak, or my favorites—hamburgers and hot dogs. Da made hamburgers like miniature meat loaves, big round patties with onion, pepper, minced celery, salt, pepper, hot sauce, and Worcestershire sauce. To go with them he roasted small white potatoes, scrubbed clean and cut in half, scored faceup like a tic-tac-toe chart, washed in oil, and sprinkled with garlic powder. Toward the end of their cooking, half of them were sprinkled with grated sharp cheddar cheese.

Cousin Patricia came over to help out while Mom was away, and she and I made chili dogs. Mom always heated up Bunker Hill canned chili, which wasn't bad for store-bought, but nothing beat Patricia's and my home-style version: chopped onions, bell peppers, and celery browned together lightly, then ground beef, finely chopped tomatoes, chili powder, salt, pepper, Worcestershire sauce, and a pinch of sugar. I liked lots of onion in mine, so when Patricia wasn't looking I'd add a little more. As the chili simmered, we'd add ketchup for a thicker sauce. We'd toast our hamburger buns in the oven, but I loved my hot dog buns steamed in a colander over boiling water. This always made them nice and soft.

Now, this was the best eating, simple and with everybody participating. As with a smorgasbord or fondue spread, the real excitement was putting your food together once it got to the table. Da, Patricia, Cynthia, Delores, and I sat at the kitchen table around mustard, mayonnaise, ketchup, pickle relish, onions, coleslaw, chili, and hot sauce, all set out on a lazy Susan we just kept spinning, making one sandwich after another. We put chili on the potatoes with cheese and garlic, or onions and sour cream too. Then we lined the table with old newspaper and ate watermelon, spitting seeds when Dad wasn't looking.

Although he didn't do much cooking, my father did make holiday and Sunday breakfasts, Low Country style, of smothered crab or oysters or shrimp, recalling his childhood in Beaufort, the continued presence of the "old country" in my life.

Breakfast was a major event in our house. When my mother cooked, there were so many items on the menu that her kitchen rivaled any diner around. Hot biscuits, toast, eggs any style, bacon, at least two kinds of sausage, ham, fish, grits, rice, and oatmeal or Cream of Wheat. Not to mention cornflakes, fruit, or cinnamon toast. Flapjacks, waffles, and sticky buns rounded out the weekend variety, and sometimes scrambled eggs with sweetbreads. But the best breakfast was Da's smothered crabmeat gravy with smoked bacon and hominy grits. He was the master of this dish.

We always had crab in the house. It was as much a staple in Low Country cooking as flour, sugar, or eggs. Like rice, crab defined who we were, just as you couldn't be Italian and not have pasta, or be French without a baguette. Every three or four months, Grandpa and Da loaded the trunk of Grandpa's car and headed down to the old country around four in the morning, returning with big bushel baskets of crabs, still alive and combative. Da boiled crate after crate of angry crabs out back in an old black wash pot. I stirred the water with a wooden paddle, like a witch's brew, while my sisters took turns fishing out the cooked crabs and placing them on a long picnic table lined with newspaper, where they were cracked and peeled and the meat picked from the shells, most of it to be frozen and stored for future meals.

Da approached his famous crab dish like a man who was hungry and in a hurry to get the job done. First he fried several pieces of hogshead bacon or fatback till well done. Then, removing the bacon, he sautéed chopped onions, minced celery, and minced bell peppers for 5 minutes or till almost shriveled. Then he put a large pat of butter into the skillet and while it was melting sprinkled flour evenly into the pan, stirring vigorously, cooking the mixture till it was a chunky golden brown paste. He had kept some stock from the big black wash pot and added a portion of this to bring out, as he said, "the flavor of the sea." Adding the crabmeat completed the dish. I am at a loss to explain why this Low Country delicacy was served only for breakfast. I would have eaten it at any time of day or night. I liked to eat it with two eggs over light, a plateful of grits, and toasted day-old biscuits with butter. With all that finally ready, my father, eager to eat and no doubt saving his best effort for Sunday dinner, would pass the last task to me, saying, "Grace the table, Son."

There is something about my father, like my grandpa, that puts me in mind of breakfast. Da could often be found in his seat, laying claim to waffles, pancakes, and cinnamon toast. His mother's recipe for sticky buns was much in demand. Yet the dish that really called him to the table was his beloved scrambled eggs with sweetbreads. Though it is a favorite of mine now, as a child I found it a bit too adult. Try serving this dish with hominy grits—a winner—and the pancakes and waffles go wonderfully with hot sorghum.

SCRAMBLED EGGS WITH SWEETBREADS

4 SERVINGS

2 pairs veal sweetbreads	2 ribs celery, minced
cold water to cover	2 tablespoons dry sherry
1 stick (¼ pound) butter, clarified (or ½ cup olive oil)	8 eggs, beaten
	salt and pepper to taste
seasoned flour for dredging	¼ cup parsley, chopped
1 small onion, minced	

Soak sweetbreads for 1 hour in cold water to cover, changing the water two or three times. Bring a pot of water to boil, add sweetbreads, and simmer 8 minutes. Plunge sweetbreads into cold water, dry, and trim by removing cartilage and tissue. Break into bite-size pieces with your hands.

In a nonstick skillet, heat clarified butter. Dredge sweetbread pieces to coat lightly with seasoned flour and sauté. When they are almost brown, add minced onion and celery and toss. Drain mixture completely in a colander and save 2 tablespoons of butter. Put sweetbreads back into skillet and deglaze with dry sherry. Place on a platter to keep warm. Put the 2 reserved tablespoons of butter into skillet. Add beaten eggs and season with salt and pepper. Cook until eggs are soft. Put on a platter and top with sweetbreads. Garnish with parsley and serve at once.

SWEET POTATO WAFFLES

❧

1 cup buttermilk

½ cup cold water

3 tablespoons butter, melted

*½ cup sweet potatoes, boiled
    and mashed*

2 eggs, beaten

2½ cups flour

4 teaspoons baking powder

½ teaspoon baking soda

1 teaspoon salt

*¼ teaspoon ground
    cinnamon*

¼ teaspoon ground nutmeg

2 tablespoons sugar

Beat all wet ingredients (this includes the sweet potatoes) in a medium-size bowl. Mix all dry ingredients in another medium-size bowl. Pour wet ingredients into dry ingredients and mix until well combined. Follow manufacturer's instructions on using waffle iron. Pour batter into greased waffle iron and cook about 5 minutes.

BUTTERMILK PANCAKES

8 SERVINGS

৵

5 cups cake flour
1½ tablespoons baking powder
1½ teaspoons salt
1½ teaspoons baking soda
¼ cup sugar
5 eggs
5 cups buttermilk
1 stick (¼ pound) unsalted
  butter, melted

In mixing bowl, stir together all dry ingredients well. Add eggs and buttermilk and mix. Some lumps will remain. Add butter in steady stream while blending. Lumps will still remain. Refrigerate for 30 minutes. Remove from refrigerator and whip or mix evenly. Prepare skillet or griddle with butter or vegetable oil application. Pour the batter onto the sizzling hot surface, about ¼ cup for each cake, cooking well until upside is firm and then flipping over and cooking for 1 to 1½ minutes.

CINNAMON TOAST

ॐ

1 tablespoon cinnamon
1 cup sugar
8 slices white bread
1 stick (½ pound) butter,
  cut in ¼-inch pieces

Mix cinnamon and sugar together in a small bowl. Lay bread out on a cookie sheet. Dot with butter. Sprinkle bread with cinnamon sugar mixture. Put under broiler until golden. Serve at once.

STICKY BUNS

8 SERVINGS

ॐ

DOUGH
2 cups milk
¼ cup shortening
¼ cup water
2 tablespoons dry active yeast
½ cup sugar
1 tablespoon salt
7 cups all-purpose flour
1 tablespoon ground nutmeg
2 tablespoons ground cinnamon
2 eggs

SUGAR FILLING
3 cups sugar
3 tablespoons ground cinnamon

2 cups currants
2 cups golden raisins
¼ cup water

GLAZE
½ pound butter
½ 11-ounce box light brown sugar
1 teaspoon vanilla

Warm milk in medium-size pot. Add shortening and stir until completely dissolved. Let stand 10 minutes. Heat water and add yeast; stir well until dissolved. Add sugar and salt and stir well. Let stand 8 to 10 minutes until yeast begins to grow. Transfer mixture to mixing bowl. With hook attachment, add flour, nutmeg, cinnamon, and eggs and mix until dough forms a ball. Dough should be sticky to the touch but should not cling to hands. Cover tightly and set in warm place. Let dough rise till it doubles in volume.

Combine 3 cups sugar with 3 tablespoons ground cinnamon. Reserve. (This will be part of the filling.)

To make glaze, mix butter, sugar, and vanilla until well combined. Reserve.

Punch dough down and turn onto floured surface. Knead dough 4 to 6 minutes until smooth. Cut into 8 equal sections.

Roll dough into long strips about 4 inches wide. Work with one strip at a time. Brush dough with water. Sprinkle sugar and cinnamon mixture onto dough and press in. Fold top side of dough down, aligning with bottom side. Roll dough again into a strip about 4 inches wide. Repeat process. Roll dough as you would a jelly roll.

Grease a large muffin tin. Put some of the currants and golden raisins, and 2 tablespoons of glaze, into bottom of each compartment of muffin tin. Place one piece of rolled dough on top of one compartment and press down to fill. Repeat process with the other 7 rolled pieces.

Cover the muffin pan and allow the dough to rise in warm place for 45 minutes. Bake in a preheated 375-degree oven for 30 to 35 minutes until brown. Remove from oven and allow to cool 5 minutes. Turn muffin tin over and allow sticky buns to fall out. Serve warm.

7 THE SINGER OF SPARKLE CITY

In Sparkle City, where I was variously known as "little Alex," "little Johnnie Mae," and "Ed Smalls's grandchild," we kids validated one another with nicknames. Mine was Bernie, a northern name for a southern boy, a gift from a northern aunt who fancied it. But a family name was most important—when at a loss, people might call me "little Smalls." There were the Hiltons, the many Gilmores, the fair-complexioned Clowneys, the particularly spottable Millens. There wasn't a face of color I couldn't recognize at shopping malls, campgrounds, county fairs, bingo games, bowling lanes, softball games, and homecoming parades.

At all these events there'd be food, of course. Every family owned a recipe or two, and there were never enough occasions for the ambitious, the seasoned, or the boisterous cook. People regarded their dishes as family heirlooms, passed down and embellished by each generation. Whenever opportunity presented itself, there were casseroles of great range, cakes of all shapes and sizes, chicken à la every which way, pies made with anything imaginable, and fried or breaded "surprise, surprise, surprise." It was impossible to eat everything—the food never ran out; you just ran out of energy. I relished these public offerings. It was all I could do to keep myself from charging Ms. Alberta's macaroni and cheese, Mrs. Collins's potato salad with sweet onions, or Mrs. Rogers's barbecue picnic that had stewed fourteen to eighteen hours.

My love of food and music grew together. When I was twelve, Aunt Laura decided that she had taught me enough and that I needed input and teaching from Miss Beatrice Cleveland, Spartanburg's most accomplished black classical musician, who sang, played piano, and conducted, and had lived in New York and traveled abroad. Miss Cleveland was big in every way. We got along great. She scheduled me at the end of the day, and I rarely arrived without cookies, a slice of pie or cake, or some experimental concoction I had labored over for her to taste. She'd giggle and gobble up those sweets, then excuse herself, go to the kitchen, and return with a large mug of ice and what she termed apple cider (revealed years later to be bourbon, lemon, and apple juice).

Miss Cleveland shaped my musical expression in a way that expanded all Uncle Joe's ideas, exposing me to my first competitive musical venues, traveling all over the state with me, performing light classical songs and the occasional spiritual in church basements, Sunday school rooms, lofty wooden chapels. The best was to sing on a revival Sunday at a rural church. Those congregations were so expressive and appreciative, they'd be amening and praising the Lord as soon as the first note left my lips. Heads bobbed and hands waved at the slightest fortissimo or high note, and at the climax of a hymn people would be dancing in the aisles— "moving on up," as the preacher could be heard saying. There was never any pay for the soloist, but with a spread of food running from one side of the church to the other, money simply didn't matter. These sisters and brothers had harvested a table fit for Baptist Pilgrims full of the holy spirit and very hungry. Platters of beans and rice, turnip greens and poke salad, butter beans with chopped tomatoes and fresh onions, yellow squash casserole with brown bread crumbs, fresh beets in orange sauce, stewed green beans and ham hocks, wild turkey in brown gravy, hams glazed in raisin sauce, all the friend young chicken a body could want, trays of deviled eggs, macaroni salad, baskets of biscuits, cornbread and hoecakes. Stacked-up pies, cakes (pineapple upside-down being my favorite), peach cobblers, and all kinds of Jell-O molds in every shade. As the guests of honor, Miss Cleveland and I would be asked to "pass the table" first. "All you could eat" was the sum for our service, and from the look of our plates, one could only say, "Well done, O faithful servant."

Family photo: the family with my sister
Cynthia's son. Thanks to Sears, we remember.

By the time I was fifteen I had become the youngest musical soloist in my high school and had excelled as well in my studies, church, Scouts, football, and baseball. Twice a year I threw a barbecue for my friends (we were a neighborhood club), deciding on the menu and, until I was fourteen, able to avoid inviting any girls. Vincent, Leslie, Ronnie, Marvin, Johnny Lee, and Butch all brought cake, ice cream, cookies, brownies, peanuts, and chips and something special from their mothers. I, of course, always cooked everything myself, relying on Mom to buy the charcoal for the grill.

Spartanburg, like all of the South at that time, was awash in waves of social and civic awareness. I had grown up climbing the stairs to the "colored section" of our segregated movie theater, knowing there were doors I could not enter, places where I could not eat. At any time now our phone might ring, or the door might be flung open by one of my sisters rushing in to announce that Raymond, Brenda, Patricia, or Howard had been arrested while sitting at the soda fountain at Woolworth's, or clubbed while clinging to a water fountain marked "Whites Only." I involved myself in a school boycott and sit-in around the issue of inferior learning materials. Taking center stage, I sang the words I'd written, while playing every octave of that piano: "Yesterday, we were chained and bound and tossed away. Now we've broken bounds and we're here to stay." Walking back to my seat, the gathered crowd still applauding, I felt as if I had crossed over to another consciousness, a new destiny. Nothing would ever be the same, ever.

At fifteen I left the familiarity of my community for Spartanburg High School—all-white, mostly affluent, highly ranked, in Spartanburg's choicest neighborhood. My life changed dramatically. There was some catching up to do (an effect of those inferior learning materials), but being the only black student in most of my classes, a Smalls, and scared of failure, I was long on determination. I became a soloist shortly after entering the music class of Mr. John Mabrey, who loved my voice and wrote arrangements to show me off. Still, being at an all-white school was as complete a cultural change as any I've experienced. As the grandson of Ed Smalls, who was the grandson of Monday Smalls, I found myself studying and socializing with the children of Spartanburg's founding fathers. We spoke the same language, but often it didn't mean the same thing. There were different rules, codes, and expectations. As I grew in this environment that had been strange and taboo, I had to juggle it and what had been my reality. Invisible railroad tracks ran between the two worlds, and there were times when I called those tracks home. It seemed too much sometimes to choose one over the other. I watched the familiarity of black small-town U.S.A. slip away. Friends, touchstones, usual habits, intimacy all seemed to go gray, change and alter. I came from this world as Bernie, but it was as Alexander that I drove the family Pontiac through Converse Heights toward Fernwood Hills. I had managed to carve a spot for myself in the white world, had become the child of progress and hope and assimilation. I had built a bridge, bringing with me the lives of Uncle Joe, Aunt Daisy, Miss Cleveland, all those who lived every moment of my challenge with me.

I sang my way through those years in auditoriums, churches, and theaters, at lunches, afternoon teas, and ladies' garden club meetings— much in demand for weddings, parties, and public assemblies. John Mabrey, my teacher, provided guidance and constant encouragement.

Since it was clear by now that my future lay in music, what possessed me to host my high school graduation bash was at that point a

At the prom with my date, Muriel Smith.

mystery. Years later this question would answer itself, but for now I just knew that I wanted to be the provider of our send-off. I had been to many of my white friends' homes, and ours could have comfortably fit into one of their garages. But I was having the party! Everybody was coming to my house, and that was that. My mother was beside herself. In a word, frantic. "Why must you do this?" For days she went on, but I was not hearing it.

At commencement, as I sang "Climb Every Mountain," all I could think about was the party, and as I looked out over the audience, I imagined that this was probably the only thing on my mother's mind as well. I couldn't get home fast enough; I wanted everything on display before the first arrival. With Mom's help I put the kitchen table out on the side porch, set out candles everywhere in the yard and driveway. Friends had earlier dropped off drinks, chips, breads, cheese, fruit, nuts, desserts. My centerpiece was a spicy gumbo turkey salad with crunchy bacon bits, around which were fresh asparagus with onion herb mayonnaise, cheese-and-rice-stuffed peppers with creole sauce, corn on the cob with lemon cayenne butter, pickled okra, vegetable crudités with scallion and crab-meat dressing, and skillet cornbread with fresh sage. A friend's mother had baked a large layered sheet cake with the school colors. This act of creativity threatened to poison us all, as the black and red dye meant only for the top layer of frosting had penetrated the top layer of her yellow cake mix.

Soon, cars lined the curbs of High Street and Woodview Avenue, music jumped through wooden speakers laced with strained static, kids

High school graduation:
Look out, world, armed and ready for ya!

who had brought blankets and pillows for picnicking were lying out on the lawn. Midway into the party, it became apparent to my mother that we had become our sleepy neighborhood's entertainment. The largest traffic parade ever was in full swing. Cars as far as you could see were slowly rolling past; some people had come out to their yards and others were strolling back and forth to watch.

I had been totally oblivious of these distractions, and as I learned later my white guests had simply thought this kind of activity took place every Saturday night in black communities. They were intrigued, having their novel black experience, while in the back room Mom, who had just sent for me, was in a panic. All she could think of was a race riot. A white kid being beaten or killed. Her responsibility. My guests by this time were making out, waving at passersby, the hippies among them dancing in the street. Mom, seeing this, went into autopilot. She called the police, Detective Ray, my father, and Grandpa. She could already see the house on fire, people fighting in the streets, the television set out the front door and rounding the corner. The police came, the detective came, and Mom settled down. The crowds left, no silverware was missing, and the dozen of us who remained sat out on the front lawn telling stories, drinking beer, and singing love songs to each other.

In Spartanburg people who didn't even know my name had begun to call me "the singer," and I felt I needed to prove myself in other ways. Awarded music scholarships at a couple of colleges, I turned them down and drifted instead into Wofford College, a local all-male school for southern gentlemen from well-heeled families.

I'll never forget my roommate's face when he opened the door to our room that Sunday morning, the first day of orientation. "You're black," he said. That may have been the first time I really needed to hear that. If there had been any doubt in my mind (and there were times), I would never forget it again. He moved out by the end of the week, and I had a room all to myself. It was in this room that Cafe Alexander took flight, aided by two hot plates, my friend Bougie's microwave (first one I ever saw), a small refrigerator, and cases of food from dear old Dad.

But after a year, missing the challenge of music, I left for Chicago to stay with my mother's brother, Uncle Roosevelt. When I was a kid, he and his wife, Roxie, a gospel composer, had owned a record store in Philadelphia. I had always thought them glamorous, interesting, and sophisticated, but this time my childhood illusions lost out. Though Uncle and his new girlfriend, Miss Reola, had a hopping southside bar-club, big cars, and fancy duds, there was no growth for me there.

So I left, this time for North Carolina School of the Arts in Winston-Salem, where during the next two years I became Alexander Smalls, singer, recitalist, opera interpreter. Miss Cleveland, when I visited her on my many trips home, treated me as a colleague and sought my advice on music and styles. I often spoke to both her students and Mr. Mabrey's classes. In Winston-Salem I moved off campus into a house where I hosted small dinners, often with my friend Denise Dickens, who had great recipes from her mother's kitchen in Valdosta, Georgia. Pecan short cookies—or wedding cookies, as they are sometimes called—were one of our favorites. My mother made these little cookies rolled in confectioners' sugar for holidays and special occasions, and Denise had an incredible recipe for them, which we made often. One night a Greek-American college student brought wedding cookies his mother had baked. (It was customary to bring something homemade to dinner in those days.) They were incredible. I insisted on the recipe at once, and the next day he brought it over. How strange one ingredient was: "¼ cup clean ash from the fireplace." But I made that recipe the very next weekend. Denise, after one bite, could not justify taste versus ingredients. Hopefully there was no lead in those ashes, since I ate nearly all of them myself. I never made those cookies again. But I never forgot them either.

At year's end, armed with a B.F.A. in music, I packed up and rolled out of Winston-Salem, northern-bound. Aunt Daisy had settled in Philadelphia with her old childhood sweetheart; Aunt Roxie, who had named me "Bernie" and always held out her arms, was still there waiting for Uncle Roosevelt to tire of the high life in Chicago and come home; and I had been accepted into the Curtis Institute of Music. So the familiar was wrapped with the unknown and the anticipated. Excitement and fear held on to me with the grip of a blue crab in June.

I guess you could say that during this time in my life I developed quite a sweet tooth. These recipes reflect my indulgence in and enjoyment of cobbler, cookies, and pineapple upside-down cake.

PEACH COBBLER

10 SERVINGS

6 cups peeled and sliced fresh or
    frozen peaches
2 tablespoons fresh lemon juice
¾ cup sugar, or to taste
pinch nutmeg
pinch cinnamon
pinch mace
3½ tablespoons flour
¼ stick (2 tablespoons) butter, cut
    into pieces
¼ cup heavy cream (optional)

DOUGH
2 cups flour
2 teaspoons baking powder
¼ teaspoon salt
½ cup vegetable shortening
½ cup buttermilk
¼ stick butter
1 tablespoon sugar

Butter a 13- by 9-inch casserole or baking dish. Put peaches in a large bowl, sprinkle with lemon juice, and toss. Add the sugar, spices, and flour and toss. Pour mixture into prepared pan, spreading evenly. Dot with butter pieces. Drizzle with cream. Set aside.

To make the dough, mix dry ingredients. Cut in shortening. Make a well, pour in buttermilk, and mix until well incorporated. Roll dough out on a floured surface and place on top of peach mixture. Cut four steam vents in dough. Dot with butter pats and sprinkle with the tablespoon of sugar evenly.

Bake 40 minutes at 350 degrees, until bubbly. Spoon into bowls and serve with ice cream.

PINEAPPLE UPSIDE-DOWN CAKE

8 SERVINGS

❦

1 stick (¼ pound) butter

1 cup sugar

2 eggs

2¼ cups cake flour

2 teaspoons baking powder

¼ teaspoon salt

TOPPING

4 slices canned pineapple
   (reserve the juice)

¼ cup (4 tablespoons, or
   ½ stick) butter

½ cup dark brown sugar

8 maraschino cherries

Cream ½ cup butter and sugar until light and fluffy. Mix in eggs one at a time. Sift dry ingredients and add to butter mixture. Add juice from pineapple slices. Mix well and set aside.

Melt ¼ cup butter in saucepan. Add brown sugar and heat until sugar is melted. Pour into baking pan and spread evenly. Arrange pineapple slices over sugar mixture. Place a cherry in the center of each pineapple slice. Place remaining four cherries in between pineapple slices. Pour batter on top and bake for 55 minutes at 350 degrees.

When cake is done, immediately turn onto a plate. Pineapple and cherries should be on top.

PECAN SHORT COOKIES

10 SERVINGS

❦

2 cups flour

½ cup confectioners' sugar, plus
more for sprinkling

¼ teaspoon salt

½ cup pecans, toasted, finely
chopped

2 sticks (½ pound) butter

Blend the dry ingredients with the butter to form a stiff dough. Shape into a log and refrigerate for 1 hour or until stiff. Cut cookies into ¼-inch slices and arrange on a cookie sheet. Bake for 30 minutes in a 325-degree oven. Cool on racks. When they are slightly cool, sprinkle with more powdered sugar.

PART 2

Other Cities, Many Tables

8 COOKING WITH GAS IN THE CITY OF BROTHERLY LOVE

*T*he Curtis Institute of Music in Philadelphia gives all its piano and special voice students a Steinway baby grand to use while they're at the school. By the time I got there, in 1974, not only was the piano grand but life was grand and so was I!

Moving to Philadelphia was like going abroad. Everything was new and different. It was as if I'd reinvented myself as a character in one of the ongoing dramas that as a child I'd played in my head, searching for an escape from my small-town blues.

No sooner had I arrived than I turned my attention to the stove. The person who'd invented the northern apartment kitchen, it seemed, had decided on it as an afterthought and just sort of threw it up against a free wall! Didn't people in small apartments have family? Friends? But after coming to my senses, I accepted the truth of my circumstances and headed out to find the nearest Winn-Dixie.

When I happened on a grocery store, my first reaction was that I would need to buy several cans, cartons, or bottles of each item, as everything was packaged too small to prepare even the most sensible meal. You would never find such small cans in South Carolina! How distraught I felt as I gathered up the best of what I could! It took me two trips and much cutting of my list to bring home the bacon that day.

Nevertheless, I was cooking with gas in the City of Brotherly Love. School was great, although very strict and infused with European concepts and training, an old world with teachers from countries I'd never heard of, strange accents, and foreign-sounding names. And competition was keen: the year I entered, ten students had been chosen out of six hundred applicants. Located on the famous Rittenhouse Square, Curtis was a large old mansion full of history and art. At the entrance parlor you were immediately struck by the ornate architectural details. A massive staircase wound its way upward. Near the front cast-iron and glass doors, as if the architect had made her a part of the foundation, sat Miss B., as we called her, behind an imposing desk of mahogany and brass, answering phones, directing visitors and students alike. No one got past her stare, her imposing "May I help you?" The words "Curtis Institute" poured out of her mouth like some rite of passage—and at times, passion. She was dear.

The gods of music walked in and out of those doors. One day I had just finished class and arrived loudly in the lobby parlor to find Joan Sutherland sitting on a sofa while her husband spoke with Maestro Rudolf Serkin, then chancellor of the school. My heart stopped and for what seemed like hours I was frozen and speechless, sure I was intruding on her quiet moment. But then she looked up and smiled and motioned me forward.

"I am Joan Sutherland," she said. "What is your name?"

Oh, if only God would speak for me, I thought. "I'm Alexander," I choked. "I'm a singer, too." (Imagine that, I would tell her I was a singer, and then add "too," as if to say, "like you, Miss Sutherland.")

She smiled again. What a large, sculptured face, and so expressive! "What are you singing?" she asked. She had noticed the score in my hand.

I had the good fortune to be working on *Traviata,* the opera she was singing that week at the Philadelphia Academy of Music. "Alfredo, Miss Sutherland," I managed to convey.

She smiled as her husband and Mr. Serkin approached. "You will do well," she said, and grabbed my hand, and with that she stood and greeted Mr. Serkin, and then she and her husband left by the great doors.

I sank deep into the arms of that stuffy old sofa, savoring my moment with the star of *The Ed Sullivan Show* that, as a boy, I had watched every Sunday night. Thank God I hadn't blurted out how, when the show was over, I used to stand in the mirror imitating her!

I was soon to meet Mr. Serkin, too. Everything at Curtis was free except room and board, and I had been promised help with that. But somehow I had trouble getting a grant, and I had nineteen dollars to my name when I made an appointment to speak with him. Mr. Serkin was a quiet person who looked as if he'd been old all his life. When I told him my situation, he began to pace the floor, then suddenly sat at his mahogany desk, staring straight at me with eyes full of compassion.

"One so gifted should not have to worry about these matters," he said. "I'm going to direct my secretary to get right onto finding you some money, and in the meantime, I'll give you whatever I have. I'll keep twenty dollars for myself."

He reached into his pocket and handed me $140.

I didn't know how to respond. "Chancellor, it's really too much," I said finally. "I'll pay you back."

But he shook his head. "No," he said, "maybe one day you'll have to give it to one of my kids, or some other kid."

In 1974, $140 could pay half your rent. The first thing I did, celebrating this newfound wealth, was buy a major steak dinner!

After sitting at the piano for hours, studying styles and phrasing, or sitting on my bed with a score, translating Italian or German or French to English, I found that the only relief I understood was to get up and cook. If I ran into a vocal problem or couldn't get a phrase properly set, or the pattern for my piano class was not coming, out of frustration I'd head for the kitchen. After a few days I had so much food in the house that there was nothing else to do but have a party.

Partly because it was also my therapy, cooking had become the way I liked to socialize. I'd cooked for friends in my dorm room at Wofford College and given my first formal dinner party in North Carolina, where I'd also hosted a fifty-guest barbecue to celebrate my senior recital. Parties were nothing new to me.

But first the issue of grocery shopping had to be dealt with. I teamed up with Peggy Barody, an old friend who was studying music at another school nearby. Shopping with her was like shopping with my dad multiplied by ten. Equipped like the emergency food squad—or better, the Red Cross—she seemed to have so many encumbrances! First her list, which resembled an inventory sheet; then pens, extra notepaper, possible coupons, a small purse with change in case we parked at a meter, and some extra canvas bags to hold smaller items from specialty stores; and last, a wheeled cart in case all those canvas bags and acquired plastic pouches got to be too heavy as we went from store to store.

So off we went in my Cutlass Supreme (a gift from Grandpa), south to Little Italy first, where the supermarket was. I don't have to tell you about Italians and food. The words are synonymous, aren't they? People hurried here and there, kissing and greeting. I found this warmth and respect familiar and had to repress the inclination to wave or blow the car horn at these strangers who felt like home.

Those doors opened onto my first real supermarket experience of Philadelphia. *Mamma mia,* the food, I thought. Endless rows of goodness, a warehouse of heavenly crops, canned, frozen, fresh. We moved about the store pushing oversize carts, running into the backsides of Italian *mammas* and *nonnas,* amid screaming children and loud-tempered stock clerks, who were nevertheless more than willing to be distracted, to ponder the shelf life of a clove of garlic or offer their mother's recipe for a *sugo bolognese.*

Like my father, Peggy smelled everything. Melons, tomatoes, lettuce, even eggs. Once I caught her smelling a jar of salad dressing through the covered top. What a nose she must have, I thought. I learned a lot from that girl—about spinach, for example. Fresh spinach wasn't something that southern people ate; you rarely even found it in a supermarket. It was treated as something exotic, not only never used fresh but never prepared well. So I'd hated spinach until Peggy made it for me, wilted so lightly with olive oil and fresh garlic. I'll never forget it.

After rolling three shopping carts through the checkout line, we packed the car, grabbed our own cart and bags, and headed for the market streets. Small store after small store appeared, with vegetable stands and just about anything else out front. It wasn't enough to have a storeful of goods, you had to take over the sidewalk too! Imported olives, herbs, olive oil (extra-virgin), peperoncini, fresh fennel, sweet peppers in colors I'd never imagined. Salads of all kinds, including arugula—weeds that one could eat and on and on. I was overwhelmed by the variety of choice. Years later, while living in Europe and shopping at open markets, I'd always recall Philadelphia and Peggy.

When it came to food preparation, she had the lightest touch. Often her dishes were Lebanese in spirit because her father was Lebanese. A typical menu would include a large garden salad with a great variety of lettuce leaves, radishes (which I hated), celery, tomatoes, spinach, carrots, fresh mint, and more garlic than I had eaten in my entire life. And I'd never had salad dressings like hers. My mother's dressings tended to be mayonnaise-based; Peggy made a true vinaigrette. I came to love salad, thanks to her. Vegetables were always lightly turned in saucepans, or steamed or broiled. The freshness and ripe goodness were there in every bite, a taste so different from the southern stewed or well-done vegetables I had grown up on. I now had a new relationship with the produce in my life: tender cooking was my motto.

I was like a magnet in those days. Everything I was exposed to seemed to cling to me. I took it all home and tried it for myself—clothes, shoes, new tips about decoration, flea markets, specialty food markets, cooking techniques. Soon I found foreign groceries; I learned to make Chinese food because I could get Chinese cabbage and eggplant. Along with freshness, herbs, and spices, presentation began to interest me. Colors and arrangements fascinated me. I began to experiment with display.

But I also wanted to use, not lose, what I knew was good about southern cuisine. I took southern ingredients to basic principles of Italian cooking. Pasta, for example: I'd make a sauce of sautéed okra and mushrooms and carrots, or I'd try a gumbo sauce—okra, corn, and tomatoes. Italians stuffed eggplants or grilled them under the broiler with olive oil and garlic, and I'd do this with yellow squash. To a marsala—veal, chicken, or turkey—I'd add a traditional southern cornbread stuffing. I kept trying to create a southern presence, a southern edge.

What was missing, I decided, from the landscape of conservatory life was a musicale, a showcase, a soiree. What better way to seize the moment? Sunday soirees at five P.M. would be perfect, and so I set out to plan one.

I wrote out my menu days before, over and over again. Now it was before me:

- Country mixed green salad with pear chunks and honey poppy-seed dressing
- Seared tuna and macaroni salad with okra bits
- Fresh tomato and mozzarella with mint on a bed of lemon-flavored succotash
- Spicy lamb meat loaf infused with currants on a bed of wilted peppery cabbage with sweet potato wedges
- Pan cracklin' cornbread
- Cheese, fruit, pound cake, and chocolate fondue

Since the organization of a party was very important to me (and to my little kitchen), I decided to do my prep work the day before. The spicy lamb meat loaf was to be my centerpiece. I had gotten the butcher to grind up a choice piece of lamb with a fattier (stewlike) cut to give balance and moistness without compromising the quality of a first-class loin. Taste, texture—I wanted it all. At home I put the meat in a large bowl, mixed in nutmeg, cloves, and a touch of mace, and let it rest. Then I put black currants, golden raisins, and a cinnamon stick to soak in warm lemon water until they were ready to be chopped and added. Next I minced celery, garlic, onions, and sweet red peppers; chopped parsley in abundance with thyme, salt, and cracked black pepper (my favorite); then combined all this in my grandmother's cast-iron skillet and sautéed it in olive oil on high heat, lightly browning the onions and garlic. The day before I had baked a pan of white cornmeal bread, leaving it in the oven to dry out and crumble. I added this to the lamb for texture along with the contents of the cast-iron pan, the fruit, and Worcestershire sauce to change the color and add flavor. The fun part was mixing, and I wasted no time getting my hands wet. Put your fingers into that bowl and mash, push, pull, grind, and smooth—what a feeling! Aunt Daisy used to mix potato salad in a large bowl like that. I always felt she was really cooking when she did it, though my mom, more proper than most, would lose her appetite at the sight of Daisy's hands all over the food.

The last ingredient was a couple of eggs to hold the whole loaf together. I have never really understood the power of the eggs in this recipe; I imagine that if I didn't put them in, the loaf would hold together anyway. Sort of like the hamburger, you know—it holds when you fry it, right? But Mom added eggs, and her mom, and on and on, so I always put one in . . . and sometimes two.

I shaped the big brown loaf in a large ring mold, wrapped it tight, and refrigerated it overnight. On Sunday I removed it from the refrigerator an hour before baking, let it stand, then put it into a 400-degree oven. On the pan around the lamb I'd placed thin wedges of sweet potato rubbed with olive oil, nutmeg, salt, and pepper. The potatoes would be placed on the platter with wilted cabbage at serving time.

The other dishes simply involved busy prep work. I marinated the tuna, first overnight with salt and pepper, lemon juice, and olive oil, on the day of cooking to be sliced into medium strips for sautéeing. I cleaned lettuce and soaked it in very cold water, cut cabbage, put cheese in milk or water to soak. I whipped vinaigrettes, seared okra well, boiled macaroni (I always used the larger kind, like ziti). I measured flour and meal for cornbread, left it waiting for buttermilk, fried cracklin', and was set to go. (I now substitute country slab ham for cracklin'.)

Dessert was a breeze. My friend Jimmy Hoback, whose apartment was next door in the same building, had just acquired fondue pots and wanted desperately to contribute to the dinner. So I left the chocolate and cheese sauces to him, reserving only the fruit and cake as my responsibilities.

I made a large bowl of punch. (Just after "How ya doin'?" "Come on in," "Sit yaself down," and "Take a load off," southerners expect to hear, "Have some punch.") And punch we had! Cola-based, mine had fresh fruit and cranberry juice with mint floating on top.

"All God's chillun" wanted to sing and play, so before the buffet we had piano, viola, and flute. Our encouragement for one another's talent was about as thick as my cornbread, which at this point seemed to be overbrowning under the broiler. I raced back to the kitchen and began to arrange all on platter and plates. I had just discovered garnishes and now included a special section on my shopping list for various leaves, weeds, greens, and flower buds. Herbs spiked, pressed, and sprinkled about added fantasy to delicious food that before had seemed to be without accessories. Now it was truly dressed.

I chose my finest platter for the lamb loaf, which had come out perfect, although a bit smaller than I'd hoped (amazing how things shrink in the oven). But that gave me a real opportunity to garnish up a storm. The loaf lay on the peppery cabbage (to which I'd added a small amount of watercress to give it more color), with some of the crispy sweet potato wedges. The remaining potatoes were put into the center of the ring with more of the dry fruit, which I had cooked down in the lemon water with a pat of butter and a taste of honey. Chopped roasted black walnuts were sprinkled over the entire dish, and a pot of Dijon mustard was placed on the side. Thyme branches formed a pyramid at the center, and *voilà!*

For some reason my bedroom was bigger than the living room and closer to the kitchen, so I made a dining area opposite the four-poster bed brought up from North Carolina. What decadence, I thought—now if only the piano fit. I was to find out later, when I moved to New York, that my bedroom concept was called a studio apartment.

"Dinner was served," so to speak. I summoned the eager masses to gather around the long table. We ate and *ate*. Much was said and wasn't said about the food, but clearly my guests enjoyed it. Peggy wanted recipes for everything or, better yet, that I come and cook for her.

Then the musical part of the evening began again, with the righteous sounds of singers who'd been lying in wait for the throne. Saving myself for last, as it seemed only fitting to do, I sprang up to re-create my rendition of Julius Caesar's "*Sveligiatevi nel core,*" by Handel. This was always a crowd pleaser, with its runs and galloping phrases. A true hero's operatic moment.

After getting those fondue pots to work properly (I had to melt both chocolate and cheese on the stove—not part of the plan) and overseeing the dipping of grapes and strawberries and the consumption of cheese and cake, I settled down, knowing that all that was left was the cleaning up. I realized that nothing excited me like a party. I was going to be the best party giver I knew.

By midafternoon the next day, everyone at Curtis knew about the party. Shouts from other students in the halls chastised me for not inviting them. But soon my coach at Curtis offered a warning: "If you don't put down that spoon," she said, "you'll never have a singing career." Ms. Silvia Lee's words haunt me to this day, and every time I think about her or see her, as I do often, I am reminded of her wisdom.

A year or so later I found an incredible apartment at 21st and Sansom Streets, a penthouse with skylights and a working fireplace—what luck! It had "party" written all over it.

Up five flights the Steinway arrived. It took four men, and they were not at all happy; it was a very hot day. But after I plied them with walnut apple spice bread, pecan molasses cookies, and a gallon of chilled iced tea, they moved the piano willingly three or four times until at last it came to rest graciously near the fireplace in front of a large window. I could sit there and play, looking out over the rooftops of the nearby town houses.

Soon Philadelphia was buzzing big-time. Old statues, memorial plaques, historic sites, and, yes, that old cracked bell in Independence Square were being polished, painted, and patched, readied for the bicentennial of 1976. All sorts of concerts were planned, one in which I was to make my debut with the Curtis Orchestra, singing publicly as a baritone for the first time. (I had up to this point been a tenor until I began studying with the Ecuadoran soprano Rachael Adonylo, who gave me my freedom as a singer, and a repertoire to sing. I will always be grateful.)

Coinciding with all this was February 7, my glorious twenty-fourth birthday. I decided to throw the largest, grandest bash I had ever thrown, and my friend Sharon Goldenberg agreed to be mistress of ceremonies and grand hostess. The printed invitations read: "Alexander Smalls (Mr. Philadelphia) invites you to attend not only the Bicentennial, but his twenty-fourth birthday party, hosted by Sharon Goldenberg." The centerpieces were turkeys and hams, in this case both seasonal and appropriate. For the turkey I created a spicy lemon-orange marmalade sauce with sherry, and for the baked ham a mustard praline sauce, with roasted pecans my father had given me at Christmas, in the traditional brown paper bag.

Surrounding this were all my hot dishes. Pork and beans, my favorite as a child, and proof that I had come a long way. Gone was the familiar Van Camp can and in its place were fine dry California small white beans, slabs of country cured bacon, tomato sauce "simmered for hours," herbs, spices, thick molasses, sautéed onions, celery with leaves, green bell peppers, and lots of garlic—a blend of tastes slow-cooked to perfection and laid out in earthenware from Carolina. Besides this, ground veal meatballs with mint on a platter of brussels sprouts slightly steamed, then sautéed with benne (sesame) seeds and bright red strips of roasted sweet pepper. A wide variety of salads, including my constantly reinvented three- to four-bean concoction with baby green beans, roasted corn, and spring red-skin potatoes (and tomatoes, depending on the season).

In discovering Chinatown, I had discovered the wok. What a frying pan, I'd thought. By this time I owned two of them. For the party I sautéed fresh broccoli, bok choy, and yellow sweet peppers with ginger, soy sauce, and sesame oil. This I put generously over rice with julienned slices of scallion that had been first sautéed (till the rice was golden) in a small amount of blended vegetable and sesame oil, and then cooked by adding the turkey stock and steaming it till the rice separated. Various other dishes rounded out the table, including my new romance, black olives, which glistened in a watercress salad washed with a citrus vinaigrette.

The tables stretched all the way across the living room adjacent to the fireplace, which roared. It was a terrific party, but the meal was almost ruined for me. I'd been experimenting with corn muffins, putting all sorts of things inside or on top of them—herbs and spices, jellies, sweet potato fillings, even fresh and dried fruit folded into the batter. That night I made cornbread muffins with rubbed sage. They were already in the muffin tins ready to fire as soon as the first guest rang, when for some reason I remembered that I had forgotten to add eggs to the mixture. Great horror! I immediately enlisted the help of Sharon and Peggy and Peggy's roommate, Susan Tilton, who had arrived early, and we got out the spatulas and put all the batter back into a large bowl, while I thanked God that I hadn't decided on the jelly-filled variety. I started cracking eggs, but having lost touch with the recipe, I had no way of knowing how many to break.

Nevertheless, the muffins came out great, as did everything about that night. Crystal Davis, a "telephone friend" in New York, decided to come down. We had never met in person, and she felt my birthday was as good a time as any. To my surprise and delight, she was fabulous. *And* she brought along her singing group, who turned out the party, performing their rendition of "Ease on Down the Road," a top-ten hit on the charts that they had recorded!

In Philadelphia it seemed as if I'd found everything I loved—music, great friends, extraordinary food. And it just overtook me. I had been seduced by the City of Brotherly Love. How could I ever leave? Why would I ever want to?

By now, there was no doubting my culinary aspirations. If for no other reason than my mastery of multiple ingredients of a varied sort, one could not overlook my ambition and my full-blown desire to cook. These recipes stimulated the limits of my imagination. "I was really cookin' big-time."

—————— ❧ ——————

SPICY LAMB LOAF WITH CURRANTS

8–10 SERVINGS

❧

1½ pounds choice lamb, ground
½ pound fatty lamb stew meat
½ teaspoon nutmeg
⅛ teaspoon (dash) mace
½ teaspoon ground cloves
¼ teaspoon cayenne pepper
⅓ cup golden raisins
¼ cup black currants
1 cinnamon stick
⅛ cup fresh lemon juice
1 cup springwater, warm
1 medium sweet onion, very finely
    chopped
1 small sweet red pepper, finely
    chopped
¼ cup celery, finely chopped
3 cloves garlic, finely chopped
¼ cup parsley (or to taste), finely
    chopped
3 sprigs fresh thyme

1 teaspoon salt
1 teaspoon coarse ground black pepper
¼ cup olive oil
1 cup dried or day-old cornbread
    crumbs
1 tablespoon Dijon mustard
1 egg (extra-large)
⅛ cup Worcestershire sauce
1 tablespoon butter
¼ cup honey

GARNISH
3 or 4 medium-size sweet potatoes
    (yams), thinly sliced and seasoned
    with salt and pepper
6 tablespoons olive oil
1 small cabbage (or ½ large)
1 bunch watercress
salt and pepper to taste
1 tablespoon cracked red peppercorns
sprigs of fresh thyme

In large bowl place ground lamb, stew meat, nutmeg, mace, cloves, and cayenne. Mix and let rest. Soak golden raisins and currants with cinnamon stick in lemon juice and water; set aside. In large (preferably cast-iron) skillet, combine onion, red pepper, celery, garlic, parsley, thyme, salt, and pepper, and sauté in olive oil on high heat until garlic and onions are lightly golden. Add to lamb mixture along with cornbread crumbs and drained fruits. Add mustard, egg, and Worcestershire sauce, and mix thoroughly.

Shape the lamb mixture into a loaf, or if you are feeling particularly creative use a ring mold or bundt cake pan. Remember that presentation is important and can set the tone of your table. When using a bundt pan or ring mold, place the pan upside down in a large, well-greased casserole or roasting pan.

Put thinly sliced sweet potatoes into a bowl with 2 tablespoons of the olive oil. Mix well, then arrange in casserole pan around molded loaf.

Bake for 30 minutes in preheated 375-degree oven. Remove from oven and remove mold (if you are using one) for remaining baking time. Baste dish and then pour off excess oil and juice into a saucepan. Heat pan on high flame to reduce the liquid. Add butter and honey, and cook to a glaze consistency. Pour over mold and return to oven for 20 minutes or until done.

Wash cabbage, slice thin, and drain in a colander. In an iron skillet or sauté pan, bring remaining olive oil (4 tablespoons) to high temperature. Just before oil smokes, throw in cabbage. At this point you will hear a lot of "snap, crackle, and pop." Immediately put a lid on skillet for 60 seconds, so as not to burn yourself and to take advantage of the natural steam for cooking the vegetable. Uncover, add watercress, salt, pepper, and peppercorns, and stir vigorously with wooden spoon for about 4 minutes or until cabbage is tender.

Distribute cabbage evenly on a large platter. Remove lamb loaf from oven and center on platter. Garnish with potatoes. Place any remaining cabbage in the center ring of the loaf and garnish with fresh thyme.

Ready!

ROAST TURKEY WITH SAGE
SAUSAGE AND VEGETABLE STUFFING

8 SERVINGS

❧

1 12-pound turkey with giblets	*2½ tablespoons grated orange rind*
1 rib celery, whole	*6 cups turkey stock (from giblets)*
1 carrot, whole	*4 cups long grain rice, uncooked*
salt and freshly ground pepper	*1 pound spicy sage sausage*
⅓ cup butter (or ⅓ cup olive oil)	*1 tablespoon fresh rubbed sage*
1 cup onions, finely chopped	*½ teaspoon cracked black pepper*
1 cup celery, chopped	*1 teaspoon thyme*
1 cup carrots, thinly sliced	*2 eggs*
½ cup parsley, chopped	*2 sprigs fresh rosemary*
1 cup orange juice	*more olive oil for rubbing on turkey*

Boil giblets until tender in water in a large stockpot with 1 celery rib, 1 carrot, and salt and pepper to taste. Add additional water as needed, reserving 6–7 cups. Chop giblets and reserve.

Clean turkey; pat cavity dry, and sprinkle with salt and pepper to taste. Melt butter in a large saucepan, add onions, chopped celery, chopped carrots, and parsley, and sauté until onions are tender (about 4 minutes). Add juice, rind, stock, and 1 teaspoon salt, and bring to a boil. Stir in rice and cook on high flame until most of liquid is absorbed. Place lid on saucepan and cook on low flame until rice is dry and tender.

Place sausage in heavy skillet and with fork or wooden spoon break apart as you sauté on high heat until it crumbles and browns. Add sage, cracked black pepper, and thyme.

In a large bowl mix together giblets, sausage, eggs, and rice mixture. Stuff body and neck cavities of turkey; reserve extra in casserole. Close neck cavity with toothpicks and tie legs under band of skin at tail. Place breast side up in shallow roasting pan. Insert rosemary sprigs under skin (breast, thighs, etc.). Rub with olive oil and more salt and pepper. Place foil tent over bird. Roast at 325 degrees for 4 hours. Remove from oven and glaze with honey mustard sauce (see page 102). Return to oven for 30 minutes.

HONEY MUSTARD SAUCE

✌

1 tablespoon butter

1 cup honey

1 teaspoon grated lemon rind

1 teaspoon grated orange rind

¼ cup orange juice

1 tablespoon Dijon mustard

½ teaspoon nutmeg

¼ cup heavy or whipping cream

In saucepan melt butter over medium heat and mix in all other ingredients except cream. Stir or whisk evenly while heating, about 3 minutes. Add cream and whip for an additional 2 to 3 minutes until sauce is hot and smooth. Pour over turkey, reserving some for a touch-up before presentation.

BARBECUED BAKED BEANS

ॐ

1 pound California small white beans
1/2 cup onions, finely chopped
1/2 cup celery with leaves, finely
    chopped
1/4 cup green bell pepper, chopped
1 tablespoon garlic, minced
3 tablespoons olive oil
1 16-ounce can tomato sauce or 6 large
    fresh tomatoes chopped and stewed
    for 1 hour
1/4 cup dark brown sugar

1/4 cup thick molasses
1 tablespoon dry mustard
3 tablespoons Worcestershire sauce
1/2 teaspoon ground cloves
chicken, veal, or pork stock
    (optional)
2 bay leaves
1 teaspoon salt
1 teaspoon cracked black pepper
1 teaspoon fresh thyme
1 cup country-cured slab bacon, diced

Wash beans, place in large pot and cover with cool water, boil for 5 minutes, and remove from heat; let sit for 1 hour with tight lid. In cast-iron skillet, sauté onions, celery, bell pepper, and garlic in olive oil on a high flame for 4 minutes or until onion is translucent. Add tomato sauce, sugar, molasses, mustard, Worcestershire sauce, and cloves, and simmer for 30 minutes. Pour off water from beans and replace with 3½ cups (approximately) fresh cool water or meat stock. Add bay leaves, salt, pepper, and thyme. Let simmer, covered, until beans are tender. Sauté bacon cubes; drain. Drain liquid from beans and reserve. Combine beans and tomato sauce in Dutch oven or bean pot. Top with bacon and bake in 300-degree oven for 3 to 5 hours. Stir beans now and then, adding reserved liquid when needed.

SEARED TUNA AND PASTA SALAD

6–8 SERVINGS

❧

TUNA

pinch salt

½ teaspoon pepper

¼ cup lemon juice

½ teaspoon nutmeg

¼ cup olive oil

1 tablespoon onion, minced

1½ teaspoons garlic, minced

1 fresh tuna steak, 1 inch thick

  (about 2 pounds)

Mix all ingredients except the tuna, then pour marinade evenly over tuna steak. Refrigerate for a minimum of 3 hours.

PASTA

1 pound large ziti or rigatoni,
  cooked

½ cup sweet pickle relish

½ cup celery, chopped fine

½ cup sweet onion, chopped fine

1 cup well-seared okra, thinly sliced

½ cup sweet yellow pepper, blanched
  and thinly sliced

1 cup mayonnaise

1 tablespoon Dijon mustard

½ teaspoon cayenne pepper

½ teaspoon celery seed

salt and pepper to taste

In large bowl mix all ingredients. Refrigerate.

FINISHING THE SALAD

Remove tuna from marinade and slice into ½-inch strips. In large, well-oiled cast-iron skillet sear strips on high flame to desired doneness (I like mine rare), about 2 to 3 minutes for each strip. Remove from heat and drain on paper towels. Arrange pasta salad on large serving platter with tuna strips around or on top.

SAGE CORNBREAD

6–8 SERVINGS

❧

3 tablespoons olive oil, plus some for
   greasing skillet
2⅔ cups white cornmeal
1 cup all-purpose flour
1½ teaspoons fresh rubbed sage
1 teaspoon salt

1 teaspoon baking powder
1 teaspoon freshly ground black pepper
3 eggs
1 cup buttermilk
1 cup milk
1 cup fresh corn kernels

Grease a 10-inch cast-iron skillet. In a mixing bowl, combine all the dry ingredients. In another bowl, combine the 3 tablespoons of olive oil, eggs, buttermilk, and milk and pour into the dry mixture. Blend quickly with a wooden spoon (do not overbeat). Stir in the corn. Pour the batter into the skillet and bake for 30 to 35 minutes. Cool for a few minutes and cut into serving-size pieces. Serve warm.

FILLINGS AND TOPPINGS

I love cornbread and often create an array of fillings and toppings for muffin tins, skillet, or sheet pans. Following are some suggestions.

FRESH HERBS: Add fresh rosemary and thyme to batter.

HOT AND SPICY: Add 1 teaspoon or more of cracked black pepper to batter with 2 tablespoons of parsley.

HAM AND CHEESE: Sprinkle a generous portion of ham chunks over batter in pan. Top with grated sharp cheddar cheese.

SWEET AND SASSY: Fold jelly, preserves, or sautéed fruit (apples, pears, berries) into batter. Good as a morning coffee cake.

SWEET POTATO: Whip one large cooked yam or sweet potato with a pinch nutmeg, 2 tablespoons butter, ¼ cup sugar, 1 egg, and dash of salt to taste. Spread lightly on top of bread and bake.

9 PORGY: FROM PHILLY TO PAREE

I might still be in Philadelphia if the Houston Grand Opera National Touring Company of *Porgy and Bess* hadn't arrived there in late spring 1976. A girlfriend had an extra ticket and invited me sort of last minute to attend that night's performance. "Clamma Dale is playing Bess," she said, and hearing that, I couldn't say yes fast enough.

While studying in North Carolina I had visited New York, and when I needed a place to stay one extra night, a professor friend who was Clamma's teacher at Juilliard had arranged for her to put me up. I couldn't have been more thrilled. I had seen Clamma having her voice lesson, and she was a rare beauty who exuded passion and power, her every gesture spellbinding.

That night in New York, full of excitement, I had rung the doorbell to her brownstone apartment. After what seemed a lifetime Clamma buzzed me in, and when I reached the last flight of stairs, she appeared solidly in place in her doorway. At the sight of me, though, her big, full, welcoming smile shrank. I had two large suitcases and two shoulder bags, enough luggage to suggest that I was moving in, and, unaccustomed to flights of stairs, I was exhausted. I hastened to press the point that one night was all I required.

The one-bedroom apartment was like a big dollhouse. Every inch of space, whether covered or not, seemed to be holding something— plaques and awards, mementos and keepsakes, photos of performances, idols, mentors, pictures of Clamma. Her ebony grand piano anchored the living room. Her bedroom brought old Hollywood to mind, with lots of fabrics soft and shiny, pillows, hats and scarfs hung from racks. Under sweet lamplight was a vanity filled with girlie stuff, and large perfume bottles with French names and exotic shapes. Clamma was tucked away in this exquisite little paradise, and she had invited me in.

"Are you hungry?" she asked. What a question, I thought. When was I *not* hungry—and how could I say anything other than yes to this, my most beautiful encounter ever!

"I'll order Chinese food," she said, and with that picked up the phone and ordered dinner for two. This we didn't do in South—or North—Carolina, and I didn't imagine that anyone else on earth did either. This was Clamma Dale magic. I could only assume that she had a Chinese friend who did anything she wanted, including cook for her at 9:30 on a Saturday night. In twenty minutes the food arrived piping hot in white boxes carried by Clamma's friend, who spoke very little English but seemed happy to see her and even happier to be paid. I was surprised when after doing all this cooking he didn't stay and dine with us—had we been rude in not setting a place for him at the table?

But I was glad to have Clamma all to myself. She emptied the contents of the white boxes into bowls, lit candles, and served iced tea in large goblets on designer place mats, with cloth napkins. Music played in the background. I had never had Chinese food like this. Sesame chicken was much like southern glazed fried lemon chicken with benne seeds. Sautéed dried green beans were spicy and delicious, seasoned with ground pork and a grated pickled cabbage, sort of like pickled chow-chow, a southern relish. The white rice was good and comforting (just right for a proper Smalls meal); there were dumplings stuffed with pork—and, of course, another southern favorite, barbecued ribs. I couldn't get over the similarities. The ribs even had the spicy citrus zest and honey found in some southern barbecue recipes. Looking back on this moment, it amazes me that despite the thrill of being with Clamma, I almost allowed the food to upstage her! How gracefully she ate. Her long, manicured hands, rings on each finger, held that rib with such poise! Her eyes danced with my every word, and her laughter brought me one step closer to heaven.

But then, after a quick cleanup, this tall, radiant woman gave me blankets and a pillow and showed me to my bed—under the piano! "Sweet dreams," heard faintly through the closed bedroom door, only encouraged my already developing fantasies.

Next morning I awoke to sounds and smells both familiar and exotic. Bedroom slippers tapped the floor, French arias by Maria Callas played faintly in the bedroom. Coffee perked in the closetlike kitchen, and the smell of cinnamon laced with the sweet fragrance of Clamma's perfume spiked the air. While I pulled myself together in her small bathroom, she set out a cinnamon bun and tea and vanished into her room to dress for her Sunday job as a church soloist. "How do I look?" is what I think she said when she emerged—more glamorous than Audrey Hepburn, Marilyn Monroe, or Lena Horne—wearing a simple dress, a soft cream shawl, and a wide-brimmed hat with a veil that covered her eyes. All I could do was stare, dumbfounded. After a time, realizing that my mouth was open, I closed it. At that point she threw her head back and let out a full-pitched yelping sound followed by the most generous laughter.

After helping me down the stairs, Clamma kissed me warmly on the cheek and made her way down Broadway in a rhythm all her own. I drove back to North Carolina full of a new itch for city life. I was twenty-one and green as grass, and from then on Clamma Dale was "city" to me.

In Philadelphia, the performance of *Porgy and Bess* was incredible and Clamma was brilliant. Afterward, she soared backstage, drained yet excited beyond restraint. When she appeared, I couldn't contain myself and rushed through the crowd yelling, "Clamma, Clamma . . . remember me? I slept under your piano!"

Well, that cleared the mob. While the room dissolved in laughter, Clamma, unshaken, kissed me on the cheek as she had before and invited me to the cast party. There I was introduced as a promising young singer; and later that week, after an audition for the Houston Grand Opera, I was invited to join the company. I was reluctant at first.

I wanted a classical career, and though *Porgy and Bess* had finally been acknowledged as the great American opera, many who joined its bandwagon arrived at a dead-end street. At that time, the only two classical musical ventures open to black male singers were *Porgy* and *Show Boat*. I was determined not to be stopped by these two barriers, as I saw them, which seemed to block promising young singers—if they were black. Once you were cast that way, it was hard to move out. But Rachael Adonylo, my teacher at Curtis, finally agreed that a few months would be good for me. The opera, which had been touring for three months, was to run for a month or so in Philadelphia and then go on to Canada and New York. It was the first time the production had been presented in its entirety, and a massive amount of money had been spent on it. Everyone in the cast was a well-trained conservatory singer with a major voice.

After a month of understudying and chorus I was offered the role of Jake, the fisherman, who sings several numbers including "A Woman Is a Sometime Thing." Without much warning, and with only one rehearsal (without the cast present), I made my debut on opening night in New York at the Uris (now the Gershwin) Theater. Just before the performance, the assistant stage manager walked me through my moves. I was twenty-four years old and terrified. I was given my own dressing room, on the same floor as the major artists, who all came by and wished me good luck. That only made things worse, and when the lights came up and the curtain opened, I thought I would die. But Steven Cole, now an established international opera singer, had befriended me. "Don't worry, just follow me," he'd said. His character, the Crab Man, could be adapted to help me out.

The rest of the chorus was not happy with the situation. Since all the singers in this production were outstanding, it had been customary to promote people within the ensemble rather than bring in new blood. I was not only new but unpopular. Some were blaming me for the sudden departure of the person who had previously sung the role of Jake. Steven's warning—"Don't eat or drink anything from anybody but me!"—seems funny now, but then it wasn't. He pulled me from one side of that stage to the other, making sure I hit all my marks, whispering encouragement and praise as the night moved slowly onward. Most of

Singing "It Takes a Long Pull to Get There" as Jake in Porgy and Bess.
(Photo courtesy of Martha Swope.)

the cast had heard me sing only the few background lines I'd been assigned. I'll never forget their faces when I began to sing. More than the roar of applause from the audience and approval from the conductor was the shock on the stage. And then Clamma made her entrance—in a bright red dress, red shoes, and wide-brimmed hat, transforming Catfish Row into her living room, challenging everyone onstage to give a hundred percent. If you couldn't sing after Clamma hit, you just couldn't sing. This ws my first glimpse into what a real performer was all about, a lesson in the art of performance. I sang.

After the first act I went back to my private dressing room up in the ivory tower, feeling very lonely among the professionals I didn't feel worthy of, and wondering what was going on in the chorus room. When I went down there to look for Steven, the room went silent. Talk about killing a party. It was only Steven's voice calling me over that put motion into my frozen steps. Then applause and bravos came from across the room. I will always be grateful to Raymond Baysmore, a big, very animated, outspoken guy, quick on his feet, who played the role of the lawyer. "I don't know what y'all's problem is," he exploded, "but, baby, this boy sang like we ain't never heard singing! And y'all just better give it up!" At once the whole chorus began to applaud. Then one by one they offered congratulations. I wanted to cry, I needed solidly to cry, I wanted to cry out loud, loudly. But I couldn't—I had to sing again in five minutes. Steven looked at me knowingly and led me through the door back out toward the stage. It doesn't get any harder than this, I thought, yet the reward couldn't be greater. I would learn later to become Jake and feel his pain, joy, and sense of salvation. But for now I was fighting for my own.

After a year my teacher at Curtis begged and pleaded with me to return to the studio. But I couldn't—not only was I singing, I was seeing the sights, meeting interesting people, making more money than I'd ever made. Even stage fright wasn't enough to send me back to Curtis. Instead of a short stint, *Porgy and Bess* became a life song. It would more than overshadow my operatic career. I was to perform in it on and off for more than seven years, and I sang the role of Jake on the Houston Grand Opera's recording, which won a Grammy. On that first tour we traveled from San Francisco to Chicago, St. Louis, and Washington, D.C., and down to Florida. They loved us in Toronto, Ottawa, and Montreal, where my own love affair—with jewelry and expensive accessories—came to an untimely end. A sleepy traveler who didn't count his bags left two thousand dollars worth of stuff at the airport.

When we hit Manhattan and I took an apartment, the parties and dinners began again. Often, after I'd taken my solo bow, I'd forgo the group curtain calls and race out the stage door for home, to put the finishing touches on whatever I'd cooked before going to the theater. My apartment, just doors from where Clamma had lived, was similar but even smaller. Its saving graces were a large bay window, twelve-foot ceilings, and a working brick fireplace that was the envy of every guest. I can't believe the number of people I packed into that space. Many of my friends from North Carolina had also migrated north, to chorus jobs or dance jobs, some living five to a studio apartment, with bunk beds— whatever it took. In New York as well were people I'd met at Curtis and the University of Pennsylvania. I was entertaining interracial, often international groups.

One Saturday night, like so many others, the gang gathered to put the week to bed. Joey, Steven, George, Bernard, Crystal, Liz, Bougie, and so on slowly piled in, throwing coats onto the bed and mixing drinks, talking trash and popping fingers to Aretha Franklin. As one of the few of us with a job—everyone was a starving artist or on alternative employment status—I felt compelled to feed everybody. My oversize rectangular oak Parsons dining table (my design) was set with an array of dips, spreads, crudités, canapés, and other finger food. We were planning to go out clubbing and carousing till the wee hours of the morning: our usual destinations were Studio 54, the Mudd Club, and the Garage. Once we got to where we were going, we'd become a part of that, but this was ours, a get-in-the-mood session, the fellowship that followed us into the night.

I had prepared a cheese and strawberry platter with a dip made of brown sugar, orange zest, grated chocolate, and sour cream for the centerpiece of the table. Country ham and spinach paste with biscuit toast and sliced pears was a great favorite. In an effort to satisfy my need to be inventive as well as impressive, I had jazzed up some old standards. Cabbage salad with quail eggs, black olives, and rosemary cornbread croutons with raspberry vinaigrette got an enthusiastic shout from Bougie (who was always too loud in his praise). But what really caught everyone's eye was the citrus-marinated chicken strips on skewers with a sweet potato and roasted garlic puree, and a dash of cayenne to bring up the temperature on our taste buds. Then I pulled out of the oven cheese corn puppies filled with herbs, which I arranged on a platter around a bowl of catfish tartar sauce with a hint of fresh mint. All this was gone in no time.

Then, having left not a morsel or crumb to an uncertain fate, we put out the fire in the fireplace and hit the streets for a wild night. There were without question too many nights like these. Under the bright lights, and with a taste of celebrity, I sought to leave my mark on the city's nightlife, in which doormen had the power to make your evening or cause you to mortgage your dignity. My freewheeling band of buddies and I considered every night we ventured out a way of preserving our noble status. When we pulled up in a Checker cab, our usual limo, Mark, the reigning doorman at Studio 54, would part the crowd. As we promenaded from the curb to the front door, screaming tourists and the night's rejects cheered us on, both we and they reinventing our lots in life for the thirty seconds or so it took to make this royal passage.

At the time it would not have entered my mind to examine what a young man with serious operatic goals was doing at those supermarket amusement palaces at four A.M., screaming at the top of his lungs, trying to outsing the massive stereophonic output from speakers bigger than his apartment; sharing glances and stories and posturing with the likes of Calvin, Bianca, Willie, Toukie, Grace, Bruce, Beverly, Catherine, Mick, and Giancarlo. Was he serious? Looking back now, having asked the question, I would respond, "Terribly serious." I was serious about me and discovering who I was and what I wanted. If this was to be found deep in the night, in the madness of the last dance, Donna Summers, and one cocktail too many, then I had given myself permission.

Porgy and Bess was off to Paris. That was a destiny I had no intention of missing. But first, having completed our run in New York, we were booked for two weeks at the opera house in Miami. Part of the allure of the *Porgy and Bess* tour was that we always performed in the best opera houses or concert halls. It was first class all the way. Miami was tropical yet familiar and a great place to be in January. The performances went well, and of course the Caribbean influence on the food was spectacular.

One night, minutes before we went on, the stage manager announced that Muhammad Ali, my longtime hero, was in the audience. When I was a boy, his appearances as Cassius Clay, an outspoken and articulate black American, had given me the courage and conviction I needed to succeed. At intermission he came backstage to take pictures with the cast. Clutching my camera tight enough to press permanent creases in my skin, unable to rise to the occasion, I started moving away as the crowd engulfed him. But as I sought to disappear, he called out to me, "Hey, Jake!" It took half the cast calling my real name—"Alexander! Alexander!"—for me to get it. I turned around to find Ali inches from my face, saying, "Jake, now let me tell you about those fishermen." For the next five minutes the world stopped and I got off. He compared

Jake's dreams to man's struggle in life. He spoke of his upbringing, of paying his dues and becoming a fighter, not only in the ring. He said that my name was a brand from the white man, gave me an Arabic name, "Ahad Sharif," told me to rediscover who I was. By this time I had forgotten my camera altogether. Ali embraced me and kissed me, then left me standing motionless and without a thought in my head.

Back in New York I waited nervously for word about Paris. I had refused the contract the producers had offered, and both sides were playing hardball. But I desperately wanted to go to Paris; I was desperate to sing in Paris. I would have done it for cost except that I needed validation, achieved only through the numbers on your paycheck, and my time had come. I had received bags of fan mail; I had been stalked by overzealous fans and groupies who begged for an audience and grace. Now I was holding out for one less performance a week at the same pay, a request I felt was justified, and I was prepared to ride to the bitter or sweet end. I decided to prepare myself as if all were well and I would be going, though my agent at Columbia Artists Management held out no hope. Two days before travel, the call came. "Pack your bags, you win!" said the company manager. I lost no composure before hanging up the phone, but then I screamed! My bags *were* packed. "I knew I was going to Paris," I shouted. "I knew it!"

To my mind I had conquered New York with my charm, my reasonable looks, my dance steps. And I'd turned out some of the best dishes in the East. So what did Paris have to offer?

Allez!

There comes a time in every big eater's life when a big appetite needs small food for a small affair. Hearty hors d'oeuvres come to mind for such an occasion. So, "these are a few of my favorite things!"

COUNTRY HAM AND SPINACH PASTE WITH BISCUIT TOAST AND SLICED PEARS

8 SERVINGS

4 cups cooked country ham, minced
6 cups spinach, wilted and drained
1 large shallot, minced
2 cloves garlic
½ cup whipping cream
½ cup sour cream
salt and freshly ground black pepper to taste

4 pears, cored and sliced (optional: peeled)
juice of ½ lemon

8 buttermilk biscuits, sliced and toasted

Put into food processor the ham, spinach, shallot, garlic, creams, and salt and pepper. Pulse until well mixed and smooth. Pour into a serving bowl and chill.

Coat the sliced pears with lemon juice (to prevent discoloring).

Put bowl in center of large platter and arrange biscuit toast and sliced pears around.

CITRUS CHICKEN STRIPS
WITH PUREE OF SWEET POTATOES
AND ROASTED GARLIC

8 SERVINGS

❧

SWEET POTATO DIP

3 large sweet potatoes (yams preferred)
5 cloves roasted garlic, mashed
½ cup sour cream
¼ mayonnaise
1 tablespoon fresh lemon juice
pinch nutmeg
pinch cinnamon
salt, pepper, and cayenne to taste

CHICKEN

8 chicken breast cutlets
zest and juice of 1 orange
¼ cup olive oil
salt and pepper

DIP

Peel potatoes, cut into quarters, and roast, covered, at 350 degrees for
1 hour. Let cool to room temperature. Add remaining ingredients. Puree
in batches in a food processor or in large bowl with a handheld mixer. Put
into bowl and serve with grilled citrus chicken.

CHICKEN

Slice chicken in strips and marinate with orange zest, orange juice, oil,
and salt and pepper for 1 hour or overnight. Put onto bamboo skewers
and grill 4 minutes on each side, brushing with marinade. Arrange on
warm platter.

CHEESE CORN PUPPIES WITH FRESH HERBS

✳

1 cup white cornmeal

½ cup flour

½ teaspoon salt

1 teaspoon sugar

1 teaspoon baking powder

½ teaspoon baking soda

1 egg

1 cup buttermilk

2 cups fresh or frozen corn kernels

½ cup sharp cheddar cheese, grated

1 teaspoon fresh tarragon, chopped fine

1 teaspoon fresh thyme, chopped fine

1 teaspoon fresh parsley, chopped fine

2 tablespoons green onion, minced

2 cloves garlic, minced

5 drops Tabasco sauce

1 quart cooking oil, for frying

Mix together all ingredients except oil to form a stiff batter.

Heat oil to 350 degrees. Drop batter by teaspoonfuls into hot fat and cook, turning, until golden brown, about 3 minutes on each side. Drain on paper towels and serve.

CATFISH TARTAR SAUCE WITH MINT

☙

2 fillets (8 to 9 ounces each) catfish,
    roasted 15 minutes
2½ cups mayonnaise
½ cup bread and butter pickles,
    minced
2 tablespoons green onion, minced
1 small red pepper, minced

1 rib celery, minced
15 leaves mint
2 teaspoons Tabasco sauce
1 teaspoon salt
1½ teaspoons sugar
1 teaspoon freshly ground black pepper
2 lemons, juiced

Put all ingredients into bowl of a food processor. Pulse until combined, but mixture should be fairly chunky. Chill and serve with crackers or biscuit toast.

CABBAGE SALAD WITH RASPBERRY VINAIGRETTE AND ROSEMARY CROUTONS

8 SERVINGS

❧

CABBAGE SALAD
See recipe for cold cabbage slaw in
Chapter 3

RASPBERRY VINAIGRETTE
¼ cup raspberry vinegar
3 tablespoons raspberry preserves
¾ cup vegetable oil
salt and freshly ground pepper to
taste

ROSEMARY CROUTONS
2 cups flour
1 cup yellow cornmeal
1 teaspoon baking powder
½ teaspoon baking soda
¼ teaspoon salt
1½ cups buttermilk
2 eggs
¼ cup vegetable oil
2 sprigs fresh rosemary

Make cold cabbage slaw, but use raspberry vinaigrette instead of mayonnaise and garnish with black olives, hard-boiled quail eggs, and rosemary croutons.

VINAIGRETTE
In a medium-size bowl, whisk together vinegar and raspberry preserves. Pour in vegetable oil in a thin stream, whisking constantly until emulsified. Season with salt and pepper.

CROUTONS
In a medium-size bowl, mix together all ingredients except rosemary sprigs.

Pick rosemary leaves from stems and finely chop. Stir rosemary into cornbread mixture. Pour batter into standard greased sheet pan. Bake in preheated 325-degree oven for 20 minutes.

Slice cornbread into cubes and put on ungreased sheet pan. Toast.

CHEESE AND STRAWBERRY PLATTER
WITH ORANGE-CHOCOLATE DIP

10 SERVINGS

ORANGE-CHOCOLATE DIP
½ cup semisweet chocolate, grated
2 teaspoons orange zest, grated
1 cup light brown sugar
2½ cups sour cream

5 dozen (60) strawberries

assorted cheeses (recommendations):
½ pound Brie
½ pound Wisconsin white cheddar
½ pound smoked Gouda
½ pound cambazola

fresh mint leaves for garnish
orange slices for garnish

Melt chocolate in a microwave for 1½ minutes or over low heat until smooth. Mix in a bowl with remaining ingredients. Pour into a serving bowl and chill.

Place serving bowl in center of a large platter. Arrange strawberries and cheese decoratively around dip. Garnish with fresh mint leaves and orange slices.

Tip: Serve with sugar wafers, graham crackers, or salt crackers.

10 POMMES FRITES AND HARICOTS VERTS

I'd never been on a plane so long in my life. I was restless with excitement, going to Europe for the first time. Years before, Bougie had spent time in Paris, and although he was very simple and predictable when it came to food, in spite of himself he still managed to convey the uniqueness and variety of French cuisine. Now it was finally my turn to see it all firsthand. And what better way to do it than as an opera star—an American in Paris with punch!

Steven Cole, deciding that the tour in Paris was not the best move for him, had opted to stay stateside. I would miss Steven, that walking textbook on how to reinvent yourself as an uppity Negro, but I'd found another source of unconventional wisdom in Bernard Thacker, who was older and better traveled than I, with a penchant for adventure and intrigue. Still, I had no idea what lay in store for me when I took the seat beside him on that plane. In truth, our large cast and crew were a sight, an array of black folks as different in our attire and experience as a can of mixed nuts.

The company's hotel was a big luxury tower in the newer section of the city. But I wanted the Paris I'd heard about and read about and seen in movies, so Bernard and I decided, after checking in, that I would explore the city and find more fashionable and bohemian accommodations. It was still quite early in the morning when I hailed a cab and said, "Left Bank, *d'accord, monsieur*?" and we were off. My French, though slightly more useful than a Berlitz phrase book, left much to be desired, although I managed to put it on the level of a complex science every time I attempted to speak. *"Ici, ici, ici! Voilà, mon ami!"* I shouted. I counted out francs, waved my happy cabdriver on, and there I was in the heart of the Paris of my dreams, right at the foot of the Boulevard Saint-Michel, staring out at Notre Dame and the Seine. Café life was awakening, waiters and porters in tight black vests, white shirts, and long white aprons were rolling out awnings and sweeping sidewalks. Vendors were readying their stations, portrait painters and booksellers positioning themselves along the river walkway.

I must have toured ten or more places before choosing the Hotel Saint-Michel, a small, unforgettable building like a New York town house with only four or five rooms to a floor. I checked in immediately and went back to the company's hotel to gather up my luggage and Bernard, who seemed reluctant to acknowledge that I, untraveled and untested, had accomplished this feat of magic. Nevertheless, we settled in on the Boulevard Saint-Michel, in the city of Hemingway, "La Baker," Richard Wright, and others. We were the Americans in Paris now.

Porgy and Bess was an enormous success. The crowds came night after night, some knowing the lyrics even though they spoke no English. "Gershwin, Gershwin," they shouted after each performance, offering their gratitude to the "American Negro Ensemble," as we came to be known. Of course the road had been paved for us by earlier productions. Sometimes you got the feeling that you were participating in a citywide spiritual revival rather than a touring opera company.

Bonjour seemed the perfect way to start the day in Paris. Midmornings, I could always be found in some small café having my *petit déjeuner,* although the French version of a hearty breakfast meant that I had to have at least two of them to satisfy me. When it comes to pastries, breads, sweet butter, and preserves, no one does it better than the French. But if you were looking for bacon, eggs, sausage, and grits, which this Carolina boy assumed he'd find in some café, you'd have to have brought it from America, prepared to make it yourself.

One morning, after an early rehearsal at the theater (the Palais de Congrès), I decided to try one of the many cafés in the building complex. Sitting at the counter bar I settled on an omelette with what had become my favorite side dish, *pommes frites,* with fresh whipped mayonnaise. Everywhere I went I'd order them until the waiters in the cafés and brasseries I frequented got to know me and when I'd say *"Pommes frites,"* they'd say, *"Avec mayonnaise, d'accord!"* Nothing like being predictable. But that morning I dared to be creative. Having observed that there were two choices, I combined them and ordered a mushroom and cheese omelette. The waiter was not amused. *"Non, non, non, ce n'est pas possible!"* he said. This was clearly my first cultural impasse.

I tried again. "But I see you have cheese, you have mushrooms . . ."

"Non, non!" He was enraged. It had to be one or the other—and how dare I not know!

Whatever I'd studied in school and my recent Berlitz class went out the window. I'd met adversity. I'd lost my ability to think, even in English!

"I'll pay extra," I offered.

But that wasn't the point. He made it clear that if I wanted such an omelette, I should go home and make it.

Calmly dining beside me was an attractive woman, very well-dressed and apparently, from the way she held her fork, meticulous to a fault. "May I be of service to you?" she said in a soft thick French accent that at once put me at ease. While the waiter, wrapped in self-righteousness, looked on, she politely explained, in English, that I could order only from the menu—no substitutions and no combinations.

Not to be outdone or put in my place I ordered both of them on the same plate. Cheese omelette and mushroom omelette. The waiter walked toward the kitchen mumbling something about *"l'américain,"* but I had just met Netty Bourgogne Berezin, a doctor of medical research and mother of two. As we shared the *pommes frites* and mayonnaise, laughing all the while at our encounter with *le garçon,* I realized that I was having my first French relationship.

Café life was full and rich in Paris—everywhere you went and nearly everything you did ultimately brought you out to a café. Netty, who took me into her comfort and company, loved this Parisian custom and introduced me to any number of places during the six-week run of *Porgy and Bess.* Night and day, people of all ages packed the small tables and chairs closely spaced inside and outside what appeared to be glass cages along the boulevards. As in dinner theater, the chairs outside were perfectly in line across the front of the café, offering the best view of the sidewalk and passersby. You could choose either to sit tightly clustered amid puffs of smoke and exaggerated gestures, or join the parade shuffling up and down the street. One of my favorite stops was the legendary Café de Flore, on the Boulevard Saint-Germain-des-Prés, not far from my hotel. Bernard and I often chatted there with people who recognized us from the show. We dressed with the objective of being seen as conservatively exotic, in classic white shirts, blazers, and English shoes. Often I added a leather-bound diary (completing the package). Holding forth day after day brought us quite a following.

One evening off from the theater, I was sitting alone with a champagne Kir Royale and writing in my diary. I hadn't noticed the gentleman behind me except to remark that he was black and spoke exquisite French yet chose to speak in English, or rather American, with an exaggerated use of southern endearments and familiarity, like a southern black woman passing out candy after Sunday service. He was like a Baptist church revival full of the gospel of James. He was in fact James Baldwin. I turned my head ever so slightly, hoping not to betray my neutral position yet attempting to satisfy my curiosity, when he yelled—loud and familiar, of course—"Hey, boy, I got to talk to you." The intimacy of his approach left me wondering for a moment if he was addressing someone else, though he stared right through me with the saddest eyes I'd ever seen. I tried to pull into focus the picture before me: Baldwin; the tall blond whose hand he was holding; and that high priestess of gloom, bad attire, and attitude beside him—Nina Simone, whose music I'd loved since I was a kid. What a lot—and what a lot to take in! Baldwin immediately insisted that I join them, and so the waiter connected us, me on one side, Nina on the other, the tall blond disappearing in the distance down the boulevard. I could not have imagined a more unlikely meeting on my journey than with those two exceptional, brilliant, accomplished, megastar black folks. They seemed, even in all their glory, at a glance homely, ordinary, and as out of place in my "gay Paree" as they would be in the White House of the America I knew. Baldwin was infectiously charming and full of boyish energy. He grabbed my hand and spoke with the urgency of one who had been waiting forever to meet me, and in less than five minutes I was on the verge of telling him more about myself than I ever knew. All this in the time it took Nina to order and drink two cocktails and roll her eyes cautiously in my direction.

"You are a singer," she said, the first thing she'd said since I sat down.

"Yes," I said, though I had the feeling that this attempt on her part was not to begin a conversation but to end it. "Like you, I attended the Curtis Institute of Music, Ms. Simone." For the first time her face showed a slight interest.

The waiter brought out another Kir and more libations for my new friends, and my sandwich, a *croque monsieur*. Baldwin insisted on paying and watched me as I engulfed this French version of a grilled ham and cheese sandwich. I went on and on about what a fan I was of Ms. Simone's music and how I'd been born thirty minutes from her hometown of Tryon, North Carolina. I even knew her real name—Eunice Waymon. This didn't win me any points, but all the attention I paid her seemed to soften her disposition toward me. We met like this often, the three of us. Years later Nina returned to New York to do a series of concerts, peddling her anger and discontent from Avery Fisher Hall to the Bottom Line, where I saw Jimmy for the last time. "Boy, we got to talk" were his last words to me when, after the show, I raced to the stage and saw him for just a moment. We never did talk again. Reading his books would be my only way to fulfill that promise.

On yet another night in Paris, Netty organized a dinner party for her husband, her two daughters, and me at the Brasserie Flo, a crowded turn-of-the-century Alsatian restaurant with a little old lady as cashier, and waiters who seemed to throw food and pitchers of good wine at people who were all talking at once, with animated gestures and cigarettes in every hand like jewelry. I was reminded of the café scene in *La Bohème* and kept feeling that at any moment a director might shout, "Cut, print, that's a wrap!" When a huge two-tier tray arrived with oysters and sweet chilled shrimp, I wasted no time getting acquainted. After this came the legendary foie gras, a specialty of the house, like chicken livers sent to heaven and back. It melted quietly and serenely in my mouth. Here was a real opportunity for unabashed gluttony, and I was resolved and committed. But to my regret the next course arrived. The waiter stood majestically over our table, his arms and hands full of plates stretched out in the open air, like a live oak beside a Low Country road. There was a sense of reverence in that still moment, like that of my father's grace. The food looked great! Netty had ordered the *choucroute,* her husband and I the steak *au poivre* (mine rare with extra sauce), and the girls had *langouste* and turbot. *Pommes frites* were passed around the table like stuffed olives. If only McDonald's made fries like the French, I thought. I wondered how they did it, it was as if they had been cooked in lard. . . .

Then the waiter placed before me a large plate of what appeared to be baby green string beans. They glistened in light olive oil and herbs. I had never seen string beans so small and delicate or prepared in this way. "Have some *haricots verts, Alexandre,*" Netty said when she noticed me eyeing what would become my second addiction. It seemed I was not alone. All around the restaurant, people were passing *haricots verts,* eating them with their fingers like *pommes frites.* Somewhere between Mom's string beans and ham hocks and Clamma's Chinese friend's dried string beans with pickled cabbage and ground spicy pork was my version to be, much like the French but with a fresh touch of mint. When I returned to the States I would prepare these beans for Uncle Joe and my father. Uncle Joe loved them; Dad insisted they be cooked again with pork until tender. I fried some bacon pieces and sprinkled them over his beans, and now he eats them this way all the time.

We finished our meal at Brasserie Flo with a generous slice of *tarte Tatin* (like deep-dish apple pie) topped with a dollop of Chantilly cream and chased down with yet another discovery, Calvados (apple brandy). Little wonder, I thought, that France attracted gifted and innovative minds—it was the food.

Often after a performance Bernard and I dashed back to the Left Bank, changed clothes, and hit the pavement. There were cafés open all night, discos, cabarets, and jazz caves down narrow alleyways. Once we went to Rue Sainte-Anne to a private club that Bougie had mentioned.

"Everyone goes there," he'd said. "Stars, intellectuals, the in crowd, all the fashionable . . . you'll see!" Indeed Club Sept, a two-story club-bar-restaurant-disco, was the hottest place in town. Gaining entrance if you were of color was difficult, unless you were a star or announced loudly, *"Je suis américain, c'est possible?"* and produced your passport. For all their love of black Americans, the French had none for Africans, Tunisians, or Frenchmen of color. But I was a welcome guest, and therefore behaved as one. Under a cloud of smoke Club Sette sizzled with excitement and intrigue, a roomful of dazzling people dancing all over the place, on tables and chairs and one another. Everyone was too glamorous or half-naked. Bernard and I made our way to the bar, where a black American designer was holding court. I greeted him and introduced myself, but my stargazing was about to go into high gear. Grace Jones had just appeared, wearing a skullcap, mad makeup, and almost nothing else. She squired a few muscle boys and a tall woman with feathers into the room. They immediately took over the dance floor. The French loved Grace Jones. Women postured in envious but respectful defiance and men simply wanted her. At one point I got close enough to start a conversation, only to have her unwary cigarette burn my new silk shirt. She departed as she had come, loudly.

That was enough for me. I was more than ready to leave, having seen and been burned by a star. But Bernard had by this time gathered a small group around him and with coy pretense was speaking the most proper English with French gestures and catchphrases, flirting and laughing operatically. Suddenly a commotion across the room revealed Diana Ross, in the most amazing dress and smile and followed closely by Rudolph Nureyev. Who could compete with that? I glanced over at Bernard to find him silent and *sans le groupe*. Thank you, Paris!

One night we were recognized and applauded at a bar and asked by the owner if we would be so kind as to render a song. My heart pounded, but I had nothing to worry about. Bernard was already on his feet, tossing his jacket back at me, all the while shaking his head, exclaiming how he couldn't possibly sing, had no voice, had not warmed up, and what a disaster it would be as he sat down at the piano. Then he played and sang for half an hour, a male version of Edith Piaf—ballads, show tunes, and even Negro spirituals. The place went wild. I always thought he should have been a nightclub performer—he sang with his heart and needed to touch people immediately. There wasn't a dry eye in the place when he sang "All the Love That I Have Known," one of his own compositions. That night, in the rain, we walked home singing at the top of our lungs, "I Love Paris."

One afternoon on the way to my room I encountered a barefoot young black man. "Hi, I'm Louis Massiah," he said softly with a big grin. He was licking his fingers, and I learned that he had been up in the attic dining with some African students who were living there while studying at the Sorbonne. Louis and I became Paris explorers together, acknowledging our common history: we both had studied in Philadelphia and lived in New York. I eventually accompanied him to one of the African students' meals. They each had cooked a dish on a hot plate and then gathered together for common dining. On this occasion there were couscous and sausage, dried beans and rice, okra and salt pork, and boiled yams. I was sure I smelled curry, but I couldn't say for sure. They were sitting around a low table, eating with their fingers out of large bowls, and Louis and I were invited to join them. For Louis, in search of Afrocentric roots by way of Ivy League schools and Black Studies programs, it was his opportunity to be one with the motherland. But as the son of Johnnie Mae Shaw Smalls, the woman who didn't allow her children to eat food prepared by certain relatives or friends she deemed strange, and as one who had just recently mastered the art of French service and proper usage of a knife and fork, any size or shape, I had a few obstacles in my way. "We have dinner plans with friends," I said, grabbing Louis's arm. He saw me as pretentious, bourgeois, and a snob. Whereas *I* thought, what better qualities could you have, being young, black, talented, and in Paris? Looking back on that experience, I'd be the first to grab a pillow and make my way through that feast.

The first thing I'd noticed about French food was its presentation. It was laid out on a plate so exquisitely, well balanced and proportioned, with form, no matter where you went to eat, even at little holes in the wall and quick-stop cafés. It seemed that everybody ate like this, especially at home. Ritual and order reigned. Walking, I'd pass charcuteries, patisseries, and *boulangeries* full of the most artful displays that were seductive and inspiring beyond the concept of "Cook it and put it on the table and let's eat, y'all." Still, this was like home to me, just fancier, each dish a signature of pride and accomplishment. I understood what the French felt because I felt it too. I began to see connections, to make comparisons. The full-bodied taste of stocks, for example: like the French, Mom boiled smoked ham hocks, and Aunt Daisy used fish heads and tails.

Ingredients impressed me. In the South we had gravies, but the French had *more* gravies—or sauces—and different kinds. I was fascinated by the use of breads and doughs in food creations. Cheeses—I'd never heard of so many. Fresh herbs were everywhere. Some were the same my mother had used—Charleston cuisine was very much inspired by the French. But once, while making dinner for a friend, I said I needed rubbed sage, and when she brought me all these leaves I didn't know what to do with them! Rather than let on, because I was selling myself as a great chef, I said, "Can you prepare them for me?" And when she took the leaves between her hands and rubbed them, I thought, "Rubbed sage!" It says that on every spice can—"rubbed sage!" As much as I finessed this incident, I'm sure she had to have caught on. To this day it's a tremendous pleasure for me to take that sage and rub it!

One night, out alone, I stopped at a dim smoke-filled speakeasy. The room was uninteresting, but I ordered a cocktail. Beside me a man smiled my way as he spoke halfheartedly to a woman of questionable intentions. (In question also was whether she could stand or not if she got up from her bar stool.) As we both made faces about her condition, we began to laugh and talk, he in a heavy, unfamiliar French accent. He introduced himself as Roland Laval, a graduate student in economics at the Sorbonne and a native of Martinique. Roland showed me a color of Paris I hadn't seen, the black Caribbean community, whose parties were mini-carnivals with Afro-Latin music, rhythmic and loud. At one, in a high-rise overlooking the city, I was treated to *acras* (codfish fritters), crabs *farcis* (land crabs stuffed with a bread crumb mixture and baked in their shells), fried plantains, *maconne* (a kidney bean and rice dish), lamb in a creole sauce, curried goat, salt fish prepared three different ways, citrus sweet potatoes, and whipped breadfruit (a potato-like starch) with caramelized onions and bacon. One table held tropical fruits; oranges and limes floated in a crystal bowl of planter's punch. But the drink that was to be my delightful undoing was 'ti punch, consisting of Martiniquan rum, cane sugar syrup, and a generous squeeze of lime. There was not a morsel of any kind that I did not taste or overindulge in, between dancing, singing, playing bongos, beating the tambourine, and being reminded of home, Aunt Daisy's feast, and Uncle Joe and Aunt Laura dancing in Grandpa's backyard. We were in Paris or South Carolina—but we were kindred throughout.

I was still in Paris when my twenty-sixth birthday rolled around. To celebrate, an American friend invited me to a concert by the much-talked-about Jessye Norman, already a big star in Europe but not yet well known at home. During the day, the conductor Michael Tilson Thomas, with whom I'd sung in the States, had called to wish me a happy birthday and encouraged me to give his regards to Madame Norman that night. Two days before, I'd hurt my big toe onstage, and I was on leave from performing, on crutches, with my foot bandaged and covered with double-thick socks. The hall was packed with people of all ages and varieties; standing room spilled over into the aisles. When la diva appeared thunderous applause greeted her every step. I had seen only head shots of Jessye Norman and had no idea of her stature or the generous amount of fabric she so graciously supported. It was as if she had deigned to grace her flock, like an evangelist on the order of Billy Graham or Father Divine. Twenty minutes later the crowd settled down, and this daughter of the South—the Peach State, Georgia—seduced, caressed, and bathed us all in the brilliance of her songs.

Backstage I waited forever on my crutches, no chair in sight, most other fans having given up and gone. Now and then an attendant asked a question, to which she responded in German, French, or Italian through her closed door. Finally, out came the beloved Jessye, in very forgettable clothes and ordinary shoes, carrying some shopping bags. She reminded me of Ms. Cleveland, my old music teacher, who if she had made it might be singing in Paris as well—after all, Spartanburg, South Carolina, was no farther from Paris than Augusta, Georgia. I bumped forward to deliver Michael's greeting.

"Oh, Michael Tilson Thomas," she cried. "How *is* he? Where *is* he!" She spoke in very broad, exaggerated tones, carefully released so as not to disturb her legato phrasing. "Do-tell-him-I-send-greetings!"

Somehow I managed to mention my birthday, though honestly I don't remember how. "Well, happy birthday—and-thank-you-for-spending-it-with-me. Hope-your-foot-is-better." And with that she was gone.

And then it was *adieu* to Paris one sunny afternoon, and a trip to Zurich by luxury train with a dining car that was exquisite, old and full of charm. I felt underdressed as I looked around at the display of fine china, white tablecloths, the biggest napkins I'd ever seen, silver trays, heavy silver place settings, and polished crystal. I had a sweet langoustine cocktail, crudités, *sole grillée Béarnaise, épinards,* and *les fromages* followed by *pêche Melba* with Earl Grey tea. Most members of the cast felt that the dining car was too expensive, too fancy, and a waste of money. Not me—I thought it was fabulous. No plate I'd ever make after that was the same, no table I'd ever set would be the same.

After Zurich came Genoa, where my host—assigned to me by the opera house, Francesco D'Amore by name—offered to show me some sights on my day off. One day we drove his red convertible to Portofino on the Riviera and dined alfresco along the shore. Here I was, Bernie Smalls, speaking Italian, twirling pasta, drinking wine on the Riviera—and getting used to it. We were leaving for Sicily the next day for a month, and that would be our last stop. Look out, Sicily, I thought, 'cause I ain't ready to go home!

These recipes in many ways not only sum up my Parisian experience but form a bridge between my native South Carolina and the Caribbean, as well as European cuisine. I think food is sometimes the best way to get from place to place. Join me!

STEAK AU POIVRE

8 SERVINGS

¼ cup black peppercorns

¼ cup pink peppercorns

¼ cup green peppercorns

8 New York strip steaks 1½ inches thick

3 tablespoons oil

1¼ sticks (10 tablespoons) butter

salt to taste

2 tablespoons shallots, minced

4 ounces bourbon

2 cups veal stock

2 teaspoons Worcestershire sauce

2 tablespoons lemon juice

2 tablespoons Dijon mustard

¼ cup heavy cream

Put peppers in a pepper mill or food processor and grind coarsely. Set aside on a plate. Coat both sides of steaks with cracked pepper and set aside.

Heat a large skillet with 3 tablespoons of oil and 2 tablespoons of the butter to hot but not smoking. Season steaks with salt and sear 5 minutes on each side. Place on a serving platter and keep warm in a 150-degree oven.

Pour off all but 1 tablespoon oil from pan. Add shallots and cook 3 minutes until translucent. Flambé with bourbon. Add veal stock, Worcestershire sauce, lemon juice, Dijon mustard, and heavy cream. Let reduce 5 minutes. Season with salt, take off flame, and whisk in 1 stick (8 tablespoons) cold butter until emulsified. Pour over steaks and serve at once.

LAMB IN CREOLE SAUCE

8 SERVINGS

❦

2 pounds leg of lamb, boned and cut
    into stewing chunks
2 tablespoons vegetable oil
salt and pepper to taste
1 large onion, minced
1 cup red wine
3 cups chicken stock
2 cups turnips, peeled and cubed
6 carrots, peeled and cut into chunks
2 large rutabagas, peeled and cut into
    chunks
3 cups Creole sauce (see recipe in
    Chapter 4)
chopped parsley

In a Dutch oven, brown lamb in vegetable oil, seasoning with salt and freshly ground pepper. Pour off all but ½ tablespoon oil. Add minced onion and cook 5 minutes. Deglaze with red wine, add chicken stock, bring to boil, and simmer ½ hour, skimming often.

Add turnips, carrots, rutabagas, and 3 cups Creole sauce and simmer another ½ hour, or until vegetables are cooked. Garnish with chopped parsley and serve at once.

CURRIED GOAT

8 SERVINGS

❧

2 pounds goat leg, boned and cut into stewing
  chunks
¾ cup curry powder
2 tablespoons allspice berries, coarse-ground
1 Scotch bonnet pepper, minced
¼ cup garlic, minced
8 bay leaves
1 tablespoon black pepper, coarse-ground
1 tablespoon salt
2 large onions, minced
4 scallions, minced
3 large potatoes, peeled and cut into chunks
juice of 4 limes
½ cup olive oil
8 cups chicken stock

Put goat meat into large bowl and add ½ cup curry powder, allspice berries, Scotch bonnet pepper, garlic, bay leaves, black pepper, salt, onions, scallions, potatoes, lime juice, and olive oil. Let stand 1 hour or, preferably, refrigerate overnight.

Heat a Dutch oven to medium-high, pour goat and marinade into pot, and brown about 15 minutes, being careful not to let meat stick. When brown, deglaze with chicken stock. Add remaining ¼ cup curry powder, bring to a boil, and simmer 2 hours. Check for seasoning. During those 2 hours, mash the potatoes to help thicken gravy. Serve with plain white rice.

FRIED PLANTAINS

8 SERVINGS

❧

4 ripe plantains
1½ cups vegetable oil

Peel plantains and slice on the diagonal ¼ inch thick.

Heat oil in a large skillet to hot but not smoking and fry plantains 3 minutes on each side until golden brown.

Drain on paper towels and serve.

HARICOTS VERTS

8 SERVINGS

❧

4 strips thick-sliced bacon, diced
   (or ¼ cup olive oil)
1 shallot, minced
3 pounds haricots verts (green beans)
½ cup chicken stock
salt and freshly ground black pepper
1 red pepper, minced

In a Dutch oven, cook bacon until almost crisp. Drain off all but 1 tablespoon of fat. Add shallot and cook 2 minutes. Add cleaned and trimmed haricots verts and toss to coat with bacon fat. Add chicken stock, salt, and black pepper and bring to a boil. Turn off heat and toss in red pepper. Put on a serving platter and serve at once. Haricots verts should be al dente.

11 MICKEY, BEPPE, CARBONARA, AND CALAMARI

Arriva a Palermo! La città della sud! Bella Sicilia, bella vita!

For my first Sicilian lunch I ordered *everything*. Why not? I was tired and hungry, and I had just found a hotel, so this was a mini-celebration. The waiter brought assorted antipasti—stuffed eggplant, zucchini, mushrooms, mozzarella and tomatoes, green beans, and roasted artichokes—all prepared with garlic and olive oil, and peasant bread as fresh as a pan of Mom's Sunday-dinner biscuits. For some that might have been a meal in itself, but then came the carbonara, pasta with big pieces of country bacon in a light cream sauce with lots of fresh black pepper. And although it was still early, I dared to have one glass of white wine, savoring the beginning of my love affair with Sicily.

The Hotel Europa's balconies overlooked the wide, well-manicured via Libertà, a lot like Park Avenue in New York, and my big, modern room, full of marble, seemed even more luxurious after six weeks of Paris bohemia. And—at last!—a bathtub big enough for a soak. I lay thinking about our arrival that morning. A hush had prevailed when the pilot announced our approach to the Palermo airport, Italy's most dangerous and most feared landing, with the sea on one side and steep rugged mountains on the other. Old ladies clutched their prayer beads, *la nonna* across from me held tightly to her grandson's hand as we confronted the tarmac. But then, as we taxied in, there were shouts of praise and loud applause, my first insight into a people devoutly passionate about everything they did. At the terminal whole families had turned out—*la nonna* was greeted by what appeared to be three generations and maybe half the village, everyone hugging, kissing, and blessing the occasion. And although only our Italian promoter and his secretary were there for us, the Sicilians did not allow all these black people from distant shores to arrive unnoticed—they waved and screamed and applauded and blew kisses. Gone was the intimidation, confusion, and condescension of the French, the indifference of the Swiss, and the polite acceptance of the northern Italians. Sicily was like Harlem, 125th Street, as regular as that.

Palermo also reminded me of the East Village of the seventies, with cobblestones, accents, and kids running the streets. Although it wasn't the fashion capital of the world, or celebrated for its sophistication and international appeal, it was a warm, comfortable, friendly city, and that made it more endearing. On my way to dinner I strolled the via Libertà just as its shops were closing, its cafés bustling. I felt like a veteran tourist—calm, cocky, no longer overexcited. I went to look at the opera house where we'd be performing. It was a perfect example of Italian architecture—ardent and self-indulgent, full of curves, ornaments, carved faces, angels, flying buttresses. And the people walking arm in arm down the boulevard seemed to grant closeness rather than distance, touch rather than polite gestures. My parents, whom I assumed loved each other, never as much as hugged either in public or at home in front of us kids. The idea of such public display, though it put me off mentally, appealed to my comfort level and sense of what I imagined to be the perfect world. I loved these people and wanted them to love me.

Sicily was like an exaggerated version of the American South, where people were so friendly and curious that everything you did in public was pure exhaustion—sort of like being the reigning Miss America in Cowpens, South Carolina. By the time I got to the theater at night I felt as if the show were already over. But the rest of the cast seemed happy, and even the chorus members signed autographs. The Italians truly loved *Porgy and Bess*. "A triumph!" one critic called it.

I immediately took up my afternoon habit of tea and cakes, at a place called Caffè Donney on the via Libertà. I would arrive shortly after lunch with book or diary and sit near the window. Recognized by the regulars as *"il cantante di America,"* I chatted with them, autographed programs, napkins, and baby pictures, wrote in my diary, and ate lots of Sicilian pastries, which were sublime. Into the fluff and puff of French pastries the Italians had managed to put soul. You imagined *la nonna* baking every bite. Every day I ate myself into sugar heaven, bound and determined to find glory in every forkful of *frittelle di mele renette* (apple fritters); Italian versions of French éclairs, full of ricotta cheese and hand-painted with chocolate; and butter cookies in every color of the rainbow, some sugar-coated and others filled with fruit jelly or nuts. There seemed to be no end to the possibilities for Italian *dolce* makers. And as if these temptations were not enough, a small bowl of *gelato* in a choice of more flavors than one could imagine was yours for the asking. Vanilla, chocolate, strawberry, and pistachio—plus watermelon, tomato, even mushroom.

One afternoon I ordered my usual bottled water, hot lemon-spiked tea, and (to start) a couple of *cannolis,* from Tancredi, the waiter who somehow managed to save my favorite seat every day. When he returned, there were more pastries on my plate than I'd asked for, and with a tentative smile he explained that *"la signora vecchia,"* an older woman across the room, had sent them with her compliments. I looked over and politely nodded acceptance.

In a short time Tancredi reappeared to announce that the generous *signora* had requested my company at her table. Well, I didn't want the interruption or the compromise of my time, but what was a southern gentleman to do? I was still my mother's boy, raised too well to kiss and tell or eat and not pay the bill. Tancredi carried me and the remains of my spoils over to the *signora,* who sat high in her chair, wrapped in faded black. Her hair was a dirty gray fashioned into a bird's nest, held together by too many clamps and pins. Black liner framed tired eyes that, afraid to focus on me, rolled around in her head like dice on a table in Vegas. She extended a large frail hand, then beat the seat beside her. Strange, I thought, as I took a deep breath and committed myself.

All eyes were on us. The *signora* spoke no English, only a dialect hard to discern and a little French. After a few minutes of niceties I realized I was in over my head. *La signora vecchia* was nuts. I knew it, Tancredi knew it, and everyone in Caffè Donney knew it. My, how my star had plummeted. She ranted on about her beauty, her fortune, and her dreams of life away from Palermo. She told me how beautiful I was and how the angels had sent me to rescue her. As the waiters passed with plates and trays, I couldn't help but wonder if they were laying bets on how long I'd last. Finally, after many attempts to disengage, and futile cries of "No . . . speak . . . Italian . . . no . . . understand," I stood and declared my need to depart for the theater.

This I thought would be the end of *la signora,* but late the next afternoon my hotel's front desk rang to say I had a visitor. I went downstairs. There in the lobby she sat, with bright red lipstick in a circle round her mouth, carrying a paper bag more wrinkled than her dress. "For you! For you!" she screamed, holding it out. Horrified, I clutched the arm of the bellman as she charged toward me yelling, "Marry me! Marry me! *Je suis beaucoup* rich, *monsieur . . . Beaucoup! Ho molto . . . molto soldi . . . "*

Stunned I was! I hurriedly put some distance between us and announced that she was not welcome. I said I was already married and had no intention of leaving my wife. "Please!" I said. "Never return!" Back in my room I peered over the balcony at the street, where the bellman had, so to speak, kicked her to the curb. Nevertheless, that evening I noticed her on my way to the theater, and again as I entered the stage door. That night I solicited the help of Henrietta Davis, a friend in the cast, who agreed to pose as my wife for a while. We went to Caffè Donney as a couple and strolled deliberately down the *via* hand in hand. But soon, out from the shadows of a marble column stepped *la signora. "Tua moglie e morta!"* she screamed with eyes of fire. Whereupon Henrietta launched into a tirade befitting a sister fighting for her man until I managed to pull her down the street, still testifying. My last image of *la signora vecchia* was a twisted figure diminishing in the distance, still shaking her battered old handbag in our direction. Aside from my mother, I don't know if anyone ever wanted me as badly as all that, and my mother of course had no choice.

Because Bernard had elected to stay at the company's hotel, I was truly on my own in Palermo, and on my first evening there had stopped to have tea at an espresso bar. Two young men in suits, driving a sleek black four-door Citroën, pulled up in front. Upon entering they paused briefly to notice me, then ordered coffee and went on talking to each other. We were all standing together at the bar, and when they paid their bill they flashed American dollars, a signal I casually acknowledged. Then they were off.

One night after the show, I went to the Studio 54 of Palermo, a club called The Speakeasy (all the clubs in Italy had American names). On the dance floor I recognized the two guys from the black Citroën, who were giving polite attention to the funky beat of the reigning disco diva of 1978, Donna . . . somebody or another. While everyone around them worked up a sweat, they simply kept the beat and protected their suits from wrinkles. (This was a crazy place, Palermo, Italy. The men mostly danced with one another and would often approach a woman in pairs.) After their turn on the dance floor, Mickey and Beppe, as I was to find out they were called, came over and introduced themselves.

"You remember me and Mickey?" Beppe managed to slowly organize this sentence. "We showed you the American dollars before," he said.

I knew that flash of green had been for my benefit, and so I responded by saying that I had at first taken them for Americans. They loved this and, fully convinced, remarked that most people did. I was amused. We spent much of the evening talking, Beppe and I. Mickey spoke no English, so it took my limited Italian and Beppe to keep him in the conversation.

After that night Mickey, Beppe, and I were inseparable. They more than took on the task of hosts, guides, and companions. They'd pick me up in the morning with plans to see monuments, churches, relics in the hills. We lunched in trattorias, rustic roadside eateries, cafés near the shore. I'd be let off by three P.M., but we'd start up again after the show and party all night. Mickey and Beppe were totally devoted—every night after my performance Mickey would be waiting at the stage door while Beppe kept the black Citroën parked conspicuously, its engine running. I was the talk if not the envy of all in the cast as stories of Mafia ties and underworld associates surfaced on the rumor mill. But as far as I was concerned, these were simply my friends, who had no jobs and no visible means of income—yet no shortage of cash. I paid for nothing, and we did everything!

I was particularly fond of Mondelo, a small seaside town a short distance from Palermo. We often drove out in the late morning, walked

With Beppe in Palermo.

along the beach, and ate a large lunch at one of the local restaurants. There I fell in love with calamari, straight from the sea, which vendors fried and wrapped in paper cones and sold from carts, with large lemon wedges to bring out the freshness—though if I'd found some hot sauce I would gladly have traded my lemons.

On my off nights I wanted to venture out to Palermo's stellar restaurants, and Mickey and Beppe, big shots that they were, were more than eager to accommodate me. This also gave them the opportunity to pull out of their closets yet another black suit, white shirt, and dark tie. Their idea of casual dress was leaving the tie at home. I told them I wanted to go to the best restaurant in town, and they both concluded that we'd go to "Charleston." My beloved Charleston had lent its name to the best restaurant in Palermo—I was excited! I raided my ever-growing wardrobe and designered down. We arrived at nine.

The Charleston was located in the Vucciria market in the old historic section of the city, where food in Palermo begins. The name is derived from the word *vociari,* which means shouts—referring to the cries of the vendors. The Charleston was exquisitely well appointed and roomy. Named, I think, for the dance of the 1920s, it was very lively and upbeat. We started dinner with an array of *antipasti,* consisting of every imaginable vegetable from the market, baked, broiled, sautéed, or steamed, and flavored with garlic, olive oil, and lemon or vinegar. Then *melanzana Charleston* (eggplant Charleston) and *involtini di pesce spada alla brace* (grilled swordfish rolls) followed by a sampling of *braciolone della nonna* (stuffed steak rolls). I ordered for my pasta course *spaghetti con sugo la granigna,* spaghetti with pieces of sweet sausage in a cream sauce with shallots and cracked black pepper.

It was Mickey and Beppe who taught me to master the art of eating spaghetti, those unruly noodles. Like every American child with 2.5 TVs, I grew up watching Italian movies and bad TV commercials selling Italian cuisine. Chef Boyardee used a spoon. As did I, Alessandro. On one of our outings, Beppe and Mickey and I ordered pasta, and as usual I asked for and received a large spoon. Beppe, who was very solicitous of me, also asked for a spoon and began to eat that way. But then Mickey, who obviously felt no inclination to conform, confronted me and went on to explain that only children use spoons. One should put a reasonable amount of pasta on the fork, separate it from the main, and twirl it around the fork against the raised rim of the plate or bowl. It was fairly simple, and was I ever relieved to be corrected. I had been to fine restaurants, been introduced to families, invited to embassy parties and the like, and here I was parading about their tables with a big old soup-spoon. It gave me real pleasure to be sitting up in the Charleston wrapping spaghetti around my fork.

By the time the veal chop came, with roasted potatoes and scented spinach, I was well into food *paradiso.* Not having the sense to stop, I challenged myself to eat everything in sight. And there was no way I was leaving the Charleston without a *dolce* from its famous *pasticceria* next door. We rolled in for tea and tangerines Charleston, a specialty of the house. We had been dining for nearly four hours—sweet delight, I say.

Despite calls from home and general concern from friends stateside about the doings of the Red Brigade, I hadn't bothered to watch much television and so was unaware of the political climate. Then one morning I got a call from the company manager reporting that Prime

Minister Aldo Moro had been kidnapped and that the evening's performance had been canceled. I tuned in to scenes of troops mobilizing, urgent "this just in" bulletins, and talk of a curfew for the entire country. The government had warned foreigners to stay in their hotels until further notice. But I had plans, didn't have sense enough to be scared, and didn't want to be cooped up. Mickey and Beppe, who felt the same way, braved the streets to get me. People were marching down the via Libertà amid sirens and racing police cars. *Un grande Cassino!* One could only wonder. Out the back door I slipped and was off with the boys.

We drove all around the seaside and up into the mountains that beautiful sunny day, and toured an old, gold-encrusted church. Occasionally we passed military convoys on the road. The *carabinieri* were by far the most frightening. They'd often come into a nightclub, stop the music, challenge people, and at times even arrest someone for no clear reason. One night in a club called Easygoing I had been pinned up against a wall, frisked, and badly dealt with, yet luckily not hauled off to jail. Still, that incident had posed little real threat.

Then Mickey, Beppe, and I came to a junction where a massive roadblock was assembled. Soldiers, after ordering us out of the car, began to search it. Suddenly I was terrified! They were mean-looking men, wearing more artillery than a Chanel jacket has buttons. And there I was with my bodyguards, who I already suspected were in the Mafia. All I could think was, Oh, my God, is this how it ends? I reach to scratch my nervous itch and buy the olive grove? But they let us go—being ordered back to my hotel seemed more a blessing than an inconvenience—and after a few days I was able to resume my tasting travels with Mickey and Beppe.

What I liked about Sicilian food was that it was warm, homey, and simple, but with a bold taste. To me, southern food in any country seems to be that way. An Italian risotto, made with rice and chicken or fish or veal stock, the stock reduced to create a creamy effect, may well be a chicken Bob in the American South. For a chicken Bob you boil an old hen, and after reducing the stock you take out the hen and add rice along with celery and onions. In Sicily I found bean dishes similar to those we cooked in the South. Also similar was the concept of smothering things, and the sense of celebration about food that southerners have—as opposed to northerners, who sometimes seem to be celebrating the custom of going out more than the food itself.

I liked the Sicilian method of simple grilling or light sautéing of meat, how they just took a piece of veal or chicken breast, threw some rosemary, a little olive oil and sage on it, and slapped it on a grill, *boom boom boom*. Also enlightening was my first experience in Italy with veal Parmesan. As a kid, anytime we went out I ordered veal or chicken or eggplant—anything Parmesan. When I finally had the real stuff, without all that cheese, I realized the cheese was why I'd liked it—because I didn't care what was under it! But in Italy, because of the purity of the dish, eating it felt extraordinary. It was like bringing two worlds together, as if I'd finally got to what the dish was all about, the essence of it.

My favorite pasta is spaghetti, which I could eat all day long, with or without sauce—just a little olive oil and garlic is enough. In Italy I learned to cook pasta in flavored stock instead of boiling water. Now I'm very particular about it. Most people think pasta is pasta. It's not! The various kinds are unbelievably different, and they even perform differently in the pot while they're boiling. I like my pasta al dente, but most American pastas don't hold up; they can't achieve that firmness and still be edible.

Beppe kept a studio apartment downtown but mostly lived at home with his mother and two sisters. After we'd known each other awhile he invited me home for dinner. From the reception you'd have thought the president himself had arrived. Mamma, in a big flower-printed dress and white apron, grabbed me, kissed me on both cheeks, and drove my head into her bosom. Released, I pulled back, only to be surrounded by Beppe's sisters. My hair, cheeks, teeth, and skin color overshadowed my personality by meters. I felt adored, though scrutinized, dissected, and analyzed, all in the time it took to walk through the door.

The meal was somewhat banquet-style, since Mamma had made an effort to prepare all my favorites. Ignoring the fact that I might not fully understand everything she said, she went on cooking and singing, talking and gesturing. I just smiled . . . and smiled . . . and nodded. Beppe, amused by this, tried at times to intervene, but it really didn't matter; the fellowship and the food made things right. We had mozzarella and tomato with olive oil, prosciutto and melon, baby shrimp with oil and lemon, and tasty carrot sticks. That was simply the beginning. Next came the *spaghetti alle vongole* (seafood pasta), and *spaghetti e pomodoro* with fresh tomatoes, garlic, basil, and olive oil. Fried calamari followed—but Beppe's mother had left the black ink sacs intact—difficult to negotiate with all eyes on me. Up until then I had thought the ink poisonous, but I was to learn the culinary joy of many wonderful pastas and risotto dishes with squid ink.

Just before the main course, a few neighbors dropped by, clearly not by accident and dressed in their Sunday best. They had known that the black American opera singer, a *straniero* from across the Atlantic, would be dining with the Ali family. In South Carolina, too, when a person thought to be important traveled through town, neighbors would "come acalling." This of course extended dinner way into the night. Little kids with big eyes stared and giggled, adults talked about me with exaggerated phrases. Beppe's mother stood over me rubbing my hair and pinching my cheeks, repeating, *"Bella, bella, la faccia."* My color fascinated them, and Beppe asked me to explain my lineage. When I said, "African, white, and Cherokee Indian," they all repeated, *"Pelle rossa,"* very impressed. After a while my face was frozen in a smile, and though I was used to this from performing—sometimes after the theater I'd have to come home and massage my face—it was something else while I was eating. But I was touched and felt anointed and accepted.

After we'd had veal and then fruit tart for dessert, out came the family photo albums, so I got to see more of Beppe, the man behind the suit. Then Mamma gave me kisses and food wrapped in foil to go. How often had Johnnie Mae sent me back to college with food in foil and kisses. It seemed as if I had traveled thousands of miles to find the familiar.

Porgy and Bess was going home, but I, in no hurry to end my European odyssey, had cashed in my ticket and was going to Florence to stay with friends. Mickey and Beppe took me to the station. We would remain friends for years, even as our lives changed, especially since I returned to Palermo regularly. But my favorite memory is of leaving them that first time—me hanging out the train window and they, in their usual black suits, running along the platform, waving.

Whether it was chicken Bob or risotto, spaghetti e pomodoro or spaghetti alla my mama, it was southern, rich, and cooked with lots of love. Imagine spaghetti in Italy made with Grandpa's sage sausage . . . hard to fathom, and too good to be true. Maybe and maybe not . . . see for yourself.

FRIED CALAMARI

8 SERVINGS

2½ pounds calamari, cleaned
½ cup cornmeal
2 cups flour
½ teaspoon salt
½ teaspoon cayenne
¼ teaspoon freshly ground black
   pepper
1 quart vegetable oil for frying
2 lemons for garnish, sliced
¼ cup parsley, chopped

Cut calamari tubes into rings and mix with tentacles.

Mix dry ingredients together in large bowl. Heat oil to 350 degrees. Dust calamari with dry ingredients, shaking off excess. Fry 3 minutes in hot oil and drain on paper towels. Put on serving platter, garnish with lemon slices and chopped parsley, and serve at once.

CHICKEN BOB

8 SERVINGS

☙

1 whole hen
2½ quarts water
1 large onion, minced
4 bay leaves
2 ribs celery, minced
1½ tablespoons olive oil
4 cups long grain rice
½ teaspoon red pepper flakes
1 teaspoon poultry seasoning
salt and freshly ground black
    pepper to taste

Using a large stockpot or Dutch oven, cook hen in 2½ quarts water. Bring to a boil and simmer 1 hour. Take hen out of liquid and skim. Let hen come to room temperature, or let it cool enough to handle. Remove all meat from chicken and reserve stock.

In a 4-quart saucepan, sauté onion, bay leaves, and celery in olive oil for 5 minutes. Add rice, pepper flakes, and poultry seasoning. Toss rice to coat with the oil and seasonings. Add 8 cups of stock from hen; if you don't have 8 cups of stock, make up the difference with water. Season with salt and pepper. Bring to a boil, add reserved chicken meat, reduce heat to low, cover tightly, and simmer 20 minutes. Fluff rice with a fork and put on a serving platter.

GRILLED SWORDFISH ROLLS

❧

2 pounds swordfish steaks
1 cup golden raisins
2 large onions, minced
4 tablespoons vegetable oil
1 cup toasted pecans, chopped
6 leaves fresh sage
4 cups bread crumbs
1 cup white cheddar, grated
juice of 4 oranges
juice of 4 lemons
salt and pepper to taste
orange slices, for garnish

Cut swordfish into ½-inch slices. Put slices between 2 sheets of plastic wrap and pound, but do not break. Put slices together, overlapping, and chill until ready to use.

Soak raisins in warm water for 10 minutes. Put onions in a saucepan with olive oil and cook 3 minutes. Add pecans, sage, and drained raisins. Cook 5 minutes. Mix half of bread crumbs with cheese and add to raisin mixture. Add juice from oranges and lemons and stir well. Mixture should be a thick paste. If not, add more bread crumbs. Let cool to room temperature.

Spread paste over swordfish pieces, roll up like a jelly roll, brush rolls with olive oil, and dredge in remaining bread crumbs. Line rolls 2 inches apart on a roasting pan and bake for 20 minutes or until brown at 400 degrees. Arrange on serving platter and garnish with orange slices.

SPAGHETTI E POMODORO WITH GARLIC, BASIL, AND OLIVE OIL

12 SERVINGS

❀

3 pounds spaghetti
¾ cup olive oil
2 tablespoons garlic, thinly sliced
15 plum tomatoes, peeled, seeded,
  and quartered
½ cup fresh basil, chopped
salt and cracked black pepper
grated cheese

Cook pasta according to package directions, to al dente. Drain and put into a large bowl. Wet with a little olive oil. Mix and keep warm.

Heat oil, add garlic, and cook 3 minutes. Toss with warm spaghetti, tomatoes, and basil. Season with salt and freshly cracked black pepper. Arrange on platter and serve. Great with Italian grated cheese.

SPAGHETTI WITH HOMEMADE SPICY SAGE SAUSAGE AND CREAM SAUCE

6 SERVINGS

⅛

½ pound spicy sage sausage
  (see recipe in Chapter 2)
1 tablespoon olive oil
2 shallots, minced
½ quart heavy cream
½ tablespoon freshly cracked
  black pepper for seasoning
salt to taste
1½ pounds spaghetti
grated cheese
¼ teaspoon nutmeg

Sauté sausage in olive oil until brown, about 20 minutes. Pour off all but 2 tablespoons of fat. Add minced shallots and continue to cook 5 minutes. Add cream, bring to a boil, check seasoning, add cracked pepper and salt, turn flame to low, and simmer for 15 minutes to reduce and thicken. Add nutmeg.

Cook pasta to al dente according to package directions. Drain and put in a large serving bowl. Pour in just enough olive oil to wet pasta and prevent sticking. Toss with sausage mixture and serve immediately. Garnish with Italian grated cheese.

OPTIONAL SOUTHERN TOUCHES:

Add ½ cup fresh sautéed sweet corn and/or ¼ cup of minced sweet red peppers, sautéed.

Garnish with 1 cup well-sautéed sliced okra.

12 LE CHANTEUR

*B*ack in New York, I felt very foreign and worldly. What was supposed to have been a weekend in Florence had turned into two months. It had been hard to leave. It seemed important for me to be in Europe. All I had to do was figure out how to get back there.

But meanwhile I was an artist in search of a canvas, a place to show off my newly acquired European sensibility. Downtown, on East 13th Street off Broadway, I found a former warehouse with a makeshift kitchen and one partially closed-off bedroom. By law it was a work space, so to present myself as a company I called it *Le Chanteur,* a theater where I would entertain ideas, philosophers, talent, and worth as I saw it. I had two more bedrooms built and expanded the kitchen. I was the first of my friends to take on loft living, and they all rallied round.

My cousin, sweet, caring, beautiful Joey McClure, a flight attendant who had lived in my apartment while I was touring, agreed to be my roommate; not as outgoing or experimental about life as I, she nevertheless enjoyed the intrigue I created. We scrubbed, scraped, plastered, and painted for days, then combed and pillaged used-furniture stores. We put posters, paintings by artist friends, and abandoned relics found on the street on the walls. A few track lights and a hodgepodge of tacky lamps decked the place everywhere. At night candles always set the dinner tone, suggesting either bohemia or an unpaid Con Ed bill.

At street level in our building, the Greenwich Auction Room sold off stuff nobody wanted, and sometimes between auctions you could make a deal. An upright piano had sat there awhile, and after persuading the owner to let me store it, I was able to buy it eventually for fifty dollars so we could have recitals. We also had poetry readings, play readings, rent parties, bingo, and theme dance parties like "Disco Fever," "Opera Night," and "Afro Day." At some parties we did, actually, roller-skate through the loft. A friend of mine, a Jehovah's Witness, gave Tupperware parties. I'd cook an elaborate feast and invite all my friends, making sure they promised to order at least twenty dollars worth of Tupperware. The Witnesses came in to sell, and we played all these games they'd created to win free items, and I got Tupperware gifts, so I'd have another party and serve it in Tupperware. There was never a shortage of ideas or a cast to play them.

All this, of course, while trying to postpone the inevitable look at my situation. In truth I was ready to sing, too, but nobody was calling or knocking. People had forgotten me, and I wasn't sure what direction my

On a Martha's Vineyard ferryboat,
just back from Europe.

musical career would take. My professional life had always been under the *Porgy* umbrella; I'd come to New York as an established performer, a "star," and didn't know how to do the rudimentary things, didn't know the business, and had no one to show me—I'd never even had to go out on my own to get a job. I'd also passed up many opportunities to take on serious management, because I didn't understand that part of the industry and thought I could negotiate my own contracts. So although I reconnected with Rachael Adonylo, my teacher in Philadelphia, and went to concerts and auditions, I was in a rut.

On my very first day in Florence I'd met Liz Gazzara, the daughter of Ben Gazzara and Janice Rule, and after a few days with my friends I'd moved to Liz's apartment and stayed with her the rest of the time I was there. About three months after I'd arrived in New York, she came back from Florence. We'd been writing, and talking on the phone, and she'd agreed to move into Le Chanteur with me and Joey, to contribute to the fixing up, and to develop her own private space. She was all excited about it, but since this arrangement meant money, it became necessary for me to meet and talk with Ben Gazzara, "Papa G.," as he dubbed himself in my life. When I was a kid I'd watched him on television and become a big fan, so I was very nervous although thrilled to be involved with one of my heroes.

Liz called me from her parents' apartment and then gave the phone to her father, who roared into my ear: "Alex*aa*nder! *Hi!* It's Papa *G.*! I know my little girl is coming to live with you! I know you're going to take good care of her, and if there are any problems, let me know, immediately! And I'm looking forward to meeting you and coming down to inspect this place!" He went on and on, and I was terrified—maybe because he was a star and so intimidating, maybe because I was suddenly involved with somebody's father—and I'd thought those days were over! All of a sudden Liz Gazzara had become not my friend, Liz, but Daddy's little girl!

But we laughed it off, and the next time Papa G. was in town he came down to the loft, and proved to be warm, friendly, attentive, interested, a great man. He loved opera and so was in awe of *me* because I could sing it! Years later, when I was working on Metropolitan Opera auditions, I called upon him as a drama coach. He never said a word, or coached me in any way, but his intense appreciation for what I did, in his silence and his facial expressions, took me further than his words might have. He beamed with a kind of appreciation and sensitivity, and by reading his face I could manipulate phrases and create a gesture that somehow seemed meaningful. After every piece he said, "That was just great, just grand!" And when I finished singing he gave me a hug and got up and left. He was always this way; whatever I was doing was "great, wonderful."

Ben and Janice took us to Elaine's, then the hangout for the Rat Pack, the crew that included Al Pacino and Merv Griffin, who that night was nearby with an entourage. Elaine, who started as a waitress, is still an institution in the hospitality industry, like Bricktop and Régine and Maxim before her. I marveled at how she worked the room, responding to everybody's need and whim, because in some basic way I knew that I wanted to have a restaurant one day, that what I really enjoyed was entertaining people. At Elaine's we were seated at the most important table, in the center at the back, with Ben Gazzara's manager, Jake Julian, and Gena Rowlands and John Cassavetes. I sat beside Papa G., who nurtured me and touted me and promoted me as a great opera singer and his daughter's friend. And the food—I can't even remember it!

Though money was tight, we always managed to eat very well. There was a gourmet shop on Broadway at 78th Street, where the Gazzara family had a charge account. Two or three times a week we took the subway uptown and charged groceries because the bills got sent to Jake Julian. For the first three or four months no one caught on, but one day a call came from Julian about these enormous bills from the gourmet shop, which seemed odd to him because Ben and Janice were spending most of their time in California. Liz finessed the situation, so we were able to charge for another month or so, until one day Ben called and said, "Liz, the account at the gourmet shop has been closed; you will have to go to the grocery store!" Well, that was that. But the dinners continued. Either we made lavish feasts or covered-dish dinners where we'd make the bulk of the meal and everybody else brought over their mom's favorite casserole or some such. We had wonderful nights, drinking wine until three in the morning, the loft lit only by candles in wine bottles.

That was our Italian period. Marsala was my big dish. The gourmet shop had wonderful veal, and I'd fallen in love with marsala—the Italian counterpart of sherry—when I was in Italy. I marsala'd everything I could; besides veal and chicken, I made a wonderful pork marsala with mixed greens—collards, mustards, turnips, kale. Either I'd serve it with rice—I'd learned to fry rice before I cooked it, like a quick pilau, fry rice with oil and get it brown, and then put water in—or I'd get small pasta like orzo. But for a French touch I used couscous, and felt I was connecting with my African roots. I cooked it with black currants, as I'd learned to do from Sylviane Quitman, a Martinican I'd met in Paris. It was a wonderful dish, an international plate at Le Chanteur.

Liz and I also used Ben Gazzara's name to get reservations all over town. Even when we were almost broke, on Saturday night we'd get dressed up, eat at home, and then go out for dessert and a glass of champagne, which always made us feel as if we were rich or grand or something marvelous was going on. One of our favorite places was One If by Land, Two If by Sea, a restaurant in the Village that used to be an old stable, owned and run by two Brazilians. They had the best-looking waiters, the best-looking room, a fireplace, and a piano player, on two levels, with an open stable effect. We also liked to go to Café des Artistes, which to this day remains my favorite restaurant room in New York. I've always taken European friends there. When I was with *Porgy,* when I wasn't rushing home to cook, a group of us sometimes got a carriage and went from the theater to the Café des Artistes, because a lot of southerners hung out at the bar there. I'd get a warm feeling, just hearing all those southern accents going through the room.

Meanwhile I did my due diligence in New York, but after many efforts to break into the industry, and feeling overwhelmed by going from somebody to just another body, I convinced myself that all my problems could be solved by getting back to Europe. And in order to do that I needed money.

I was still commuting to Philadelphia every week or two to study, and I decided that, to reestablish myself as a singer and to get some money, I had to win a competition. I went into a strict regimen of practice, coaching, and voice lessons, with the goal of winning the Baltimore Opera Competition, a very difficult contest that everyone felt was rigged, the first place seemingly always reflecting some kind of political situation. I was nervous and upset and emotional about the whole thing, but I geared myself up.

The competition was in three stages: elimination, semifinals, and finals. Rachael Adonylo's son drove me down to Baltimore with strict instructions not to allow me to talk during the journey. Talking was very bad for the voice. Not talking was very bad for me—but I wanted to win, so I shut up. I made the semifinals, which meant returning to Baltimore the next week for two nights and earned me the right to chat on the way home.

The other singers, a broad range of performers from across the globe, were incredibly talented. I felt uncomfortable around them, since I'd never been as absorbed in the *act* of singing as in the pure emotion of the art. I couldn't stand around talking about my voice as if it were my wife or a badly behaved child. It wasn't a thing, a life coexisting with me, it was *my* joy, *my* pain, *my* confusion, and *my* freedom.

I was chosen for the finals, and that night I was a wreck. I hated myself for wanting something so much, and for subjecting myself to the odds of success or failure that could be devastating. What was "good" singing anyway, and who could judge? I was indifferent to all the grandstanding as singer after singer rewrapped their vocal cords around a difficult, familiar aria. I followed yet another baritone, who'd wowed the crowd with an interpolated high note. Show-off, I thought.

One of the judges had said to me after the semifinals, "Where's the fire? Sing out—don't sleepwalk through this!" During my long walk to the middle of the stage, remembering his words, I challenged myself to go the distance. And I finished second—a huge triumph, given what was assumed about the competition! I was elated!

My friends Michael and Denise Dickens, he being in the hotel business, had arranged a suite for me in the Lord Baltimore Hotel. We celebrated at a small, elegant restaurant over Maryland crab cakes, oyster and corn stew, fried Smithfield ham with redeye gravy, wilted dandelion greens, and hot buttered cornbread. Then ice cream, pecan pie, and berry cobbler. Champagne flowed as we recaptured the evening—from bad hair to good hair, bad gowns to good gowns, diva to dump her. I couldn't help but think of the moment as a major victory, that I was beginning to understand the power of focus and perseverance. I knew I could do anything I wanted; I just had to figure out what I wanted. This would prove to be the real issue.

Back in New York, friends gathered at Le Chanteur to congratulate me and send me off to Rome for the summer. Liz, who also loved to cook and would sometimes fight me for oven and stovetop space, helped me orchestrate a grand buffet, as did Joey, who brought a kind of stability to our household and saw Liz and me as dreamers hanging on a thin string like chimes in the wind. You could always count on Joey to make some vegetable organic something, or brown rice with baked chicken, or—if she really felt naughty and a little self-indulgent—a macaroni and cheese casserole.

So the gang assembled—Alfredo in leather, even though it was summer, with his mom's lasagna dish; Chip, an actor, with cheese and crackers and an unrecognizable attempt at cooking that got pushed to a back counter; Daniel from California, a designer of discos, Mexican passing as a Spanish aristocrat, bringing wine and booze. Mossa Bildner, who'd grown up in Brazil studying opera and acting, had her housekeeper make something; Gwendolyn Bradley, my Carolina diva and now the principal soprano at the Berlin Opera, brought cakes and pies (store-bought). With Raul, Stella, Donna, Karen, Roger, and the rest we ate and danced and talked through the night. Every bite of my Low Country–inspired *pasta vongole alla creole* was consumed and the bowl mopped clean by diehard diners armed with peasant bread. Liz's lemon chicken with rubbed sage and rosemary twigs vanished.

Before taking another mouthful of cake, I strolled to the piano to reenact my triumph in Baltimore, first imitating all the singers, from the heavyset soprano to the tenor who reached for and missed a high C. I then rearranged my posture for my aria, *"Avant de quitter."* My piano playing was questionable, but my remedy for this was to sing louder. That night I said good-bye to the best people I knew, my New York family. There was no need for Tupperware; we ate everything—even the garnishes.

Mossa Bildner and Gwendolyn Bradley were also going to Rome, all of us planning to study with Ricci, the famous Italian coach who had written and preserved a lot of the cadenzas—the riffs—in Italian opera. Mossa, who came from a wealthy family, managed, through Gianni Bulgari of Bulgari jewels, to secure a duplex penthouse for us. A woman who claimed to be a patron of the arts had taken a liking to me and had promised support. When summoned to the Plaza for breakfast, I got all dressed up and arrived with my résumé and my RCA album of *Porgy*. She ordered me two breakfasts, then took me to her travel agent to make the reservation. Then we went for a walk in the park while she told me about her isolated life and her marriage of convenience. In my naiveté I thought she only wanted reassurance; I didn't realize how far she was from Mother Teresa. What frustration she must have felt that I didn't get it. Three days before I was supposed to leave, she still hadn't paid for the very expensive ticket. Mossa and Gwen were already gone. At the last minute I took half my prize money, bought this very expensive ticket myself, and got on the plane.

I arrived early on a Sunday morning. No one answered the phone. For what seemed like hours I waited on the street with all my suitcases, until finally someone from the building let me put the luggage inside, while I walked the streets and kept calling. When I finally found Gwen and Mossa, it was almost six o'clock. They had taken the only two bedrooms, so I dragged a mattress into the dining room and went to bed under the table.

I woke very early the next morning, about five-thirty. Below me the city was starting to come alive, and I lay there for a moment unsure of where I was, listening to the rustle of street vendors. Foreign sounds. Then I came awake realizing that, yes, I was here. The house was still. I opened the shutters and looked out the window at the architecture of Rome, the steeples, in the distance all those domes. I had done what I said I was going to do. I'd come back, I had made it, what a journey.

---❧---

Interestingly enough, these recipes, starting with the oyster and corn stew as a first course, come together nicely for dinner or a simple, elegant buffet. Helping yourself to southern crab cakes atop dandelion greens, pork marsala of Italian origin, and African couscous instead of rice is like taking a trip halfway around the world with the help of your kitchen.

---❧---

PORK MARSALA WITH MIXED GREENS

8 SERVINGS
❧

PORK AND SAUCE
2 pounds pork loin
salt and freshly ground black pepper
  to taste
3 tablespoons olive oil
4 tablespoons shallots or scallions,
  minced
½ cup marsala wine
2 tablespoons vinegar
2 tablespoons lemon juice
3 cups veal stock
½ stick (4 tablespoons) butter

GREENS
1 pound collard greens
1 pound mustard greens
1 pound turnip greens
1 pound kale
2 strips bacon (or ¼ cup olive oil)
2 cloves garlic, minced
1 cup chicken stock
salt and freshly ground black pepper
  to taste

Slice pork into ¾-inch slices. Season with salt and pepper. Brown pork in 3 tablespoons olive oil, cooking 5 minutes on each side. Keep on a warm platter in a 150-degree oven until greens and sauce are ready.

To make sauce, pour off all but ½ tablespoon of oil. Add shallots and brown for 8 minutes. Deglaze with marsala, vinegar, and lemon juice. Add veal stock, bring to a boil and simmer 5 minutes. Take off fire and whisk in 4 tablespoons butter. Pour over pork and serve at once.

GREENS

Chop all greens into bite-sized pieces.

In a stockpot, fry bacon until almost crispy. Drain all but 1 tablespoon of fat. Add garlic and cook 2 minutes. Add greens and toss to coat. Add chicken stock, salt, and pepper. Bring to a boil and cook 15 minutes. Serve with pork as a side dish.

MARYLAND CRAB CAKES

8 SERVINGS

&

3 cups bread crumbs

2 pounds lump crabmeat

1 large onion, minced

1 large red bell pepper, minced

2 eggs, beaten

¾ cup mayonnaise

juice of 1 large lemon

2 teaspoons Dijon mustard

1 teaspoon salt

1 teaspoon cayenne

2 ribs celery, minced

¼ cup parsley, chopped

2 cups vegetable oil

Reserve 2 cups of bread crumbs for dredging. Mix remaining cup of crumbs with all other ingredients except oil.

Refrigerate 2½ to 3 hours. Put reserved bread crumbs on a flat plate. Using ice cream scoop, shape crab mixture into cakes. Coat on both sides with bread crumbs and lay on a large pan lined with wax paper. Chill 1 hour.

Heat oil in a large skillet to 325 degrees. Take cakes directly from refrigerator and fry until golden on both sides. Drain on paper towels and serve at once. Great with tartar sauce or herb mayonnaise.

OYSTER AND CORN STEW

❧

1½ sticks (12 tablespoons) butter

1 large onion, minced

1 clove garlic, minced

1 rib celery, minced

1 leek, cleaned, sliced, and chopped

4 ears fresh corn, kernels removed

3 tablespoons flour

4½ cups milk

½ cup cream

1 teaspoon salt

freshly ground black pepper

5 pints oysters with liquor

¼ cup parsley, chopped

Melt butter, add onion and garlic, and cook until translucent, 4 minutes. Add celery, leek, corn kernels, and flour. Cook, stirring often, 5 minutes. Add milk, cream, and seasonings. Bring to a simmer and cook 5 minutes. Add oysters and liquor and cook 4 minutes. Mix in chopped parsley and serve at once.

COUSCOUS WITH BLACK CURRANTS

8 SERVINGS

2 cups couscous

1 cup black currants

3 cups hot water

½ stick (4 tablespoons) butter
* (or ¼ cup olive oil)*

1 teaspoon orange rind

½ cup toasted pecans, chopped

3 scallions, minced

¼ cup parsley, chopped

salt and freshly ground black
* pepper*

Put couscous in a medium-size bowl with currants. Bring water to a boil with butter. Pour boiling water over couscous and toss to coat grains evenly. Cover with plastic wrap and let steam for 15 minutes.

Uncover, fluff, and add rest of ingredients. Serve warm or chilled.

WILTED DANDELION GREENS

❧

3 quarts dandelion greens (stems
discarded), coarsely chopped
1 cup slab bacon, cubed
1 clove garlic, minced
1 tablespoon shallot, minced
½ cup Dijon mustard
¼ cup Champagne wine vinegar
¼ cup sorghum
salt and pepper

Place washed and dried dandelion greens in a large serving bowl. Cook bacon until crisp. Add garlic and shallot and cook 3 minutes until transparent. Whisk in mustard, vinegar, sorghum, salt, and pepper and cook 2 minutes. Pour over dandelion greens and toss well. Serve immediately.

13 CASSIUS CLAY AND IMPORTED OKRA

*I*n Rome *La Dolce Vita* was more than a great movie; it was most certainly my theme song, and not knowing how long I'd be there, I planned to *dolce* myself to death. I felt different this time in Europe. Not a star but still a curiosity, I was more an accepted *straniero* sharing the space. I made fast friends of everyone. Mornings, in the piazza in front of the Pantheon, the ever-there and ever-ready Tony served me weak tea, blood orange juice, and *panni.* Gwendolyn Bradley and Mossa Bildner often joined me for *caffè latte* and a short walk across the river to a *scuola Italiano,* where Gwendolyn and I had enrolled in the vain hope of speaking fluent Italian in six weeks.

After school I usually strolled through the market in the Campo dei Fiori, a beautiful square framed by ornate palazzos, an oasis at the end of several long, narrow, winding cobblestone streets. Vast quantities and varieties of food lay on makeshift wooden tables and filled rows and rows of crates and paper cartons. Vendors shouted to shoppers, who rambled through with poised indifference, bantering back and forth, matching the sellers grunt for grunt. Shopping there was not a job for the timid—a raised voice could make all the difference. But one always behaved graciously after a battle and was often rewarded by the vendor's offering to close the sale with an extra pepper or zucchini.

Mossa Bildner, insider to the Italian social mafia, wasted no time putting her list of friends and contacts to use. Our first few weeks were like one coming-out party after another as we presented ourselves freshly scrubbed, polished, and charmingly interested to a long line of strangers. We were displayed at luncheons, cocktails, dinners, concerts.

Most memorable, though, was our Saturday luncheon at the home of Emma Bisconti, a tall, attractive woman, originally from Mexico, who would, by her generosity, become our godmother and sponsor. Her husband, always referred to as "him," was a very successful international attorney, and they lived on the outskirts of Rome in a large compound surrounded by high walls. It was explained to me that due to the fear of terrorism and the threat of kidnapping, which had become the job of choice for many, wealthy and influential Italians were at great risk. When Emma's driver, whom she had sent for us, pulled up to the Bisconti fortress, we were greeted by huge black Great Danes, trained attack dogs galloping about salivating—over the taste of my leg, I imagined, or worse. Young Mexican girls struggled to contain them and put them away, as we all agreed not to put one foot on soil until they were well out of sight.

Safely inside, we were treated to warm hospitality and made to feel as if the occasion were for us. Already present were other guests—a single gentleman about forty, introduced as a prince (fair game for Mossa, who I felt secretly sought to bring a title home with her), and to our great surprise, neighbors of Emma's, the celebrated baritone Tito Gobbi and his lovely wife. Clearly this was not to be an ordinary luncheon. Sitting very calmly in a corner was a beautiful older lady with the most remarkable face, perfect posture, and impeccable attire. How soft she appeared, not a rude gesture in her repertoire. I was drawn to her. "Allow me to present the Contessa Bonmartini," said Emma. There could have been trumpets, the moment definitely called for them. A princess, not a queen, something still naive about her. The problem was that I had simply no reference for an old princess. To my good fortune she was seated across from me at the table.

Emma's china was beautiful, and polished silver framed each place setting. Light yellow napkins, pressed and specifically placed over each plate, added a warm softness. Crystal glasses, handblown and almost too fragile to grasp, held water and white wine. Emma, who loved to entertain and was one of Rome's prominent hosts, had found ways to marry the best of her heritage with the Italian foods she loved. Up to this moment my exposure to Mexican food had been fast-food joints, canned goods, and overdone beans with ground chili. Taco Villa, Bella, or Bell just didn't work for me. But Emma's cooking did. Some of the dishes were foreign and hard to place, but extraordinary. I remember an array of relishes and corn cakes, sweet and peppery. A chilled soup of tomatoes, sweet peppers, celery, roasted corn, and spices. Then what appeared to be polenta cakes with beans and chicken in a spiced tomato sauce with a taste of coriander, and a small grilled paillard of beef, with a well-seasoned salad washed down by a Chianti reserve (in different, wider crystal glasses).

Tito Gobbi, who sat at the head of the table next to me, was impressive and loud, as if onstage developing a character before my eyes. At last the feared subject presented itself with a roar from his chest. "You are a singer, I understand."

I began to grow smaller in my chair, and finally said, "Yes," in a nearly inaudible whisper. I was seldom at a loss for words, but this was Tito Gobbi. I had learned recital songs, arias, entire operas from his recordings. I'd seen him, as Germont, take on Violetta in *La Traviata,* and watched him die at the hand of Maria Callas in *Tosca.* I figured I didn't have much to say that he wanted to hear. But sensing my reticence, he became gentle and kind, his voice quieter as we spoke of music and the business of the performing arts. I got over my shyness and talked on for hours, exhausting both him and the party, I'm sure. Somehow the idea of my singing for him arose, and it was decided that I would call him.

Contessa Bonmartini also asked me to call. She wanted me to meet a special friend, an artist she knew. Tea at her home was a Sunday affair I anxiously anticipated, having been told that Puccini's nieces, keepers of the family flame, would be present. The Bonmartini palazzo on via San Teodoro, a small street not far from the Colosseum, seemed tucked away, remote and private. As I paid my cabdriver, an Asian gentleman leading two beautiful boxer dogs exited the front door and waved at me. This had to be the artist the contessa had spoken of, Thomas Concepcion. Dressed in white, as I would see him most days, he approached, saying, "You're the opera singer, Alexander." Whether that was a question or a statement I don't remember, but then he assumed a heroic posture and burst into song. I stood there unsure of what to do—was I being challenged to a duel of voices, or was this his way of asking for a voice lesson? "Bravo, bravo" came out of my mouth finally. Laughing at the top of his lungs, he gave me a bear hug, the dogs were led away by a gentleman whom I surmised was the butler, and Thomas took me into the house.

The private quarters of the contessa were on the third floor, and by the time we got there, he and I were old friends. He was Filipino, well-educated, sophisticated, traveled, and celebrated. He was also the companion of the contessa's son, Count Sebastiano Bonmartini, and that more than explained why he was so much at home here. The sitting room we entered was spacious and elegantly decorated with art and antiques that reminded me of the Curtis Mansion. If ever there was a moment to thank Mrs. Bok and the society ladies who poured tea and taught the proper way to eat cookies, it was now. Perched on a silk pillow in the window, the contessa was like a songbird smiling a song. She blushed girlishly, called me forward, and took my hand. I remember thinking she held it a little longer than seemed proper (but in reality it took her other hand to disengage the hand I clung to). Then she rose (as she did only once the entire afternoon) to introduce me personally to each of the three other ladies present.

The contessa's sister, Contessa Barberini, managed to offer a smile and gentle welcome. The bigger challenge waited for me behind the stiff posture and stares of the two remaining fluffed-up dowagers, who had no doubt been told I was coming to tea. The air was thick, even with Thomas's playful antics. The old girls were giving up nothing in my direction. It appeared to be a contest to see who could make the American more uncomfortable, and I felt as if I were about to be exposed as a fraud, with only borrowed musical ability. The word *terror* does little to convey the weight of my feet on my approach, the loss of steadiness in my hands, and my immediate need to potty.

"*Cantante di opera lirica . . . huh!*" Her head unmoving, the elder sister directed her charge.

"Sì!" The word was just coming across my lips when she fired round two: *"Quale aria di Puccini lei piace . . . huh?"* Still no movement in her upper body; I never saw her breathe.

"Mi piace tutto, caro . . . prego" were the words of my saint, Contessa Bonmartini, as she sat me down, poured me tea, and signaled Thomas to engage the ladies. Time to recover, I thought. Finally I got my wings back and we chatted about opera, art, Rome, and New York. As a special thank-you I sang *"Amarille mia bella,"* an Italian art song, but only after declaring Puccini my favorite composer and *La Bohème* my all-time favorite opera.

The first day I arrived at Tito Gobbi's I was shown into a large sitting room with a grand piano and evidence everywhere of an illustrious musical career. I don't remember learning any vocal technique during our sessions, but I did learn how to attack a note, turn a musical phrase, and exaggerate my facial expressions, and sometimes the Gobbis—his wife always accompanied the maestro—would invite me to lunch. On these joyful days we'd dine alfresco in their garden amid fruit and olive trees. Signora Gobbi was the daughter of a famous musician who had helped launch the maestro, and she had given up her own career as a pianist to ensure his. They filled me with pasta and stories and were wonderful to watch together—so affectionate, a real team in every way, starting and finishing each other's sentences, knowing when to prop up a dying tale and pull the other one through. They were like Uncle Joe and Aunt Laura, and I was lucky enough to know both couples.

Thomas Concepcion and I stayed in touch, and one evening en route to his atelier in Trastevere, I lost my way. It was dusk and the winding cobblestone road was unfamiliar and growing more and more tedious. What suddenly distracted me from this concern was an extraordinary smell, thick in the air, of sweet goodness—sugar, nutmeg, cinnamon, bread, cakes, cookies, and candy. Several feet away people were gathered in front of a small shop. Coming closer I noticed not one but several specialty shops full of a variety of sweets, breads, meats, and prepared foods. It was as if this were a separate village contained in the walls of Rome, and I was amazed by the sense of community. Feeling as if I'd stumbled onto a secret, I purchased a few morsels, got some directions from the shopkeeper, and arrived at the atelier in good time, where Thomas explained to me that I had come upon the Jewish quarter and that the pastry, the breads, and even the old restaurant there were exceptional. For obvious reasons, from then on I was often in the neighborhood.

Shortly after my arrival at Thomas's, the door opened and in came a thin, distinguished gentleman in his late forties, with grayish hair and thick black-framed glasses. Smiling, he walked straight toward me. "You're Alexander, and I've heard all about you from my mother and Thomas," he said. "I'm Sebastiano Bonmartini." I greeted him with an answering smile, a big wide one, having heard so much about this amazing man, who ran the family business, traveled throughout the world, kept an apartment in New York, tended the family vineyard, and was a devoted patron of the opera.

That night we dined just two blocks off the viale Trastevere at Alberto Ciarla. Here was amazing food, an entire menu devoted to fish and reigned over by a passionate, driven perfectionist. Alberto Ciarla created dishes with imagination and color, yet subtle, innovative, and beyond delicious. Sebastiano knew everyone who mattered in Rome, and dining with him meant the best table, special dishes, and welcoming glances. We drank an assortment of wines with tasting plates of *seviche di pesce, zuppa di fagioli con frutti di mare, calamari fritti, spiedini di gamberi, risotto con le vongole,* and *branzino al cartoccio.*

For dessert we strolled back across the Tiber to the great masterpiece of piazzas, Navona, where we settled at a small outdoor café. Sweet cakes, ice cream, and coffee arrived, and then Sebastiano had the waiter bring an after-dinner drink with the appearance of still water. One whiff of it made the distinction obvious. I drank my first and second grappa that night, feeling no pain, while Thomas and Sebastiano told me all about a wonderful black American soprano whom they'd once known well and loved. She had come to Rome seeking peace and quiet and time to reassess her extraordinary career. Thomas had painted the album cover for Leontyne Price's *Prima Donna* recording, and their stories allowed me to relate to her in some small way—another American in Rome.

Though my studies were going well and I felt I was advancing, I still wasn't sure if my voice and I wanted the same thing. I loved the club scene and joined the glitterati night crowd, and sometimes after suffi-cient wine and stroking I would take to the mike and sing a popular song. As in Sicily, the people of Rome really went out of their way to respond, which gave me self-assurance and power unequaled in my American experience. I was no longer America's dirty linen problem; my every step was not dogged by a sense of apology for living or by the embarrassment of a nation too arrogant to make peace with its unfor-givable past. I felt freer in Italy than on a dirt road in South Carolina or on Broadway in New York. So for all of my studying, I was seduced by the people, the food, the *dolce vita*. I wanted to live in this heaven on earth, be grand, and sit in piazzas day and night. Maybe give a perfor-mance now and then. I wanted Rome, and I went out and got it.

One morning I fought and won a hard battle in the market, and for my verbal work was given a ripe melon by a much humbled vendor—once I'd finished with him! To share my spoils, I decided to cook dinner for Gwendolyn and Mossa. While Mossa practiced, though sometimes it seemed her efforts were directed at raising the dead, I threw pots and pans around and made a simple meal—my favorite, *spaghetti alla carbonara*, with the addition of fresh peas, sweet red peppers, and frozen corn I found at the supermarket (a novelty from America). My main course was a real experiment on a two-fisted theme, *pollo e gamberi nel sugo di marsala*, and maybe that's how you say it in Italian. Chicken and shrimp in a marsala sauce. This was slightly over the top, as I could not imagine any Italian *mamma* laying claim to it. I finished the dish with toasted almonds and a bit of lemon zest added to the marsala sauce. For my *contorno*, the side dish, I decided on *dadini di patate arrostiti* with lots of rosemary. *Per le verdure, gli spinaci saltati con pomodori*. Wonderfully sun-ripened egg tomatoes with center pulp removed, sliced in strips and sautéed with garlic before adding the spinach. A little freshly grated nutmeg, salt, pepper, and you're eating at eight. Lost in the madness of invention, I failed to hear the front door open, and so was somewhat shaken when a vaguely familiar voice asked, "What's for dinner, Alexander?"

Standing next to Gwendolyn, who was about to burst out of her dental braces, was LeVar Burton—LeVar, of course, was the star of the megahit *Roots*, which had just revolutionized the black presence on TV.

With Gwendolyn Bradley (Berlin Opera star)
and LeVar Burton (actor) in Rome.

We had all sat glued to our screens as Kunta Kinte, a young African, was sold into slavery. Now a free man, he stood graciously in my kitchen.

"Look who I brought home!" Gwendolyn managed to exclaim. The shock on my face said it all. Unruffled, LeVar made his way into our apartment that day and into my life, and we remain the best of friends. He and Gwen had met in the piazza of the Pantheon, our favorite watering hole. We dined that night on delicious multicultural creations of Italian descent. What a summer I was having. I knew I'd be telling somebody about it someday.

There was no easy way to go from Florence to Spoleto by train, but I was in Florence and had to get to Spoleto, where the Festival was in full swing, as was everybody who was anybody. I was joining Mossa and Gwendolyn, and had detoured to Florence to study with Maestro Gobbi, who was heading a month-long opera workshop. I had sung *Eri tu*" from the opera *Un Ballo in Maschera,* and *"Bella siccome un angelo"* from *Don Pasquale.* He had seemed more than pleased, and patted me on the

Agonizing over the menu in Rome at Tàvola Caldo.

head, and now I was off. I could have taken a bus or even a train back to Rome, and then another to Spoleto, but oh, no. All night I traveled, on three different local trains, and I arrived the next morning around eight. I could have walked the route faster.

But then I got my chance to walk, as there were no cabs to be had at that hour. Tired, hungry, pissed off, and loaded with more luggage than the situation called for, I began to walk up the hill through the town toward the festival. A group of kids out playing noticed me and after some hesitation ran toward me. Coming closer, they began to chant, "Cassius Clay, Cassius Clay, Cassius Clay!" (This was before I became the bearded wonder I now am.) I would say there was some resemblance, and having had my own private moment with the champ only a year before in Florida, I was not insulted by the attention. Singing and chanting, helping me with my bags, the kids walked me the rest of the way, enjoying their time with the person they thought was the greatest boxer on the planet. People came out of their homes waving and shouting and blowing kisses, all of which I accepted on behalf of my brother Muhammad Ali.

. . .

The next weekend Gwendolyn and Mossa went to Spoleto without me, and since a friend was coming for a two-day visit I decided to give a party. I had befriended a flight attendant for Pan Am who flew New York–Rome on a regular basis, and after one night on the town she had agreed to furnish me with fresh or frozen okra every time she visited. (Okra was the one thing I greatly missed in Rome.) For the party she came through with a big supply, as well as a smoked ham and Domino brown sugar. I was set to treat the Italians to Low Country goodness *alla italiano,* so to speak.

For hors d'oeuvres I fried up all my okra and made a sweet red pepper creole mayonnaise for dipping. The ham I prepared *alla* Johnnie Mae Smalls, glazed in her paste of brown sugar, mustard, and lemon, with pineapples and cherries and cloves spiked everywhere, rising up in the center of the table like an offering from Miss Wilkes's front-room restaurant, run out of her house off Church Street. The only thing missing was the aluminum foil around the broiler pan. Southern fried chicken; Uncle Joe's potato salad with ginger snap peas and pickled quail eggs; macaroni and cheese with ziti instead of elbow macaroni, some added Parmesan cheese, and sliced tomatoes baked on top. I combined the *insalata* and the *verdure* into one dish by making a mixed bean succotash with fresh tomatoes, mozzarella, arugula, and shaved Parmesan cheese. The cut corn in the succotash caused a little hesitation—but not much. A light fresh mint vinaigrette with herbs gave the salad a summer freshness. For dessert, a coconut fresh berry upside-down cake waited in the wings. I set the table lavishly, and having (overly) garnished every dish, stepped back to admire my handiwork. French and Italian food was so visually exciting to me. Aside from the taste, it emphasized what Uncle Joe had taught me about cooking—imagination, color, and presentation.

The guests, an assortment of who's who and what's what, piled in, fashionable and fashionably late. I had expected twenty-five but got twice that and then some. Many were my club and disco buddies. There was Tzghe (pronounced ?), a beautiful Ethiopian woman whom I adored and even considered marrying so that she could come to the States. She introduced me to the Contessa Augusta, a beautiful blonde from Milano who had a fine appreciation for the darker persuasion and who became my partner on the dance floor more often than was coincidental. She had been married twice to men of color and found her preference a cause for public celebration. Kali, Fabio, Alessandro, Adrian, Gisela, and Joseph, an American med-school dropout turned gossip columnist and gadabout—all partners in partying till dawn; not a very dependable crowd, but lots of fun when they'd show. The food was at first shocking to them—clearly a palate adjustment would have to be made. Italians never eat salt and sugar together (e.g., meat with a sweet sauce), and the ham was a little inconceivable. Undaunted, I sliced it and served it. They of course loved it. Case closed: they ate everything, including the okra. But they trashed the apartment—now I knew why Europeans ate out all the time; it was easier on the furniture. First and last party in Rome.

The summer ended too fast. Gwendolyn returned home to marry, Mossa and I remained and missed the wedding, clinging to Rome, fearful of the lives we'd left behind. In New York we'd be lost and confronted with our particular realities; here we were exotic, magical, spirited dropouts. She with her trust fund moved to another apartment, I with the cash-in value of my return ticket moved into Pensione Brotzky. Through the grace of Emma Bisconti and others I began giving English conversation lessons to the children of her wealthy friends. I also hired myself out to cater events for friends and friends of friends who wanted American southern fare, often finding myself the main course of entertainment. Since my services weren't cheap and they were intent on getting their money's worth, it was not uncommon for me to cook, host, decorate, and, yes, sing at one of these affairs, not to mention clean up. But I was in Italy, and that was enough. What better place to be missing in action.

One day in December, Michael Tilson Thomas, the wunderkind, called to say he was in town. We had dinner alfresco at La Carbonara in the Campo dei Fiori. Under the stars the palazzos surrounding the piazza seemed more like a movie set than the real thing. Over plates of fried artichokes, zucchini flowers, antipasto, pollo arosto, and pasta, pasta, Michael took a break from telling me about himself and his glorious career to ask about me. "What are you doing?" he said with a concerned, bewildered sigh.

My first response was simply to proclaim how fabulous I was, life was, my work, my music, and all my plans were. I spoke of my upcom-

At a sidewalk café in Rome.

ing tour of Germany to get into an opera house and how the big payoff was around the corner. It was convincing. I almost believed it. I certainly needed to if I were to continue like this.

The look on Michael's face was that of one who had just either had a great talk with God or looked a dreamer squarely in the eye. His pregnant pause was clearly a substitute for his inability or reluctance to respond. The choices were both bleak: to feed the masquerade or expose the truth under the skin of the tale. "I don't know what I'm doing," I blurted out to save him the choice. In Michael's simple and to-the-point way, on returning to the States he sent me a one-way ticket home for Christmas.

I left everything in Rome at Mossa's apartment. I knew I'd be back; I had lots of unfinished business. Mossa and I flew home together. It was great to be in New York, but the future was so unsure. In a matter of weeks friends gathered and the parties started at Le Chanteur. But I was forlorn and unsettled. I would have to do something—and soon.

―――――― ❧ ――――――

The Italian presence in my food was well developed by this point.
"When in Rome do as the Romans do . . ." with a few South Carolina
intentions. Just cook everything, set the table, call in some friends, and
dine on these recipes until you pop.

―――――― ❧ ――――――

CHICKEN AND SHRIMP IN MARSALA SAUCE

8 SERVINGS

❧

4 tablespoons butter
4 tablespoons shallots or scallions, minced
½ cup marsala wine
3 cups veal stock
2 tablespoons lemon juice
2 tablespoons vinegar
salt and freshly ground black pepper
    to taste
2 pounds (24) large shrimp
1 pound chicken cutlets, cut into strips
2 tablespoons olive oil

Melt 1 tablespoon of the butter. Add shallots and cook 4 minutes. Deglaze with marsala wine, scraping bottom of pan. Add veal stock, lemon juice, and vinegar. Season with salt and pepper. Reduce 3 minutes. Take off flame and whisk in the remaining 3 tablespoons butter. Set aside.

Shell and devein shrimp, leaving tails intact. Wash well. Season chicken cutlets and shrimp with salt and pepper. Sauté in large skillet in 2 tablespoons olive oil, tossing well. When shrimp is nearly done, add marsala sauce and cook 2 minutes more. Pour onto platter and serve immediately.

CHICKEN IN SPICED TOMATO SAUCE

6 SERVINGS

ॐ

1 3-pound chicken, cut into 8 pieces

1 teaspoon salt

1 teaspoon freshly ground black pepper

1 large onion, minced

¼ cup olive oil

4 cloves garlic, minced

1 large green pepper, minced

*2 tablespoons coriander seed, freshly
    ground*

*4 cups plum tomatoes, peeled and
    pureed*

2 tablespoons tomato paste

Clean chicken pieces and season with salt and pepper. Set aside.

Put all other ingredients into a large bowl. Lay chicken pieces in a casserole pan and brush with this basting mixture. Bake in a preheated 375-degree oven for 1½ hours, basting frequently with mixture until all mixture is used up. Lay on a large platter, pour pan drippings over chicken, and serve at once.

SPAGHETTI ALLA CARBONARA

❀

2 pounds spaghetti

1½ cups fresh peas

1 cup of fresh corn kernels

1 cup slab bacon, cubed

2 shallots, minced

3 cloves garlic, minced

1½ pints heavy cream

2 large sweet red peppers, julienned

¼ cup fresh parsley, chopped

2 tablespoons fresh basil, chopped

2 teaspoons salt

1 teaspoon freshly ground black pepper

¾ cup freshly grated Parmesan

Cook pasta according to package directions. When pasta has 5 minutes to go, add green peas and corn to pasta water.

Meanwhile, sauté cubed bacon until crisp. Add shallots and garlic and cook 2 minutes. Add heavy cream, bring to a boil, then simmer 4 minutes. Add sweet red peppers, herbs, salt, and pepper.

Drain pasta and put into large bowl. Toss with sauce and put on serving platter. Sprinkle with grated cheese and serve at once.

MIXED BEAN SUCCOTASH WITH FRESH TOMATOES AND MOZZARELLA

8 SERVINGS

❦

1 cup lima beans, cooked

1 cup red beans, cooked

2 cups string beans, steamed

3 ears corn on the cob, cut into 2-inch pieces, cooked

6 plum tomatoes, peeled, seeded, and chopped

8 slices mozzarella cheese

¼ cup red wine vinegar

1 teaspoon mustard

1 clove garlic, minced

2 teaspoons freshly ground black pepper

1 teaspoon salt

¼ cup fresh basil, chopped

1 cup olive oil

2 pounds arugula, cleaned and dried

½ cup Parmesan cheese, shaved

Mix beans, corn, tomatoes, and mozzarella in a large bowl.

In a small bowl, mix vinegar, mustard, garlic, black pepper, salt, and basil. Whisk in olive oil in thin stream until emulsified. Pour over beans and let marinate 30 minutes in refrigerator. Arrange arugula on large platter. Lay mozzarella on top of arugula in center of platter. Pour bean and corn mixture over mozzarella, top with shaved Parmesan, and serve at once.

CHILLED TOMATO SOUP WITH SWEET PEPPERS AND ROASTED CORN

8 SERVINGS

❧

4 ears corn, in husk

8 large tomatoes, seeded, peeled, and chopped

2 large sweet red peppers, minced

3 cloves garlic, minced

1 stalk celery, minced

1½ quarts tomato juice

3 leaves fresh sage, chopped

¼ cup parsley, chopped

1 tablespoon fresh tarragon, chopped

½ cup olive oil

3 lemons, juiced

1 small onion, minced

2 tablespoons Tabasco sauce

1 teaspoon salt

freshly ground black pepper

Roast corn for 10 minutes in husk under broiler or on a grill, turning often. Cut kernels from cobs and reserve.

Mix rest of ingredients in order listed, using a large bowl. Mix in corn kernels and chill 2 hours.

SWEET AND PEPPERY CORN CAKES

8 SERVINGS

8 ears corn, kernels removed
1 small onion, finely chopped
2 ribs celery, minced
1 small red pepper, minced
2 jalapeños, minced
4 tablespoons sherry
3 large eggs, beaten
2 tablespoons Tabasco sauce
1 cup buttermilk

1½ cups flour
1¼ teaspoons baking powder
2 tablespoons cornmeal
1 tablespoon sugar
1 teaspoon salt
4 teaspoons freshly ground black
 pepper
¼ cup vegetable oil

In a large bowl, mix all ingredients except oil in order listed, mixing well after each addition. Mixture should be the consistency of thick pancake batter. Chill 10 minutes. Heat oil in large skillet until hot but not smoking. Ladle batter into oil, forming round cakes. Fry until golden on each side. Drain on paper towels and serve at once.

14 THE RELUCTANT OVEN

*B*err . . . nie . . . " The southern accent on the other end of the line was unmistakable, but she introduced herself anyway: "Berrnie . . . this is Ann . . . Allen . . . from Spartanburg . . . How ya doin'?" Ann was a great friend and supporter, president of the local arts council, which had established an Alexander Smalls Scholarship Fund. She was calling to ask if an exchange student from Paris living in Spartanburg could come to New York for a few days and stay with me. I hesitated—a *college* student, female—but I could never say no to Ann.

So Claudine Chambovet—wild, spoiled, wanting to be worldly-wise, and gorgeous—arrived at Le Chanteur. She spoke English with a thick southern accent, was easily excitable, and felt the need to share that with anybody. I liked her immediately, and her wit and easy charm endeared her to all my friends. Years later she would tell me how Ann had prepared her for her visit with a big black man: "Really nice and friendly. . . . Don't be scared." The afternoon of her arrival, I took Claudine to Washington Square, that mecca for college kids, tourists, bench warmers, and dropouts. On the way we passed Les Trois Petits Cochons, a French-style deli where she decided a picnic was in order and proceeded to buy the place out. Several pâtés, cheeses, sausages, salads, breads, and cakes later, we found a park bench and shared experiences, and sometime during her five-day visit she dubbed me "Mr. Fruit Cake Baby," a name she still calls me. I was to follow Claudine back to Europe later that year. Despite my efforts to settle back into New York and resume voice lessons and coaching, things were still hit-or-miss and I was missing my lifestyle across the Atlantic. Claudine's visit did much to disturb my tenuous situation.

My dear friend Bougie had moved to New York to study acting and was living in a Village loft very near mine. We spent a lot of time propping each other up and made it a point to have dinner at a good restaurant once a month, just to balance the ups and downs of trying to make it: the lost jobs, lost roles, lost friends, no money, bleak prospects, the usual. Often we'd go to La Chaumière, a great little French place that served couscous and amazing lamb sausages with hot spice paste. Sitting in this storefront parlor with overblown French posters and French doors with half-curtains, sipping Veuve Cliquot, we could address each other's strengths and weaknesses and offer comfort. On one of our outings Bougie showed up sharp and suave in a three-piece suit, the problem being that no matter how great he looked in a suit you always felt he was off to bury somebody—undertaking was his family's business.

I'd been taken aback at first sight of Bougie, walking toward me across the commons at Wofford College in 1970. There he was, sporting a huge unruly Afro that seemed to tilt from side to side, a large young man wearing an old dashiki, baggy jeans, and gold wire-rim eyeglass frames, which, as he came closer, were revealed to be empty of lenses. At Wofford there was deep concern that the twelve students of color (out of fifteen hundred) create strong ties, and Bougie had been talked up to me as a kindred spirit and mirror image. Well, the mirror cracked!

"I'm Gregory Leevy, but most folks call me Bougie," he said. Stunned at his getup, I missed the person entirely, and proceeded to avoid him. Then one afternoon, approaching the campus auditorium, where the greatest piano I'd ever seen or played was kept, I heard the amazing sounds of a soul running up and down those eighty-eights. I opened the door, and there, hair swaying wildly atop his head, sat Bougie tearing through some mean Beethoven. The Bösendorfer was completely at the mercy of his wild fingers, jumping around as if on an old typewriter instead of this magnificent music box. Still, music and heart came through.

Bougie and me after a joint recital I'd just sung in New York City.

And that was it—all it took for Bougie and me to find our common denominator. We became the talented two and took over the Glee Club, he as pianist and I as solo singer. It should be said that Bougie was totally self-taught on the piano. All my lessons only helped me talk intelligently about playing music—Bougie actually played it. We toured North Carolina, Virginia, and Washington, D.C., performing in white churches, country clubs, and auditoriums. At one place, when none of the white families would house us, a black family on the other side of the tracks (literally) was found to take us in. The two old sisters that Bougie and I stayed with were terrific. I ate the best meal of that tour in the kitchen of a small four-room house on a Virginia dirt road (within city limits). The elder sister fried up a mess of catfish, and besides chicken and stewed green beans served fried fresh white corn and cabbage salad with homemade mayonnaise and fresh coconut (a first) grated into the salad. Her sister, who lived down the road, brought cornbread, the kind Uncle Joe made, rising high out of the pan and swimming in churned butter. And biscuits like angel puffs that disappeared after two bites. Huge slices of chocolate cake with sugar and sweet butter frosting and toasted pecans and fresh-churned vanilla ice cream with the salt cap taste still lingering.

"Salvation is ours," said Bougie. (You could always count on him for a benediction; it was in his genes.) And since our motherly sisters of care and nurture had not been invited to our performance before an all-white audience, we sang a tune or two for them, to say thank you and to remember and celebrate our humble beginnings. "To be young gifted and black with your soul intact" was how Nina Simone recorded it. That was good enough for us, too.

It was one of those nights, years later, at La Chaumière that I announced to Bougie my plans to return to Europe once again. I had been in touch with Patrick McLaughlin, an elderly English gentleman I'd befriended, who was offering free room and board in his large apartment in Rome in exchange for some cooking, marketing, and light house chores. I was going to Paris first. All I needed now was spending money and a plane ticket, some good wishes, and a packed bag.

Bougie heaved a great sigh. He hated to say good-bye. He hated change. Eventually he would buy himself a new suit, put a part in his hair, and become at once the president and CEO of his family's business. What a great role for an actor. But like most inherited stages, it wasn't enough. Bougie got himself an agent, became a character actor, and has gone on to perform small roles in a number of movies.

In Paris, a stone's throw from my friend Howard Dickenson's apartment, was Les Halles with its shops and cafés and sidewalk seating. I made a beeline for the heart of this hub—it was the best way to convince myself that I was really back, really here, really French again! Howard was a fashion designer with Nino Cerruti, who one day joined us for lunch at La Poularde Landaise, a cozy spot with fireplace, dark beams, and an attentive owner. Over plates of *confit de canard, haricots verts, salade niçoise, pommes frites,* black olives, and crudités, along with a good regional wine and Évian, Monsieur Cerruti graciously allowed me to quiz him about his fashion empire. As one designer, model, and mogul after another passed by to say hi, I felt I had the world on a string. I wondered what everybody in the States was doing for lunch, but I was sure it couldn't beat this.

My carte orange *mug shots—*
Paris style.

I reconnected with Roland Laval, whose great gift to me was to share his dear aunt Gerard Damblant, a strong-looking island woman with dark skin, sharp weary eyes that had seen too much (like Grandpa's), and a smile that betrayed her hard, frozen, timeless face. She made me at once her boy, for six weeks pulling me into her family of two kids and husband, a white Frenchman who kept a separate residence but often came for dinner. Auntie Gerard adopted not only me but my adventure as well; she loved the idea that I was an opera singer, that I dreamed of greatness. The ease of our communication was a wonder. My French was in its pure infancy while her English was the result of two brief trips to England and a dictionary. These odds would daunt even the well-intended, but the spirit of Aunt Gerard predominated, and once or twice a week she would take me to movies, the museum, or a concert.

Before calling me on the phone she'd practice her English conversation, ever so brief but nonetheless courageous. Believing restaurants a waste of money and a compromise of comfort, she'd pack a nice lunch of sandwiches, cakes, cookies, and fruit for our outings. She was a good salt-and-pepper cook, like my mom, and once a week at least I took the métro to Porte de Vanves, a suburb of Paris, where in a large apartment complex Auntie Gerard laid out her fine china and silver, her best linens and goblets, placed amid silk flower arrangements. The smell of herbs, spices, and fresh lime lingered full in the air.

Auntie Gerard, who didn't drink, would make me a 'ti punch of her best Martinican rum, lime, and cane sugar syrup. Her food was simple, fresh, and appealing, with no unrecognizable dishes or sauces that caught you off-center. A typical meal might start with a huge green salad of baby lettuce, marinated cucumbers, tomatoes, and avocados with olive oil and lemon. Next would be escoveitched fish, a fillet of fish skillet-fried crisp, drained, and put into a vinegar-based marinade for a couple of hours before serving. Then pigeon peas and rice, fried plantains, green tomatoes, and roast chicken with a curry gravy for the main course. All the while we pulled from loaves of crunchy French bread. For dessert there'd be a spice cake or dark bread pudding, which often went home with me. But first I'd read English stories to the kids, Michel and Marie Gabriel. Auntie Gerard, who had traveled in Europe, the Caribbean, and Africa, knew few Americans and little of American culture, but felt an enormous kindred connection to all of us. She wanted desperately to give that gift to her kids, and I'm pleased to say she has succeeded—her son Michel, now an adult who speaks English and travels throughout the world, has often visited me here in New York.

At Patrick's spacious, quaintly overdecorated apartment in Rome there wasn't a table, mantel, or counter that didn't have too many things on it. The place was a thinking man's abode, and Patrick, well into his seventies, had done a lot of that. From his generous base I was able to reenter the life I knew and loved, studying and coaching, teaching my English conversation classes, partying till dawn. Patrick was solicitous of all my friends and encouraged their presence at lunches and dinners. Sort of an English Uncle Joe, he was a great patron of the arts, in search of a stage even at his age, and not one to be too far separated from his brandy. After a dinner party or a fat lunch that drifted into early afternoon, he would pull a book off a shelf or from a pile on the floor, and with brandy in hand he'd read Shakespeare, Byron, or Browning with the concentration of a child lost in an ice cream cone. Smacking his lips with delight, he'd call up the images on those pages like old friends come to play cards on a Saturday night. I loved how he loved this moment; I'd been here before. I looked forward to floating on the words of those whose only hope of continued life was in the passion of men like Patrick and Uncle Joe.

For a time, all was well. Beppe, who had enlisted in the army, was stationed in Rome, so we saw a lot of each other, and some weekends we'd fly down to Palermo. But then the day came when Patrick, with life threatening to abandon him, decided to return to London and put his house in order. I found my way back to the Pensione Brotzky—to my old room!—on the top floor of a beautiful palazzo on via del Corso, in the heart of Rome near the piazza del Popolo. Entering past wrought-iron gates and through a large courtyard, you'd take an elevator up to the penthouse and there, decorated like someone's oversize apartment with several bedrooms, was home.

Early one morning, coming in after a night with friends, I encountered a stunningly beautiful black woman unlocking the gates of the pensione. Engaging her in conversation, I detected an accent of no particular origin but one to suggest that English was her second language. In short time we discovered common ground, both black and exotic in Rome, both living in the Brotzky temporarily due to some unfortunate circumstances—while funds were being wired, or we were out of money and Mommy and Daddy couldn't be reached while sailing the Pacific Islands. It was clear that we had exceptional pedigrees and were much grander than our present surroundings but as a testament to our character were negotiating our separate situations well and with dignity.

But after hanging out until daybreak, we discovered we were both working hard to pull off similar capers. Who was zooming who, I might have asked. My new friend, who went by an African name, turned out to be Trent Hargrave from Bridgeport, Connecticut. A naive aspiring model, she had been persuaded, by an ambitious Nordic hairdresser seeking to endear himself to Rome's chic and trendy, to assume the identity of a princess, the adopted daughter of Idi Amin. Night after night he paraded her to parties, dinners, clubs, and concerts, translating for her and presenting her to all who would be welcoming. Italian gossip papers, outrageous in their coverage, sought her out and featured both her and her unscrupulous patron.

At first I think Trent saw this little game as a fun and exciting way to see Europe—everyone wanted to have Idi Amin's princess in hiding, fearing for her life, at their next party. Outfit after outfit was meticulously selected, and after we became friends, I was frequently called upon to button the back of a dress or fasten a necklace. At the end of the night Trent would have herself dropped off near the piazza del Popolo, pretending to be staying in an exclusive palazzo nearby. Then she'd sit in the all-night café for a while before hiking the one block up via del Corso. Often I'd meet her and we'd spend hours walking around the Spanish Steps, tripping over American expatriates who'd been there since the sixties playing bad guitar. Sometimes we'd take a bottle of wine over to the Piazza Navona to sit with our feet in the fountain, and if we ran into people who knew her as the princess she would transform herself instantly.

I would always know Trent. Over the years she has come into and out of my life wearing more hats than imaginable. She has appeared as a high-fashion model, real estate broker, importer-exporter, nutritionist, junior guru designer, writer, and wife of an Italian diplomat. But she's always a princess to me.

Midsummer approaching, I decided to go to the south of France and spend time with Claudine Chambovet, my wonderful French girlfriend with the southern accent. Michael Tilson Thomas and his personal manager Joshua Robison were also planning to be in France, at the Orange Music Festival, a yearly event that attracted grand musicians from all over the world. Michael was guest-conducting the opera *Rigoletto* with the beautiful and talented black American soprano Barbara Hendricks, a new face on the international music scene. So I arranged with Claudine for all of us to stay at Château Domaine de Lestagnol, her family's winery in the countryside, in exchange for her brother François's use of Michael's New York apartment.

Claudine picked me up at the station, and we stopped by L'Arais, her parents' sprawling estate in Orange, where they got their first look at me. They were wealthy pillars of society who basically didn't approve of anyone who wasn't French, and the fact that their little daughter had spent several nights with a black man, who was much older, was disturbing enough—and then the black man came to visit!

But the Chambovets, it seemed, were as fascinated with me as I with them, and even though they spoke no English, found ways to make me feel at home. Hospitality, I found out, could easily be expressed when words failed—a lesson I'd learned the moment I first set foot on European soil. In fact, I'd argue that there were times when words got in the way.

The grounds of the estate were lush and carefully landscaped. Pool house, guest house, gardens, duck pond, barn, a good-size chicken coop that provided fresh eggs daily, and a small kennel at the edge of the property. Years later, visiting Martha Stewart's Westport compound, I would be reminded of L'Arais.

Madame Chambovet had planned a simple luncheon in the dining salon with Claudine and her three brothers, a sister-in-law, M. Chambovet, and me. I was nervous about speaking so little French, and only Claudine and her brother François spoke English. But once the food arrived, it didn't matter much. Madame Chambovet, seated at the head of a long dining table draped in white linen, conducted the service of the meal by ringing a small bell, which signaled the kitchen when appropriate. On the table, aside from bottled water and a few bottles of the family wine, were small trays of black olives, celery sticks, and sour pickles; crocks filled with rillettes; and a crunchy baguette at each place setting. We had fresh tomatoes and cucumber slices with seasoned olive oil, and a main course of sea bass wrapped in lettuce leaves in a flavored stock. This was followed by a small green salad, assorted cheeses, a light fruit tart, and tea and coffee. Not being able to keep up with the language or the family dynamics, I lost myself in the food and these perfect surroundings, imagining life in the south of France as my typical day, with not a care in the world, not even the language.

Later that day, en route to the winery, we packed goodies and supplies into Claudine's car and left Mom and Dad waving in the long driveway. Some twenty well-driven minutes later, we turned off the highway onto a private dirt road, then rode for another ten minutes or so past vineyards and workmen, then arrived suddenly in a wooded area with an old-as-stone small castle, three stories of house and an attic, with large windows and movable shutters and a massive wooden door at the entrance. A set for *Carmen* came immediately to mind.

"We'ah *home,* Mistah Fruit Cake Baby!" How out of sync Claudine's southern accent seemed here, or maybe it was just to remind me that I was never too far from home.

We unloaded the car and moved ourselves in. Ruggedly grand and masculine would be the way to describe the decor. Heavy furniture everywhere, on a stone floor that wore its age well. Most impressive was the oversize wooden table that easily seated twenty. Off the dining room was a country kitchen with utensils and pots and pans that seemed to be the first ones on earth, a large, beautiful room that for me took "country" to another level. I couldn't wait to lose myself in it, and it turned out I didn't have to. Shortly after our arrival François showed up with the news that in three hours six friends would be coming for dinner. He turned to Claudine for assistance, pleased by the visit but not pleased to be cooking. Assessing the situation, I volunteered to prepare a southern treat.

François, who suffered from a strong dose of French arrogance and indifference toward any but French food, was not as warm on the idea and strained himself in gracious protest, but Claudine overruled him. A forced *"Bon"* pushed out of his tightly held lips, and he hastened off to create a task for himself. Highly amused, Claudine drove me to market, where we bought all kinds of things because everything I saw I wanted.

Back at the house I realized there was not a lot of time to prepare, so I went into high production. Claudine set the table, laid out breads and pâté, created a field salad of various greens with a standard vinaigrette, and went to bathe for an hour. Singing and humming my way through the prep work (much like Johnnie Mae), I cleaned and plucked off forgotten feathers from my chickens, cut them up, salt-and-peppered and laid them to rest. Potatoes boiled with eggs, sliced vegetables set in marinade waiting to be grilled, little white beans cooked in rapid liquid spiked with herbs of Provence that grew wild outside on a hill near the kitchen door—and I put the finishing touches on my shrimp paste recipe, to which I had added a little hot pepper to bring out the color in my French friends. In a large roasting pan I threw the chicken into the oven on what I felt was a modest heat and then busied myself with a barbecue sauce. It was to be a creation, since the ingredients I needed were not the ones I had found, but I felt that enough honey, lemon, mustard powder, hot pepper, onions, celery, chili powder, ground cloves, soy sauce, garlic, and peppers should suggest more than the idea and I'd just wing it.

The guests, very much on time, were old friends of Claudine and her brother who lived in a nearby town. At first or even second glance they all seemed a loving French family, nothing out of the norm, what appeared to be mother, father, older daughter with boyfriend, younger daughter with dog, and family friend, a guy who was the organist at the church they all went to. But as the evening evolved I was to learn a new lesson about what it meant to be French. After the introductions, and the opening of the first case of wine, I was told that it was not unlikely that we'd go through a case and a half. I returned to inspect things in the kitchen. All was ready except that the chicken seemed to be cooking a little slowly. I turned up the heat on the old and somewhat reluctant oven, grabbed the shrimp paste and crudités, and returned to our guests, who were in earnest conversation. The shrimp paste was a hit—the pepper, as I had imagined, a little surprising and worth mentioning by some. Most of the family spoke English, and it was shortly into the wine and conversation that odd exchanges and couplings began to happen that challenged my understanding of the evening, not to mention my southern sensibilities. Sensing my sudden confusion about the formula defining and grouping this lovely family, Claudine ushered me into the kitchen, where my poor chicken was barely sweating in the oven, and with muffled laughter explained the peculiarities of our guests. This was a family divided and then reassembled: the mother who was once with the father now lived with the former boyfriend of her elder daughter. The father now lived with the church organist but had bought a house across the street from the mother so that the daughters might live between the two homes. Whew! Not your normal evening at dinner with the Cleavers or the Huxtables. And nobody cared about any of it for a second.

As the shrimp dip began to vanish, I discovered not only that my chicken was uncooked but that I had exhausted the propane gas oven and only the burners on the stove had any juice. Panic overtook me— dinner was well into overtime, and still no food. Trying not to alarm the guests, who looked very different to me now, I alerted Claudine, who informed François, who found a large electric toaster oven. I shoved as much of my half-baked chicken as I could in under the blistering-hot coils, hoping to cook a portion at a time just to get things going, while François and Claudine made light jokes about the slow cooking of the South and who had forgotten to buy the propane. But I was aware that in my zeal to whip up a state meal as an American ambassador, I'd failed to assess the limitations of the kitchen. I should have parboiled the birds first and then roasted them with sauce, but you know what they say about hindsight.

The toaster oven succeeded in burning the skin right off my chicken but did little for the rare quality of the meat within. In great desperation I spotted a large cast-iron skillet, greased it, packed in the chicken, and with a timely dropping of water steamed it done in minutes. Claudine hurried out all the fixings as I ladled heated sauce over every piece of those chickens. The dinner was a huge success, or a huge relief. It had taken almost two hours to get it to the table. Sick of chicken by that time I passed on it, to the delight of our guests, who left not a morsel, but who departed in haste with barely emptied mouths. Fast eating—by no means a French tradition but rather an American one upheld.

The next day everyone arrived from everywhere! Michael and Josh from Marseilles; Claudine's three acting buddies from Paris; and Urs Kasser, a Swiss pianist friend, from Zurich. It was as if we'd started an artists' colony. Late mornings and early afternoons we all went off to study. Michael Tilson—with his music scores, suntan lotion, and iced tea—set up in the clay courtyard in front of the house; I and my opera score (I was preparing for that audition tour of Germany) went to sit under a big old tree near the fragrant herb garden; Urs with tape recorder and headphones and his recital music found solace down near the vineyard close to the water well; and my dear Claudine, who sought fame and completion on the stage as a way to distance herself from family conventionality, rallied her acting troupe in the great room of the château.

I was in sweet bliss here. My imagination wandered freely as I proposed the future to myself, the small-town boy from South Carolina feeding on the fat of Europe's past and present prosperity. Somehow I was writing myself into the pages of all that. But no longer did I feel that music was my only option; the direction it laid out for me was being challenged by other interests and talents—discovered, developed, and loved. I was excited and scared all at once. How could my heart and spirit do justice to my changing desires? Was this my eclipse or my fork in the road? Had I come full circle or belly-up? The courage to respond was not yet within me, so for now I would pause. No need to rock the boat.

Very early one morning, I dressed and made my way down to a not yet awakened living room, where the smells and thick air of the night before still hung, which explained the taste of garlic passing through my mind. Opening the shutters, I noticed the morning dew heavy on the vines and remembered the honeysuckle that grew wildly and undisturbed in my parents' backyard. It scaled the fence, passed my clubhouse, climbed toward the gate on the way to Grandpa's. We'd suck on that honeysuckle, my sisters and I, till dizziness set in. Grandma called it the breath of angels, and the bees protected it with great fervor.

I fixed an oversize cup of piping-hot tea and went out to walk about the grounds, wishing that I could roust the sleeping house into the morning. Suddenly a brilliant notion seized me: I would go to market, bring back vittles, and prepare a country breakfast. The market was only about five minutes from the house and, thanks to a farmers' schedule, it opened at six A.M. I ran over, selected my purchases, and raced back to the familiar pots and pans and the stove, which I'd now mastered.

Michael Tilson, first downstairs, came joyfully into the kitchen. With cinnamon French toast cooking, sautéed apples in butter and honey and sizzling sausages with fresh sage on their way to the table, he sipped his coffee patiently so as not to be accused of preempting the feast. I scrambled eggs with sweet onions, tomatoes, cheese, and herbs and then set it all out with syrup, jams, and berries. By eight there was no waiting for sleepyheads who had not found their way, and I sat down with Josh and Michael. I remember the latter chuckling about how he couldn't imagine that the others would want much of this meal. I didn't get it just then, in fact not until Claudine came down and began to laugh.

"Mistah Fruit Cake Baby, whut ah you doin'?" she drawled affectionately. "They don' wannah eat this big food, they'ah *French,* baby."

It was at last clear. As Michael and Josh struggled to stay in their chairs, unable to contain their laughter, one by one the others appeared, shocked by the scene and trying to find something to eat that didn't offend them. Most settled on a cup of coffee and a slice of French toast. A towering lesson learned, another of life's moments summed up in a phrase, "I'm American, what do you want from me?"

Back at the Brodzky I immediately packed my bags and went off to Frankfurt, Munich, Kassel, Düsseldorf, Hamburg, and Cologne in search of an opera house, a contract, a lifeline. It was hard, frantic, and fast, but Germany left me longing for Italy. After a month I returned to Rome tired of bratwurst, liverwurst, potatoes, blood sausage, sweet white wines, and Germans who didn't appreciate my colorfulness. I had auditioned well and had been offered two possible contracts. Kassel had promised to make me a great star, but I couldn't for the life of me find one good reason to want to be there. After some considerable thought I realized I'd once again have to return to the States and confront my demons. I needed divine guidance to sort through the wealth I'd built and the focus I'd lost. I needed a small miracle—and home was where I had to find it.

—❧—

These recipes remind me so much of Auntie Gerard at home in her apartment outside Paris. She nurtured me with her cooking and family stories of her childhood. She was never one to overdo; simplicity and abundance ruled. She was reverent in that way.

—❧—

SEA BASS WRAPPED IN LETTUCE LEAVES

8 SERVINGS

❧

3 heads romaine lettuce
2 quarts water
2 quarts ice water
1 tablespoon olive oil
1 small onion, minced
2 cloves garlic, minced
1 carrot, minced

1 teaspoon fresh thyme
4 leaves fresh sage, chopped
1 stick (¼ pound) butter, softened
8 fillets (8 to 10 ounces each) sea bass
salt and freshly ground black pepper
1 cup chicken stock
juice of 3 lemons

Wash and core romaine lettuce. Bring 2 quarts water to a boil. Using outer leaves only, drop four at a time, for 45 seconds, into water. Using tongs, gently take out and plunge into ice water. Drain on kitchen towels. Set aside.

Heat olive oil in saucepan. Add onion, garlic, and carrot and cook 8 minutes. Turn off flame and add herbs. Cool mixture. Mix into softened butter.

Arrange two large leaves of lettuce, overlapping, on a work surface. Top with one fillet of salted and peppered sea bass, skin side up. Using a butter knife, spread skin with seasoned butter. Fold over lettuce leaves and put into a nonstick baking pan. Finish rest of fillets, arranging in single layer. Pour in chicken stock and sprinkle with lemon juice. Bake covered in a 400-degree oven for 20 minutes. Arrange on platter and serve at once.

FRIED CATFISH

ॐ

1½ cups flour

¼ cup cornmeal

1 tablespoon sage, rubbed

1 tablespoon cayenne pepper

1 teaspoon garlic powder

1 teaspoon onion powder

½ teaspoon ground nutmeg

1 teaspoon salt

1 teaspoon freshly ground black pepper

3 cups vegetable oil for frying

8 fillets catfish, washed and patted dry

4 large eggs, beaten

lemon wedges for garnish

Mix flour, cornmeal, sage, spices, salt, and pepper in medium-size bowl. Heat oil in large skillet to hot but not smoking. Dip catfish pieces in beaten eggs. Dredge in seasoned flour, shaking off excess. Fry until golden on both sides. Arrange on platter and garnish with lemon wedges.

SHRIMP PASTE WITH HOT PEPPER

8 SERVINGS

&

½ pound large shrimp, peeled,
   deveined, and poached
1 cup black-eyed peas, cooked
   (or similar dried beans, cooked)
3 cloves garlic, minced
1 jalapeño, minced
½ teaspoon cayenne pepper
juice of 4 small lemons
½ teaspoon salt
½ cup mayonnaise
¼ cup cilantro, chopped
¾ cup olive oil

Place all ingredients except olive oil in large bowl of a food processor. Pulse until of smooth consistency. With machine running, pour in olive oil. Check seasoning. Serve in a medium-size bowl, accompanied by a breadbasket.

STEWED GREEN BEANS

8 SERVINGS

❧

2½ pounds green beans
4 slices bacon, diced (or ¼ cup olive oil)
1 small onion, minced
1½ cups chicken stock
1½ teaspoons salt
½ teaspoon freshly ground black pepper
¼ stick (2 tablespoons) butter
2 tablespoons fresh chopped tarragon

Snap ends off beans, wash, and pat dry.

Fry bacon until crisp. Drain off all but ½ teaspoon of fat. Add onion and cook until transparent. Add beans and toss to coat with fat. Add chicken stock, salt, and pepper. Bring to a boil and simmer 3 minutes. Toss in butter and tarragon. Put onto platter and serve at once.

SALAD OF BABY LETTUCE, MARINATED CUCUMBERS, AND AVOCADOS

8 SERVINGS

❧

1 seedless cucumber, peeled
¼ cup Champagne wine vinegar
3 tablespoons honey
½ teaspoon cayenne pepper
1 teaspoon benne (sesame) seeds
½ teaspoon salt
4 heads Boston lettuce
6 plum tomatoes, sliced
3 avocados
juice of 2 lemons
½ cup olive oil

Thin-slice cucumber on the diagonal. Put into medium-size bowl and toss with vinegar, honey, cayenne, benne seeds, and salt. Refrigerate 10 minutes.

Meanwhile, core, wash, and dry lettuce, taking care not to bruise it. Arrange on large platter. Arrange tomatoes around leaves. Halve, core, and slice avocados. Arrange avocados around tomatoes. Arrange cucumbers in center of platter. Sprinkle mixture with lemon juice and drizzle with olive oil. Serve immediately.

DARK BREAD PUDDING

6 SERVINGS

❧

2 cups buttermilk
1 cup granulated sugar
½ cup dark brown sugar
1 tablespoon cinnamon
1 teaspoon nutmeg
2 tablespoons bourbon
2 large eggs
1 loaf bread
½ cup currants

Whisk buttermilk, granulated sugar, ¼ cup of the brown sugar, cinnamon, nutmeg, bourbon, and eggs well in medium-size mixing bowl.

Crumble bread in large chunks into buttermilk mixture, add currants, and let stand in refrigerator for at least 30 minutes.

Grease a large muffin tin. Place saturated bread chunks in muffin cups. Pour in remaining buttermilk and loose bread crumb mixture. Crumble the remaining ¼ cup brown sugar on top. Bake in water bath in preheated 325-degree oven for 40 minutes or until liquid is solidified and bread pudding begins to pull from sides of muffin tin. Cool in refrigerator for 30 minutes. Run knife around sides of muffin cups and turn out. Serve with whipped cream.

CHOCOLATE CAKE WITH
BUTTER FROSTING AND TOASTED PECANS

10 SERVINGS

&

CAKE

2 ounces semisweet chocolate

2 ounces bitter chocolate

2½ cups cake flour

1 teaspoon baking soda

½ teaspoon baking powder

½ teaspoon salt

2 sticks (½ pound) butter

2 cups sugar

6 large eggs, separated

1 teaspoon vanilla

1 teaspoon bourbon

1 cup buttermilk

4 cups pecans, chopped

butter frosting (see recipe in Chapter 5)

CAKE

Melt chocolates over boiling water and cool. Set aside.

Sift together flour, baking soda, baking powder, and salt. Set aside.

Cream butter and sugar until light and fluffy. Add egg yolks one at a time until each is incorporated. Add vanilla and bourbon and mix well. Add cooled chocolates and mix well. Add flour mixture and buttermilk alternately in thirds, scraping sides of bowl after each addition.

In mixing bowl, whip egg whites until stiff but not dry. Fold into chocolate cake mixture. Pour evenly into two greased 9-inch round cake pans. Bake in center of preheated 350-degree oven for 25 minutes or until springy to the touch.

Remove from oven and cool in pans 5 minutes. Turn out onto cooling rack and allow to come to room temperature.

FROSTING

Arrange chopped pecans on cookie sheet. Bake in 325-degree oven for 10 minutes. Allow to cool.

ASSEMBLY

Ice top of one layer. Place second layer on top and ice. If necessary, use toothpicks to hold layers steady. Ice sides. With palm of hand, spread toasted pecans on sides of cake, completely covering icing.

PART 3

Small Miracle

15 ASSISTANT, LIGHT HOUSEKEEPING

I had sublet Le Chanteur to someone who had sub-sublet every corner, including the room that was supposed to have been left vacant for me. After a week of sleeping on a mattress behind a partition, I packed up what I needed, hailed a cab, and moved myself to the Upper West Side, where Madeline René, Luciano Pavarotti's personal secretary, had offered her apartment while she traveled with him.

Most of the teachers, coaches, and students of classical music assembled daily in this part of town. Thanks to the generosity and support of Matthew Epstein, vice president of Columbia Artists Management, I landed an agent. Gwendolyn Bradley, who was singing regularly at the Metropolitan Opera House, brought me to the studio of Marlena Malas, at that time the reigning diva teacher whose studio boasted the most gifted and promising young singers. I studied every day (I would not let myself party at night if I hadn't), went on auditions, and did a bit of recital work; but no one was looking for me and no one was passing out contracts. One audition after another fell short of a job.

When Pavarotti sang at the Met, Madeline introduced us, and from then on whenever we met he always greeted me with great kindness. One day Madeline called to suggest that, since I spoke Italian, I might chaperone his daughters around the city. Delighted, I dressed and went to Central Park South to meet them. Signora Pavarotti greeted me with surprise, but behind her appeared Luciano, pulling me into the apartment.

"Alessandro, my daughters Titti, Christina, and Giuliana," he said, and after some fatherly advice disappeared into one of the other rooms. The girls were great, each with a very different temperament but all three with a great desire to see the Village, so we headed for the nearest subway station. On the train it became apparent that people were staring at us. I began to feel really uncomfortable. In retrospect, the idea of entering a subway with Luciano Pavarotti's daughters was already somewhat over the top—but what was the problem? It occurred to me that a black man with three white girls from twelve to seventeen was possibly of interest. Or maybe, having been in Europe so long, I had acquired a European air? Surely all these people hadn't seen me in *Porgy and Bess.* Finally it struck me—I had been totally oblivious of the fact that among them these girls must have been wearing tens of thousands of dollars worth of gold, diamonds, and other precious stones! When I realized I was responsible not just for their lives but for their jewelry, I panicked. "We're getting off at the next stop!" I managed to announce, then rushed us up to the street and into a cab.

That same week a friend of Luciano's threw a birthday party for Giuliana, the eldest. By this time the girls and I were buddies. The hostess had gone all-out to prepare a lavish feast. All kinds of Italian delicacies lay on every available counter, table, and sideboard. Servants with trays passed around zucchini flowers, meatballs, shrimp cocktail, prosciutto-wrapped vegetables, and canapés. There were dips, breads, cheeses, pâtés, and platters of crudités with sculptured vegetables. The party—about fifteen of us—wandered around the house, trying to get comfortable.

Black and green olives, cheese sticks, and anchovies on toasted garlic bread lay on a table in a downstairs music room with games, stereo, a TV, and big, full furniture. The girls and I settled in. After we played solos and duets on the piano, Giuliana asked me to sing something for her. I felt terribly nervous about this, and with Pavarotti in the house there was no way I'd sing opera. But a part of me wanted the big guy to hear my voice, and so I began playing the introduction to that old favorite of mine, "Yesterday." Halfway through the first part of the song, Luciano—followed by the entire party—came barreling down the staircase. It was just at this point that Giuliana gave me a big smile, as if to say, "Sing, Alexander—the way you know you can!" So I did, and as I finished the last note Luciano began to applaud, shouting, "*Bella voce* . . . incredible . . . so musical . . . You are a musician . . . This is music, this is a musician!" He kept repeating this over and over, until I became not just the baby-sitter or a friend of Madeline's, but the singer Alexander Smalls, who'd just sung for Pavarotti. I would always remember his generosity that night, a much-needed boost from an unlikely source that has remained with me over the years.

When Madeline returned from traveling, another friend invited me to share his apartment downtown, and so I packed up again and headed south. It was fun to be in the Village, but I had too much time on my hands. (For an income I was subletting not only Le Chanteur but my first New York apartment on West 80th Street, and I also relied on occasional help from the Spartanburg Arts Council's scholarship fund.) Still, life just didn't seem real, together, or in sync. A job, I felt, might give me stability, a sense of routine and order that was now missing. My friend J.J. (Jerriese Johnson) suggested I become a private chef for a family or a rich successful couple on the fast track. J.J., from Atlanta, was a combination of every wonderful southerner I'd ever met and the unauthorized pope of the East Village, who blessed his flock with humor, warmth, cheer, and a belief in the salvation of everything and everyone. He, Bougie, and I put together a résumé and reference letters, all fabricated of course, and for several Sundays we met over the *New York Times*'s help-wanted ads. Finally I spotted one: "Part-time assistant, light housekeeping and occasional cooking, for professional couple on Upper East Side." Why this ad and not the other hundred or so, I couldn't say.

Laura Torbet, frizzy-blond and a little frantic, opened the door. She and I were instant, that is to say we were old friends in minutes. She was a true Renaissance woman—painter, illustrator, jewelry designer, writer (with several books to her credit). I sold myself as a rare jewel between appearances at one opera house or another. I promised that if La Scala or the Met called I'd find a replacement, and then return following all my applause. Laura bought the whole thing—it was clear that she liked me, the dreamer, and she'd take whatever came with it.

The job was great, the hours flexible, the apartment just beautiful. Laura was as easy as they come as long as I kept up my end of the deal. She had a strong, earthy background but felt at home in an Armani pants suit or Capezio dance shoes (her signature footwear). In no time at all we were going to shows, lunches, and dinners together, even calling each other on the phone to gossip. Many of Laura's friends became my friends and my friends hers. Peter, her husband, was always warm and gracious toward me, though I rarely saw him. It was clear that I worked for Laura. I began cooking and catering parties for them on a regular basis. This was the most fun—especially for birthdays and anniversaries or big client dinners, when Peter would bring home the VIPs. But it was one thing to cook, another to pace and present beautifully and on time. Laura's kitchen was my training ground, where I learned to facilitate cooking, preparation, and timing.

One of the first meals I made was a disaster. Laura had asked me to prepare a country beef stew for the weekend. Simple enough, I thought. Ignoring my instinct to select cubes of chuck, I decided on the leanest beef in D'Agostino's. Big mistake! Back at Laura's apartment I used veal bones to make a stock flavored with fresh thyme and rosemary leaves. While this was cooking I cut up carrots, parsnips, onions, celery, and potatoes, and seared it all in an extremely hot skillet with a little salt, pepper, and garlic-infused olive oil. I seasoned my tender beef sirloin with herbs and light flour, seared this in the same pan till golden brown, then combined these wonderful ingredients and simmered the concoction while busying myself with other chores. Laura mentioned the intense aroma, and I assured her that the stew would be as delicious as it smelled. "You can't cook it enough" were my parting words that Friday afternoon, and I could only imagine the praise I'd encounter after the weekend.

But by midday Monday Laura had not breathed one compliment in my direction. I finally had to inquire. "Oh, Alexander." She paused. "We had to throw it out, the meat was dry as a bone." I was horrified. "The gravy wasn't bad, but we ended up ordering steaks in." No more was ever said about it. I knew I should not have attempted to get fancy. I would eventually make beef stew to a fanfare of praise. But you can blame the butcher only once.

One of Laura's good friends, Barbara Johnson, who with her husband, Don, was a partner in a midtown search firm, hired me to cook dinners for them a couple of times a week. I'd shop the night before, leave Laura's around one, cook up a dinner for two to four people in my kitchen, and deliver it by cab with warming instructions. This arrangement suited me well. Barbara and I consulted about menus, and occasionally she'd find recipes for me to try.

Overnight I was in the catering business, it seemed, so I gave the business a name: Small Miracle, Inc. My friend Denise Dickens designed a business card, a basket of food on a blue-gray background with lettering the color of red wine. Soon there were so many requests that I had to develop a crew of waiters, bartenders, and cooks to assist me. J.J., who had worked for large catering concerns and in restaurants as a waiter, maître d', and manager, was my number one, generously warm, accommodating assistant and director. No one could work the room better.

Since things were going reasonably well, I threw myself a thirtieth birthday bash. Randy Jones, my roommate in North Carolina, had moved to New York and become the cowboy in the singing group The Village People. He offered me his very large loft (Le Chanteur had by now been repossessed). I organized, arranged, and cooked for days. Each of the hundred or so guests was asked to bring roses and bottles of Stolichnaya. I made all sorts of cold dishes: salmon and spinach rice salad; a sherry-glazed corned beef and green bean plate; sweet potato and cranberry salad with toasted pecans; turnip, parsnip, and white bean salad tossed with thin-sliced cabbage and black olives in a vinaigrette of Dijon mustard and garlic. Of course, there were the usual dips, chips, pickles, crudités, nuts, and powerful fruit punches I'd become famous for. People drank vodka and danced with roses in their hair, behind their ears, or clutched in their teeth like Carmens of the night. It was romantic and joyously celebratory. It was also the sounding of the drum, the blowing of the bugle, the ever-pressing need to answer, "What am I going to be when I grow up?"

Peter and Laura had bought an old schoolhouse in Carmel, only an hour from Manhattan, and one weekend J.J. and I agreed to go up for a few days to clean the place. It was Easter, so we invited some friends as well, figuring we'd clean after they left. In Spartanburg the food at Easter was like two Sunday dinners rolled into one, with special surprises, including whipped sweet potatoes with toasted marshmallow topping or strawberry Jell-O with fruit cocktail and fresh mint in a mold. My mom also arranged big baskets with green, yellow, pink, and sometimes blue straw, and filled them with eggs she'd dyed as well as chocolate rabbits and chocolate chicks filled with caramel or jelly, and my favorite candy, jelly beans.

In Carmel I was inspired by the countryside (two acres surrounded by a national reserve) and Peter and Laura's warm, beautifully decorated house with its large eat-in kitchen and outdoor patios. I decided to serve a meal worthy of the setting. Besides the traditional glazed ham I roasted Cornish hens with a lemon, pineapple, and brandy sauce, their stuffing a blend of sautéed spinach, caramelized onions, cornbread, and sautéed duck livers with a pinch of salt, pepper, and nutmeg to lift the flavor. A platter of assorted colored deviled eggs—made with saffron, puree of beets, spinach, mustard, and curry powder—sat atop a nest of colored straw and flower blooms. Spring potatoes, asparagus tips, red onions, and cherry tomatoes with chives and a light tarragon vinaigrette rested in one of Laura's hand-painted bowls. Friends brought red wine, French bread, sweet butter, and cheeses from the city. Dinner was served in the kitchen, and we adjourned to the patio for coffee and tea. J.J. organized·a game of croquet, putting wickets all over the back lawn, in lieu of an Easter egg hunt, I thought. While the others played, I remained in the kitchen putting together one of my favorite desserts, coconut cake. I had taken my mother's recipe and added sweet potatoes to the batter, piled lots of seven-minute frosting between each layer with generous amounts of fresh coconut, and dropped jelly beans all over the top and sides. Everybody loved it—in fact, the croquet players took time-outs for seconds and thirds. After everyone left, J.J. and I reminisced and cleaned, but I remember we had to go back a second time as the first cleaning was not exactly satisfactory—little wonder.

One day Peter called from his office about Laura's fortieth birthday. He wanted to pull out all the stops and have me cater a party in Carmel.

I was delighted, though I was still learning the ropes of catering: how to charge, order, organize, time myself, and generally pull it off. What is now second nature to me was like pulling teeth before, one by one. The pain of knowledge, you might say. I told Peter that a party like the one he was describing would be really expensive. A man of Peter's wealth and arrogance did not appreciate this suggestion. However, always prepared to humor the clueless and unsophisticated, he was cool. "Well now, Alexander . . . how expensive, really?" he said. "Just figure out everything and let me know."

A party for fifty people or so. Outside tent, tables, chairs, station wagon, rental plates, glasses, silverware, serving utensils, bowls, platters, grills, napkins, waiters, beverages, ice, payroll, and last but not least, food! I wore a lot of hats before that party was over. But I was excited. I felt good; I loved this as much as singing, and that should have been a warning light. My catering kitchen was no bigger than a four-by-five square in my small apartment. But through coordination and timing I got the most out of those four burners. First I made the foods that required no refrigeration: cakes, pies, smoked hams, starches, and breads. For additional cold storage I filled portable coolers and my bathtub with ice. The day of the party I was up—or up again—at dawn, having set the clock all through the night to get up and put something in the oven, sleep for an hour, then wake up again to take it out and put something else in. J.J. arrived early to help pack and run last-minute errands. Tito and Enzo, my waiters, arrived by late morning looking dashing in black trousers and white shirts with bow ties. We piled the food, in large bags, boxes, and cartons, into the big rented station wagon; collected booze and the rented supplies from Peter's office; set out for the adventure; got lost a few times; and arrived only an hour before the guests. Peter and Laura were, well, you can guess.

We threw the party together at record speed. This is where J.J. shone. He whipped the situation into shape in minutes and calmed the fears of the fearful hosts in no time at all. The boy was good. While he organized the mechanics, I laid out all the appetizers and hors d'oeuvres so as to buy time as the eager crowd arrived. J.J. set up the bar and waiter stations, which allowed Tito and Enzo to service the rush that soon followed. The waiters passed little slices of spinach, gorgonzola, and egg pies made with cornmeal crust; spicy salmon and onion salad canapés on toasted biscuit chips; frankfurter hush puppies with hot mustard dip; and jumbo shrimp cocktail with garlic and poppy-seed mayonnaise. Meanwhile, I was arms deep in preparation for the main course. I needed another set of hands as well as a bouncer at the door to keep out all of Laura's friends, who never thought twice about coming into the kitchen and holding me hostage.

The grill out on the lawn at first refused to cooperate. With a hefty amount of lamb kebabs in marinade waiting (on skewers with okra, tomatoes, corn, and onions), I did the only thing I could do—started running them under the broiler. When Peter finally got the grill going, I used it just to get the charcoal flavor through. The main course I laid out under the tent on a long table Laura herself had decorated. Besides the lamb there was a seafood rice pilau with little clams and mussels in their shells; a platter of snow peas with roasted shallots, garlic, and sliced carrots; a field salad with endive; roasted red peppers in a lemon vinaigrette; and two of Laura's requests—a tomato and cucumber salad with fresh mint and a bowl of orzo seasoned with garlic, olive oil, and feta cheese, with chopped black olives and some lemongrass thrown in for color. We served nearly every bite of food and almost ran out of aluminum foil to make packages for those who knew not when the party was over. I remember thinking, "And they say only black folks get it to go."

The party indeed over, I sat outside on the front step, all packed up and ready to head back to town. Only one glass of Champagne for me—I was driving. Peter handed me a big check. "A little extra for a fine job," he said.

I don't know if I knew then that I was creating my career, that I'd begun to think of myself as a food person. It was as if it were waiting in the wings. How often we stumble over the obvious truths. In a sense, by a certain time in your life you are what you are, not what you're going to be. But when we got home the four of us unloaded our gear and then headed for the last few turns on the dance floor at a downtown club. Who wanted to think about growing up?

Nevertheless, catering jobs just kept coming and I got better and better at it. I organized menus and price lists, and my team was ready when I called. J.J. was often the booking agent and the advance person. We did parties for private clients and small companies and offered a special service where we'd hire ourselves out as cook and butler for a night. We'd bring everything with us, including the pots and pans. Sometimes we'd create ambience, calling in out-of-work artists to decorate or musicians to play piano, violin—even, once, a trumpet. People gave us as gifts to friends, family, and business associates. One night I cooked dinner and J.J. served, after which we came out and sang solos and duets before cleaning up and departing.

Things were comfortable during this time, and I felt hopeful about my direction. At the invitation of a friend who was giving a recital, I joined her in a duet from *La Traviata*. The recital hall was packed. Michael Tilson and Josh came and had much to say about me as well as all the things in the world they'd been doing. Michael continued to be amazing, and I continued to be trying to continue. I secretly wished he'd take me and my big unfocused talent, mold it, and present it to the world. But meanwhile I'd moved back into my 80th Street apartment and was happy to be on my own again and settled in that familiar space. I still dreamed of greatness on the stage—with a paring knife in my hand. I knew something was just around the bend; I was just waiting for it to appear. But while I waited, I cooked and cooked and cooked.

———— ❧ ————

As you can see, I was cooking up a storm during this period. A regular show-off in the kitchen, I had a lot to prove. Any one of these dishes would make a delicious centerpiece at any meal—especially the sweet potato coconut cake.

———— ❧ ————

COUNTRY BEEF STEW

8 SERVINGS

❧

¼ cup flour

1 teaspoon salt

¼ teaspoon freshly ground black
  pepper

2 pounds beef chuck, cubed

3 tablespoons vegetable oil

1 large onion, chopped

3 ribs celery, chopped

6 cloves garlic, minced

1 cup red wine

6 bay leaves

1 tablespoon fresh thyme

2 sprigs fresh rosemary, chopped

1 tablespoon brown sugar

¼ cup tomato paste

6 cups beef broth

1 large green pepper, chopped

3 carrots, peeled and cut into chunks

3 parsnips, peeled and cut into chunks

2 large potatoes, peeled and cut into
  chunks

additional salt and pepper to taste

Combine the flour, salt, and pepper. Dredge the beef in the seasoned flour. Heat the oil in a Dutch oven and brown the beef on all sides. Add onion, celery, and garlic. Cook 5 minutes. Deglaze with red wine. Add herbs, brown sugar, and tomato paste and cook 5 minutes. Add 1 tablespoon of the dredging flour and mix well. Add beef broth, bring to a boil, and simmer 1½ hours. Add vegetables, and salt and pepper to taste, bring to a boil, and simmer for 30 minutes. Serve with rice or noodles.

ROAST STUFFED CORNISH HENS WITH LEMON-BRANDY PINEAPPLE SAUCE

8 SERVINGS

❧

4 Cornish game hens, cleaned
salt and freshly ground black pepper
2 cups chicken stock for basting

STUFFING
1 cup spinach, chopped, sautéed
1 cup onions, chopped, caramelized
2 cups cornbread, cubed
1 cup duck livers, sautéed
1 tablespoon fresh thyme
1 teaspoon sage, rubbed
1 teaspoon nutmeg

1 teaspoon salt
¼ teaspoon freshly ground black pepper
2 large eggs, beaten

SAUCE
2 shallots, minced
2 shots brandy
juice of 5 lemons
⅛ cup brown sugar
2 cups pineapple chunks in juice
1 cup chicken stock
1 stick (¼ pound) butter, cut into pats

Season game hens with salt and pepper and lay in roasting pan.

STUFFING

In a medium-size bowl, mix stuffing ingredients. Loosely stuff birds. Bake in a 350-degree oven 1 hour, basting frequently with 2 cups chicken stock. Set aside to cool.

SAUCE

Using pan drippings, in a medium saucepan sauté shallots for 5 minutes. Flambé with brandy. Add lemon juice, brown sugar, and pineapple chunks and reduce for 3 minutes. Add 1 cup chicken stock and reduce 5 minutes. Take off flame and whisk in butter until emulsified.

Slice hens lengthwise in half and arrange on platter. Pour sauce over hens and serve at once.

SALMON AND SPINACH RICE SALAD

❧

3 cups long grain rice

3 tablespoons olive oil

salt

freshly ground black pepper

½ cup white wine

1 cup water

1 bay leaf

2 salmon fillets, 8 ounces each

1 large onion, minced

3 stalks scallion, minced

¼ cup parsley, minced

2 ribs celery, minced

1 large red bell pepper, minced

2 cups wilted spinach, minced

¼ cup fresh dill, minced

¼ cup mayonnaise

¼ cup red wine vinegar

salt

freshly ground black pepper

lettuce leaves for platter

Cook rice according to package directions, using olive oil, salt, and black pepper to season. Chill.

Bring white wine and water to a boil. Add 1 teaspoon salt and bay leaf. Poach salmon fillets until firm, about 15 minutes, in simmering broth. Cool. Scrape off skin and break salmon apart into small pieces.

Mix onion, scallion, parsley, celery, red pepper, spinach, and dill. Toss with mayonnaise, vinegar, ½ teaspoon salt, and black pepper to taste.

Put chilled rice in a large bowl and fluff to separate. Add vegetable and herb mixture and salmon, and toss until well mixed. Chill 10 minutes; arrange on platter lined with lettuce leaves.

SPINACH, GORGONZOLA, AND EGG PIE

8 SERVINGS

❧

½ cup shortening
2 cups sifted flour
½ cup cornmeal
water
1 egg white
4 cups fresh spinach,
    cleaned, dried, and
    chopped
1½ cups gorgonzola,
    crumbled
6 large eggs
3 cups milk
1 cup sour cream
pinch nutmeg
½ teaspoon salt
freshly ground black pepper

In a bowl, cut shortening into flour and cornmeal. Add enough water to make a firm dough. Roll out on a floured surface and line a 10-inch pie pan with dough. Brush edges with egg white. Place spinach on top of pastry. Top with gorgonzola.

In a small bowl, mix eggs, milk, sour cream, nutmeg, salt, and pepper. Pour over cheese and spinach. Bake for 10 minutes in preheated 400-degree oven. Reduce oven to 325 degrees and bake 30 minutes more, until knife comes out clean when inserted into center. Slice and serve.

TURNIP, PARSNIP, AND WHITE BEAN SALAD

10 SERVINGS

∞

3 cups turnips, peeled and cubed

3 cups parsnips, peeled and cubed

2 cups white beans, cooked

1 large green cabbage, sliced thin

2 cups whole pitted black olives,
   halved

DRESSING

3 cloves garlic, minced

¼ cup Dijon mustard

¼ cup red wine vinegar

1 tablespoon fresh mint, chopped

½ teaspoon salt

½ teaspoon freshly ground black
   pepper

1 cup olive oil

In a vegetable steamer, steam turnips and parsnips about 15 minutes. Chill. Mix turnips, parsnips, white beans, cabbage, and olives in a large bowl. Toss with dressing and chill 15 minutes before serving.

DRESSING

In a blender, combine garlic, mustard, vinegar, mint leaves, salt, and pepper. With motor running, add oil in a thin stream until emulsified.

FIELD SALAD WITH
ENDIVE AND ROASTED PEPPERS

8 SERVINGS

❧

3 cups black-eyed peas, firm-cooked
2 large heads endive, cut into ½-inch circles
1½ cups roasted red peppers, cut into strips

LEMON VINAIGRETTE
juice of 4 lemons
1 teaspoon Dijon mustard
2 teaspoons honey
1 teaspoon fresh thyme
½ teaspoon salt
¼ teaspoon freshly ground black pepper
1 cup olive oil

lettuce leaves, for platter
¼ cup fresh parsley, chopped, for garnish

In a large bowl, mix peas, endive, and red peppers.

VINAIGRETTE
In a blender, combine lemon juice, mustard, honey, thyme, salt, and pepper. With machine running, add oil in a thin stream until emulsified.

Toss vinaigrette with peas, endive, and peppers until well mixed. Chill 15 minutes, then invert onto a lettuce-lined serving platter. Garnish with parsley.

SWEET POTATO COCONUT CAKE

10 SERVINGS

❦

CAKE

2 sticks (½ pound) butter

2 cups sugar

1 teaspoon vanilla

3 cups cake flour

3 teaspoons baking powder

1 teaspoon salt

½ cup milk

½ cup buttermilk

½ cup fresh coconut, grated

½ cup roasted sweet potato, pureed

6 large egg whites

FROSTING

1½ cups sugar

½ cup water

2 large egg whites

1 teaspoon vanilla

¼ teaspoon salt

1 tablespoon light corn syrup

2 cups fresh coconut, grated

2 cups assorted jelly beans

CAKE

Cream butter and sugar until light and fluffy. Add vanilla and mix well. Sift together flour, baking powder, and salt. Mix milk and buttermilk. Add flour mixture and milk mixture to butter mixture alternately in thirds, scraping down the sides of the bowl after each addition. Add coconut and sweet potato and mix well. Pour into medium-size bowl. Whip egg whites until stiff but not dry. Fold into cake batter using over-under motion. Pour batter evenly into two greased 9-inch round cake pans.

Bake in preheated 350-degree oven for 25 minutes, or until springy to the touch. Remove from oven and cool 5 minutes. Turn cakes out onto cooling rack and allow to cool to room temperature.

FROSTING

Whisk sugar and water together, dissolving sugar completely. Place on high heat and allow to come to rapid boil.

While water is boiling, whip egg whites on high speed. When whites are stiff but not dry, add vanilla and salt. Remove boiling sugar water from heat and pour into egg whites in a slow, thin stream. Continue whipping until mixture reaches room temperature. Add corn syrup and continue whipping on high speed until icing reaches spreading consistency. Refrigerate 30 minutes.

ASSEMBLY

When cake layers reach room temperature, assemble the cake. Sprinkle the outside of the frosted cake with coconut, covering it completely. Garnish with jelly beans.

16 PORGY AND PARIS REDUX

One morning as I prepared to leave for Laura's, the phone rang. I'd been balancing working for her, catering, voice lessons, opera coaching, auditions, dinner parties, and wild nightclubbing. Now it was Sherwin Goldman's office with news of a new production of *Porgy and Bess* to run at Radio City Music Hall after a six-week tryout in Chicago. I danced around the apartment shouting, "Count me in!"

I found a replacement to work for Laura and put Small Miracle, Inc., on hold. Within the month we were well into rehearsals, and then we opened in Chicago.

It was exciting to hear the old voices, and the new, among them Veronica Tyler, legendary among opera veterans and aficionados, who for some reason had chosen this vehicle for her comeback. An extraordinary soprano with a voice like spun gold, she had wowed the public for years, then mysteriously disappeared. To the first rehearsal she wore a leopard coat and hat, causing quite a stir, and she followed this with one lavish outfit after another, rivaling the theatrics of Bess herself. I learned so much from Veronica. She sang the role of Serena and brought the house down every night. She was my new Clamma Dale at a time when I had to really understand my position in the music business. We became great friends, both of us running against the clock.

Opening night at Radio City was thunderous! Backstage drama, dressing room chitchat, fluffed costumes with a crew of dressers, and

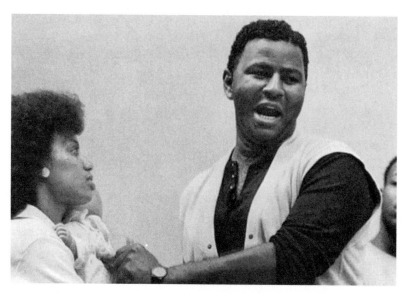

Rehearsing for our first run of Porgy and Bess *in Charleston with singer Harolyn Blackwell (Metropolitan Opera singer).*

everywhere opening night jitters. It felt so good to be working, and the feeling was infectious. In Chicago the cast had bonded over a whole lot of barbecued chicken and ribs, fried potatoes, hush puppies, baked beans, slaw, and sweet potato pie. Jackie O'Brien, *Porgy's* original director, had teamed up this time with the extremely talented George Faison, who choreographed our every beat and shake. George was wild energy from a background in theater, dance, and popular music, with roots in black music. He was also a great guy who responded to my talent and pulled more out of me than I knew was there. Through George my life got richer, fuller, blacker. I met Alvin Ailey, Arthur Mitchell, Stevie Wonder, Ashford and Simpson, the members of Earth, Wind & Fire, Miles Davis, Chaka Khan, Eartha Kitt, and later Maya Angelou, just to name a few—people whose struggles often resembled my own. George gave the most incredible parties; on his birthday Roberta Flack arrived, and then Patty Austin followed by Debbie Allen and Judith Jamison. And Jennifer Holliday brought the party to its knees with "You Were Always on My Mind."

*My second parents, Jeanie and David Goodman,
in Carmel, New York.*

A long run in Boston and an extensive tour of Canada were supposed to follow Radio City, so I rented out my apartment. But after six
weeks in Boston the rest of the tour was canceled (my luck). Marc
Goodman, a friend, suggested his parents' place, which was empty; and
his mother, Jeanie, gave me the go-ahead. Once again I was in residence
on 80th Street, just next door to my old apartment.

Jeanie Goodman, tall, blond, blue-eyed, and in your face, was a
breath of fresh air and a cozy comfort. She knew what she liked, and in
this case she seemed to like me as much as I liked her. David, her husband, who had been dragged to the opera since his childhood, still main-
tained season tickets at the Met and was thrilled to have an opera singer
in-house. These two invincible wonders of another generation, as different as they were alike, and as close to each other in spirit and partnership
as Uncle Joe and Aunt Laura, took me into their hearts and home, and I
lived in their shadow and grace off and on for ten years. Besides their
beautiful apartment they had a big, funky pink beach house on Long
Island where they spent much of their time. My relationship with my

own parents grew tremendously because of the friendship I shared with Jeanie and David. I was fortunate to have two sets of parents, each different in their approach but both wanting the best for me.

Like me, Jeanie loved to entertain. David would grumble about not wanting to see anyone ("Don't invite those people. Why do we have to have them? I'm not going to talk to her anymore"), but then he couldn't wait till the first guest arrived. I was in heaven. All I had to say was "dinner party," and we'd be scurrying off to the supermarket, Zabar's, Fairway, the nut and candy store, and of course Carroll's, the wine and spirits shop. Several trips with double plastic bags later, classical music blasting, we were burning metal. Jeanie had a couple of specialties; beyond those, her idea of getting creative was to mix everything together that she'd ever made or liked. "If the sauce is good the hell with the rest" was her point of view. I loved her orange spice chicken dish. You seldom tasted any orange in it despite all the slices she put in there, but it was always juicy and the overcooked chicken would just fall off the bone. Her green salads consisted of whatever she bought and whatever she found in the refrigerator going slowly south. "Just add a little more dressing on that," she'd say.

Soon these parties were talked about, the place you wanted to be, the most colorful and integrated and with the most surprising guest list, from the pizza boy on the corner to the reigning diva at the Met. On my thirty-first birthday the large oak dining table looked as if it would buckle from the weight. (When entertaining more than twenty I always tried to put all the food on the table before the first guest arrived. This meant food that was chilled or at room temperature, unless chafing dishes or hot plates were used.) My friend Kevin had smoked two turkeys for me. Beside those were Jeanie's orange chicken and her vegetable stir-fry surprise, as well as a large platter of seared tuna, red potato, and wilted cabbage with fresh fennel in a creamy dill dressing. In a large bowl I had piled high my latest creation, a spicy beet salad with scallions, charred sliced okra, roasted sweet peppers, mushrooms, fried corn, and black beans, tossed in a vinaigrette with sesame seed and cracked pepper and served over shredded iceberg lettuce (savoy cabbage works, too). Grilled vegetable rice salad, with chunks of squash, zucchini, peppers, eggplant, tomatoes, onions, and black olives, rested beside wedges of sage cornbread, bacon-and-onion cornbread, and hot-pepper-and-cheese cornbread. And there was no such thing as a party without Alexander's famous ham, melting in your mouth, good with that old mustard and brown sugar smack that left you panting for more. My friend Freddie Clark always said, "That ham has the taste vegetarians stand in line to get." It's hard to recall the number of people who came, but the party got so good that at one point there was cause for concern as to whether the swaying floor beams could support them.

One guest was the fabulous eighty-something Ruth Dubonnet, an amazing sipper of martinis, who had been and done everything, had known everyone, and had the age and state of mind to prove it. Her ideas about life, love, sex, and career were well beyond her generation and mine. Rumor had it that she'd been romantically linked with Rudolph Valentino, and her motto was simple and to the point: "Just do it, do it, and do it again!"

Ruth and my pal Wendy Burden were well into a conversation when I approached them. Wendy, the great-granddaughter of Florence Vanderbilt and William Burden, came from the kind of family Uncle Joe would have worked for or wanted me to marry into. She shared my love of food, wine, parties, France, and Italy. Over the years we'd given parties and dinners together, including barbecues at her grandparents' estate. I was always in charge of the barbecue sauce, which I'd spike with generous amounts of bourbon and cayenne pepper. Wendy tackled the side dishes and created mouthwatering desserts. She loved grits—odd for a northern girl. Now, panicked that she was about to turn thirty, she had decided to marry. But before she did she wanted a last fling. One of her dreams had been to go to cooking school, and to live in Paris. "Just do it!" Ruth yelled at the top of her lungs, well into martini five or six. Wendy, as calm and willful as she could be, turned to me as if to say, "It's in your hands; I'll do it if you'll do it," and with that our fate was sealed.

So after a one-month stint with *Porgy and Bess* in Italy—at the Teatro Communale in Florence—and a stop in Rome, I flew to Paris. The grant money I had been assured was mine had fallen through, but

Jeanie and David—ever-ready—came to my rescue. A couple of weeks later Wendy and Pearl, her English bull terrier, arrived, and in no time we were the lovely Parisian couple with the strange white dog (which some Frenchmen referred to as a pig on a leash) who followed them everywhere and chased other dogs away. I studied, sang, soaked up art and French music style. But something was still missing, and always there was that inner voice that understood my doubts, crying: "Please let *me* want this as much as I've convinced everybody else I do!"

My longtime friend Sharon Goldenberg had organized an evening at Carnegie Hall to benefit One To One, an agency to protect abused and neglected children. She had managed to throw me a bone and include me on the program, which featured Renata Scotto, Anna Moffo, the Alvin Ailey Ensemble, and many more. George Faison, one of the hosts of the evening, had gotten Phyllis Hyman to present me. I left Paris for a week on a round-trip first-class ticket, compliments of the organization. The night of the event, full up with fear, I thought my stomach would leave the building. But when my turn came, and after the first few measures it was clear to me that the voice wouldn't desert me, I relaxed and sang the count's aria from Mozart's *Le Nozze di Figaro,* and then the crowd pleaser, "A Woman Is a Sometime Thing." The audience was so generous as I stood on one of the greatest stages in the world, bowing, waving, and mouthing thank-yous. It could all end here, I thought; maybe this could be enough.

Back in Paris at the studio of Madame Aitoff, one of the leading coaches at the Paris Opera, I was vocalizing all over the pages of Gounod's *Faust.* Poor Madame Aitoff's desperate attempts to teach me had sent us well into overtime, since my heart and head were anywhere but there, and her frustration at my lack of focus was reaching the boiling point. "Saved by the bell," she must have thought as the arrival of another student ended our session. I shared her relief as I thought of the food shopping I needed to do for dinner. But when the door opened, to my surprise there stood Kathleen Battle. We had met during the first Broadway run of *Porgy and Bess,* when I joined her and Steven Cole for lunch. She was soft-spoken, warm, and attentive, and I had liked her immediately, though she spoke about two sentences to my ten, and for a diva in training I thought she could use a little more tiger in her tank. I even wondered to Steven whether she was strong enough to make it in this business or not—what a joke that turned out to be—and here we were in Madame Aitoff's living room.

That night, in honor of old times we dined at the famous Leroy Haynes restaurant, the soul food capital of Paris. Leroy, a black American veteran of World War II, had married a Frenchwoman and opened the restaurant in Pigalle. The place was jumping with lively music, old expatriates, and well-dressed Frenchmen, and full of the smell of southern vittles boiling, cornbread baking, and collard greens braising. We ordered everything on the menu that spelled home. After months of French sauces, French waiters, and lots of savoir faire, this was great stuff. We ended the evening laughing and singing and dancing down the Champs-Élysées toward Kathleen's hotel. For the next two months or so the two of us spent a lot of time together. She was performing the role of Susanna in *Le Nozze di Figaro,* with Daniel Barenboim conducting. Sitting through one grueling rehearsal after another I witnessed firsthand her pure genius, her strategy as she built her character and brought it to life. Her commitment and focus caused me to tremble. I had never, ever given that much of myself to music study, or to anything for that matter. I feared that it wasn't in me to do so, and I felt I had let us all down—Aunt Laura and Uncle Joe, Miss Cleveland, myself especially. But even through this momentary indulgence, I found a way to hang on to Kathleen's every note. I had never known it possible to put fire, hail, wind, and the sun, moon, and stars in a voice until I heard her. I was to grow in amazing ways with Kathleen. I would sit over the years, as I still do, through countless rehearsals, concerts, operas, recording sessions, ceremonies, and family gatherings (hers and mine). We would share the expected and unexpected, but Paris of '84 gave us each other.

Every Sunday night, with few exceptions, Wendy, Pearl, and I would venture out to La Coupole for dinner. There Pearl was treated like visiting royalty. She always had steak, compliments of the house, while Wendy and I dined on cold chicken and *pommes frites.* We took Pearl to nightclubs and concerts and on boat trips down the Seine, though we did leave her home when Wendy, through family connections, got us reservations at Taillevent, the best restaurant in Paris. From the genuinely gracious welcome committee to the foot waiter, hand waiter, maître d', manager, and warmly solicitous owner, the experience was extraordinary. There were so many courses it was hard to tell when dinner was over. I remember being completely blown away by the cheese course. How could cheese be so special? A dinner like that called for an after-dinner celebration, so we hailed a cab and headed for the Palace, where Dee Dee Bridgewater was holding court. Dee Dee became a regular, like so many others, at our apartment off Saint-Germain.

The best southern fried chicken in all of Paris was made by Patrick Kelly, then a struggling designer, later to become one of the most celebrated French couturiers. If you had chicken, Patrick would fry it. He sold chicken dinners out of his apartment to those in the know, between sewing buttons, running seams, and fitting models and society ladies. I shared many a chicken wishbone with all who adored him, including my old friend Toukie Smith, model, actress, and no stranger to the kitchen either.

When the Bill T. Jones and Arnie Zane dance company arrived in town, we were all aflutter. Bill T. was the biggest dancer I'd ever seen and Arnie the smallest. They were warm, humble, and breathtaking, yet powerful and unconventional. I threw a southern cocktail party in their honor. Patrick fried the chicken, Wendy made the guacamole, I created hot chili dip, herb corn pancakes with crème fraîche, seafood puppies, pimento cheese spread with jalapeño peppers, mini veal-peanut meatballs in mustard sauce, spinach dip, and assorted breads and cheeses. Wendy's brother had shipped us a whole case of Cheez Doodles, I'd gone to the Tex Mex restaurant on the Right Bank and bought a huge bag of taco chips, and last but hardly least I made the first barbecued ribs that many of my guests had ever seen.

Finding those ribs, however, was an odyssey. After visiting three or four meat markets, I was at a loss. What was the conspiracy, I wondered, behind the fact that the ribs of the *cochon* never made it to market? Walking back toward the apartment, I noticed a small market with rabbits still dressed in fur, turtles, and baby goats hanging from hooks in the window. This had to be it, I thought, surely ribs couldn't be more exotic than this. But I found none. Frustrated, I began to query, with my broken French and masterful sign language. The butcher showed me all sorts of hog parts, hoping to identify my request. Well into this exercise he finally pulled out the rib cage I longed for, but rather than being over, the battle had just begun. He refused to sell it to me. This was not a product to be sold, explained a nice, slightly amused middle-aged lady, who spoke English and had witnessed it all. This was sold in large quantities to producers of pet food, she said; there was simply no retail value.

I could have chosen to be insulted, but with my quest in sight I chose to value the purchase, and with a hundred francs I sealed the deal for more ribs than Leroy Haynes was serving that night in Pigalle. After a day of soaking in vinegar, onions, and spices, these sought-after bones of spicy bliss rested well-wrapped in my famous honey barbecue sauce. After the party, not a one was left on a plate anywhere. As usual, Wendy and I more than did our share for French-American relations.

Just before we left Paris, I went to visit friends in Lucca, Italy—ten days of Italian countryside, fabulous food, and a chance to ponder the landscape of my life. I knew only too well there was work to be done in my garden, metaphorically speaking.

What had I accomplished? What had Paris been about, and what the hell did I do now? Was there a genuine strategy guiding me, or was it time to call a spade a spade?

I would mount one more major effort in pursuit of an operatic career—a Metropolitan Opera audition. Preparing for it, back on 80th Street, awakened all the old wounds. At so many auditions the color of my skin had overshadowed any musical sound I could possibly have made.

Once, Joel Black, my first agent, after some discussion with the director I was singing for, asked in a brash, forceful way, "Alex, do you know any gospel you could sing for us?" My voice had frozen somewhere below my vocal cords. "I'm sorry, I've never sung gospel in my life, and I'm unprepared to do justice to that particular form," I answered finally. Joel, who was made to feel smaller by the antics of an uppity black man, said, "Oh, come on, Al, you know you know some gospel tunes. . . . Sing it a cappella, pat your foot, and really get into it."

This was just a symptom of the problems of opera and black men. There were no role models other than Paul Robeson, Seth McCoy, and Simon Estes, and among those only Robeson became world-renowned—and not for his singing. I was now being represented by Betsy Crittenden, who had negotiated a triumphant return to South Carolina for me, once again singing the role of Jake, this time with the Charleston Symphony. I loved being in Charleston, where the secret receipts of Low Country dwellers were served up all over town. I ate from morning till night, and the kitchen in my rented house became a lab where I sought to continue my experiments to marry southern Low Country cooking with European style and techniques. Between rehearsals and, later, performances, I lived and slept the food arts of the region. I bought cookbooks, history books, literature, and any magazine that attempted to unravel the myth of southern food, and accumulated a notebook full of recipes.

I returned to New York just weeks before the much anticipated Met audition. Kathleen threw her support behind me, always championing my vocal ability to anyone who'd listen, and offering advice that did much to prepare me. Gwendolyn had never missed an important moment, and this was no exception. I was as ready as I was going to be. With Betsy Crittenden I waited my turn outside the small hall at the Met, and once shown inside I wasted no time taking charge, singing through phrase after phrase of *Bella siccome un angelo* from *Don Pasquale*. I was singing for my musical life and identity. Sure, I had not always been the perfect student, and I was not without my considerations, but I was a fine singer and I wanted the Met to admit it.

At the end of the aria I stood motionless onstage, assured of the impression I'd made. "That was wonderful," came a voice from out there. Someone commented on how much I'd grown as a singer since last they'd heard me. I felt good—a turning point, hopefully. I glanced at my agent, who smiled encouragingly.

"We'd like to offer you the role of Jim, and a part in the chorus of the opera *Porgy and Bess*. Would you be interested?"

Jim—a two-line part. This seemed to me an awful joke, one I had nothing left inside me to respond to. I had sung on the Grammy Award recording. Often, with *Porgy*, I was the only one who got reviewed. As I went light-headed, I heard my grandfather saying what he always said, "Own your own way, son; take charge of your destiny."

"No, I would not be interested," I said, and wandered out of the hall. Behind me, faintly, I heard the voice of my agent trying to get my attention.

"Why did you turn down the Met?" she screamed. "That's a great opportunity to get in the door, and then who knows? I can fix this if you want it. Just tell me."

I turned to her, wanting to know one thing. "Did you know they were going to make this offer to me?" I asked quietly.

"Well, yes . . ."

Everything else she said fell on deaf ears. A few weeks later Veronica Tyler called with the news that the Met had hired several black Broadway singers to sing *Porgy and Bess* and had offered them, as well, major roles in classic opera. That was the slap in the face I could not survive. After drinking all the booze in the house, I said good-bye. All the decisions in my musical life had been made for me, but this was the one I felt I controlled. Out of a sense of survival, I threw in the towel, buried my voice, and hurried on to Small Miracle, Inc.

---⸿---

Whether at a party on 80th Street in New York City or on the Left Bank in Paris, I would serve these dishes to a waiting and willing audience. Sometimes it's simply the food that makes the party, but don't forget to call some great people over to help you eat.

---⸿---

BARBECUED CHICKEN OR RIBS

4 SERVINGS

⸿

2 cups white vinegar

4 cups water

1 teaspoon whole cloves

salt and freshly ground black pepper
    to taste

1 3-pound chicken, washed, cleaned,
    and patted dry; or 4 pounds pork
    spareribs

¼ cup vegetable oil

3 cloves garlic, minced

¼ teaspoon ground cloves

3 cups ketchup

1 cup dark brown sugar

½ cup mustard

1 cup honey

¼ cup Worcestershire sauce

juice of 1 lemon

1 small onion, minced

2 tablespoons Tabasco sauce

3 teaspoons chili powder

1 teaspoon celery seed

Combine vinegar, water, and whole cloves. Season with salt and pepper. Add chicken or ribs and marinate in refrigerator overnight.

Heat oil in large pan and sauté garlic until golden. Add remaining ingredients and a dash of salt; bring to a simmer, stirring constantly. Cook over medium-low heat for 45 minutes, stirring occasionally. Remove and cool.

Remove chicken or ribs and discard marinade. Place chicken or ribs in large roasting pan and season with salt and pepper and bake 15 minutes in preheated 375-degree oven. Then start basting and brushing with barbecue sauce every 15 minutes, and cook 1 hour, turning occasionally.

Serve hot or at room temperature with remaining sauce on the side.

SEAFOOD PUPPIES

12 SERVINGS

❧

1 cup flour

½ teaspoon salt

1 teaspoon sugar

1 teaspoon baking powder

½ teaspoon baking soda

1 egg

1 cup buttermilk

1 teaspoon fresh tarragon, chopped

1 teaspoon fresh thyme, chopped

1 teaspoon fresh parsley, chopped

2 tablespoons green onion, minced

2 cloves garlic, minced

5 drops Tabasco

½ cup shrimp, poached and chopped

½ cup bay scallops, poached and chopped

½ cup lump crabmeat

1 quart cooking oil, for frying

Mix together all ingredients except oil, to form a stiff batter.

Heat oil to 350 degrees. Drop batter by teaspoonfuls into hot fat and cook, turning, until golden brown, about 3 minutes on each side. Place on paper towels to drain. Serve immediately.

SPICY BEEF SALAD

8 SERVINGS

❧

VINAIGRETTE

2 tablespoons sesame seeds, toasted

1 tablespoon freshly ground black
  pepper

¼ cup Champagne wine vinegar

1 teaspoon Dijon mustard

1 teaspoon salt

1 cup olive oil

1 pound boneless sirloin

¼ pound fresh okra

1 tablespoon olive oil for sprinkling

on okra, plus 1 tablespoon for
  sautéing corn

1 teaspoon salt

1 teaspoon freshly ground black
  pepper

1 cup fresh corn

1 head savoy cabbage, shredded

4 scallions, chopped

1 cup black beans, cooked

2 cups mushrooms, sliced

½ cup roasted sweet peppers, cut into
  strips

VINAIGRETTE

In a small bowl, combine sesame seeds, pepper, vinegar, mustard, and salt. Whisk, adding oil in thin stream, until emulsified. Set aside.

SALAD

Roast beef in 400-degree oven for 40 minutes, to medium rare. Set aside to cool.

Slice okra lengthwise, sprinkle with 1 tablespoon olive oil, salt, and pepper, and char in large cast-iron pan. Remove from pan and set aside.

Add 1 tablespoon of oil to the cast-iron pan. Add the corn and sauté for 5 minutes.

ASSEMBLY

Lay shredded savoy cabbage on large platter. Slice roast beef thin and arrange on top of cabbage. Toss okra, fried corn, scallions, black beans, mushrooms, and sweet peppers with vinaigrette in a large bowl. Arrange on top of roast beef.

GRILLED VEGETABLE AND RICE SALAD

10 SERVINGS

❧

2 yellow squash

2 zucchini

4 Japanese eggplants

6 plum tomatoes

3 sweet red peppers

2 Vidalia onions

olive oil

salt and freshly ground black
    pepper

2 tablespoons fresh rosemary,
    chopped

1 tablespoon fresh thyme, chopped

4 cups cooked long grain rice

1 cup black olives, halved

¼ cup fresh parsley, chopped

¼ cup fresh basil, chopped

Halve yellow squash, zucchini, eggplants, and tomatoes. Cut red peppers in half and seed. Slice Vidalia onions in half, then in wedges, making six pieces out of each onion. Skewer onions and set aside.

Lay all vegetables on a cookie sheet. Season with olive oil, salt, and black pepper. Sprinkle with rosemary and thyme. Over hot coals, grill all vegetables four minutes on each side. Set aside to cool.

Chop vegetables into bite-size pieces and toss with cooked rice, olives, parsley, and basil. Arrange on a large platter.

SPINACH DIP

ॐ

1 pound cream cheese

¼ cup sour cream

3 cups spinach, cleaned and wilted

3 tablespoons green onion, minced

4 shallots, minced

2 ribs celery, minced

¼ cup mayonnaise

1 tablespoon Dijon mustard

juice of 1 small lemon

3 cloves garlic, minced

½ teaspoon cayenne pepper

¼ teaspoon freshly ground black pepper

½ teaspoon salt

Mix all ingredients together in large bowl and puree in two batches in a food processor. Chill several hours and serve with assorted vegetable crudités and crackers.

17 BUTLERED WATERMELON

*M*any of Small Miracle's old friends and clients were all too eager to use me again and to tell their friends about me. So J.J. and I, he in white shirt and tux and I with aprons and bag of spices, would troop in and take over people's kitchens, some of which needed desperately to be brought into the twentieth century. Often when we did affairs for my friends, I was not only the caterer but expected to sit as a guest as well. This took great organization, but J.J. was incredibly versatile and adept; we were the best two-man team I knew. He assembled and dealt with the appetizers once the bar was set up, so that I had only to concentrate on the main course and preparation for the other courses. J.J. heated, served, and cleared. Boy, did he make me look good.

Sometimes we'd find ourselves in strained situations. One evening, given as a present, we arrived ready to cook and serve dinner for eight. J.J. put votive candles everywhere, hoping to add romance to a dining room that hadn't seen much of it in a while. At seven we passed miniature crab pies, stuffed cherry tomatoes with spicy pimento cheese spread, salmon dill spread on sliced cucumbers, and puff pastry shells stuffed with sage sausage and gorgonzola cheese—to the host and the only two guests who had shown up. By nine the count was up to five, including the obviously disappointed host, who gave the signal to serve the main course, stuffed veal chops with sage sausage and a cornbread stuffing topped with an orange relish cranberry sauce and garnished with a spicy poached pear. A side dish of sautéed spinach finished off the plate. J.J., who wanted so much for the occasion to match the food, kept trying to liven things up with jokes and stories, but the party just dragged. I pushed plates of pecan pie out of the dining room, cleaned up, and rallied us out the door. All I could think was "Glad I got paid!"

I didn't think about opera much. Every now and then I'd run into a friend from that world, or read in the news about someone I knew and wonder "what if," or something. Then out of the blue a call came from the Indiana Opera Theater asking me to sing the lead role in their production of *Lost in the Stars*. I was flattered to be asked and pleased that somebody out there remembered me. My role carried the entire drama, I had a great deal of speaking and acting as well as singing, and I was able to put to use everything I'd learned about being an actor and opera singer. *Lost in the Stars* proved to be one of my proudest achievements. The reviews were some of my best. I felt fulfilled and truly vindicated, and returned to New York ready to take on the world. But for me the world seemed to be on vacation, possibly a permanent vacation, so I continued to cater, usually a couple of dinner parties a week and one big affair a month—not setting the world afire, but keeping the wolves at bay.

One night a friend invited me to a wine-tasting party at the home of a friend of his. I volunteered to bring dessert, and so arrived promptly at half past seven with a large peach and toasted pecan upside-down cake. What I found was party preparation in chaos, but a nice guy as host. Bill Bolton's sense of humor put me immediately at ease despite the lack of order and focus of the dinner at hand. From the bags of groceries still unpacked on the counter, it appeared he had arrived home only minutes before I rang the bell. I got involved at once. There were potatoes that needed peeling, asparagus to trim and steam, salad that needed fixing, a leg of lamb to be dressed, and a host who needed to *get* dressed. The dinner—eventually—was superb, the table laid with fine china and big white napkins with Bill's family crest, which embarrassed him but which I saw as a warning of great pedigree, classic kitsch. Not bad for a blue blood off Park Avenue. Even the mushroom soufflé for ten that Bill attempted almost worked—or worked well enough. We must have drunk a bottle of wine and a bottle of Champagne, each, and so I was feeling no pain when we adjourned to the living room for brandy, port, and more Champagne. I had had my eye on Bill's Steinway piano and couldn't resist it, and a bottle of Champagne later I was holding the party hostage with songs, stories, and operatic highlights.

Bill had a large camp in the Adirondacks with a swimming pool and a rushing river that ran right through the property about fifty yards from the house. Four to six of us would fly up in his private plane about once a month during the season. Mealtime was our entertainment; we all helped out, but I would of course put myself in charge. I was also the willing audience and barometer for the many dates Bill brought along, feeling out their girlfriend potential. This he called the acid test. His success rate was not even close to good, but the food was.

Bill, who owned his own investment company, was looking to put more of himself into ventures that represented his creative side (he was an active member of a Gilbert and Sullivan troupe). He could find no better partner in creative entrepreneurship than me. We talked about restaurants, catering operations, and music performance projects. I had the idea of recording ballads and love songs, possibly to carve a niche as a romantic classic singer. I also wanted to adapt traditional German lieder, orchestrating the music in a jazz idiom and writing my own lyrics. So I wrote a proposal and Bill backed the project for a year and a half. I wrote a great deal of music and recorded some, working with the very talented arranger and pianist Daryl Waters, leader of the Eartha Kitt Trio. Aside from a great cleansing for me, we netted very little, but Bill had no problem chalking it up to nothing ventured, nothing gained.

By now I was catering everything! No party too large or too small or too particular. If you could pay, we would play. I did dinner parties, large buffets, weddings, divorces, office parties, art gallery bashes, recording company lunches, and even a few corporate accounts. But my promotional party for PolyGram Records, to celebrate the group Tony Toni Tone, was the highlight of my catering career. The group's new album *Revival* was hot, and PolyGram wanted to throw a party that people would be talking about for years. I figured that if it was going to be a "revival" party I had only to think back to all those church basements of my childhood. As boys, on the church steps, we'd sing, "What a fellowship, cornbread and buttermilk, black-eyed peas and skeeter meat." Miss Cleveland and I had had revival fever, our temperatures brought down by a vigorous passion for the vittles accompanying the service. I wanted those buffet tables for six hundred plus guests to speak to them the same way.

And that's what I did. We passed assorted hush puppies around the room—oyster; cheese and jalapeño; crab and blue cheese; turnip greens and ham puppies—on silver trays garnished with roasted corn. On tables decorated with baskets of dried flowers and vegetables from the garden were platters of carved Black Angus beef, barbecued chicken, shrimp and seafood rice pilau, green beans sautéed with roasted spring potatoes, pecan praline hams, and potato salad garnished with roasted sweet red peppers and bread and butter pickles. Butlered Watermelon, my inspiration for the evening, caused a stir even before the party started. No one wanted to admit never having heard of such a thing. It sounded so familiar and yet foreign at the same time. I had the melon cut into triangular wedges, no more than two to three bites to a piece, and served on silver trays decorated with flowers, carried by waiters properly attired with white gloves, a twist on the old stereotype. It was the hit of the night—at one point someone grabbed a mike and yelled, "Have you had your Butlered Watermelon? Get yourself some Butlered Watermelon!"

I had been hired as the food consultant and thus oversaw the preparations by the chef. This was power, kitchen power, something I'd not yet had. The kitchen (at Bridgewater, in the Fulton Market) was huge. So many people ran around doing things that it was hard to take it all in. I remember being happy that I was not the chef, coordinator, or pot scrubber. Better, I was the man about to have his recipes, his status, and his concepts elevated. I was on the map.

When Laura Torbet filed for divorce, she laid claim to the beautiful mini country estate in Carmel. I moved into the guest house to be there for her, and for the next few years that was where I felt most at home.

Cherry Hill Road was my Camelot, where I was lord of the manor and head honcho. I was party planning and catering (the house had a large, well-equipped kitchen, and the guest cottage had another), and the ride to the city by car or train was under an hour. With five extra bedrooms and no shortage of couches and sleeping porches, we had guests almost every weekend.

But something was missing. Trying to lose the desire to sing, I'd been abusing my voice and had developed chronic hoarseness. I could see the look on people's faces as they'd discover that my once hearty laugh was dry and strained. Desperate, yet afraid to confront my fear of irreversible damage, I finally went with Veronica Tyler to see her doctor, who found nodes on my vocal cords that would require laser surgery. After the diagnosis was made, I sat, shocked, staring at the white walls, the antiseptic decor. I had never before done any harm to myself. How could I have let this happen? I agreed to have the operation three weeks later.

It was much like having my tonsils out again. I was forbidden to talk for a week. Jeanie and David were in New York and took delight in feeding me ice cream and sorbet. Roberta Flack, whose determination is legendary, got me into the best vocal studios in town. Joan Lader, known for mending some of the most famous voices, became my teacher, savior, mother, protector, and friend. There were times I'd drive from Carmel down to Manhattan just to cry in her arms for the thirty-minute session we normally worked. Joan gave me back my voice, but I had to discover all those things like courage, conviction, and tenacity all over again. This time they were hard-won.

Camp Carmel was quite a handful to take care of. There were chores, pool to be cleaned, yard to manage, house, and then some. Certainly more than a city slicker like me wanted to take on. But one afternoon shortly after we moved in, Craig Muraszewski from down the street stopped by to inquire about odd jobs. God-sent, I thought, and so sixteen-year-old Craig became our man Friday, a special kid who added tremendously to our lives. And, happily, our influence on him was profound: he went from being classified a troubled youth with learning disabilities to college prep, from shy and limited in scope to boisterous, creative, opinionated, and self-assured. He cleaned, did yard work, loved the garden, and kept tabs

With Anita, David, and Craig in the kitchen in Carmel.

on the lawn service. He not only served our guests but hung on their every word. He began to like new foods. During the winter months when we'd come up Thursday through Sunday, he'd have a fire in the fireplace and sometimes a pasta dish in the oven. When he was seventeen, his mother allowed him to come into the city with us for a long weekend at Christmastime. Craig, Laura, and I and a couple of other friends, along with Champagne, juice for Craig, smoked salmon, cheese, and breads from Zabar's, piled into a stretch car and did the town big. Craig's eyes just popped out of his head. The next day I dressed us both in black tie and took him to a formal cocktail party. Extending myself to him was more rewarding for me than even I knew at the time. The way he looked up to me did much to restore my sense of worth. Craig went on to college and majored in restaurant and hotel management, and is now Night Room Service Manager at the Four Seasons Hotel.

The Lord giveth . . . and the shepherd of the Lord taketh away. In other words, I had two weeks to vacate Camp Carmel. Within a few months,

With Kathleen Battle after her concert with
Jessye Norman at Carnegie Hall.

Laura had completed her divorce, Peter had died, his kids had taken possession of the house, and Eden was over.

But back in New York, life began beating fast and furiously. Small Miracle was alive and well. I was studying with Joan Lader and teaching voice, mostly musical theater, to other singers. Recovered, I was able to sing at the wedding of two dear friends, André Balazs and Katie Ford (of the Ford Model Agency), at St. Thomas Episcopal Church. At my parties you never knew who might show up—a count, an Arab oil baron, the new hot director, the most famous recluse on the Upper East Side.

Kathleen Battle and I had remained the best of friends since Paris, and now her career was about to rocket right off the planet. She had given classical music a new glamour, and a new audience to go with it. I was so proud of her. And every time she stepped onstage she carried my unachieved ambitions along. She had very broad shoulders.

Kathleen and Jessye Norman's groundbreaking recital of Negro spirituals at Carnegie Hall did much to encourage recognition of the spiritual as classical song. We had decided on a special celebration in honor of the event. I would of course do the food. This was the first of our many collaborations. We went over every detail, more than once. Kathleen being as thorough as she is about everything, even I, the caterer, took notes. We planned the perfect party: no casserole dish left unturned, no platter of surprises, no drink too sweet or too bitter. After we decided what *I* was going to make, then we decided what *she* was going to make—there was not about to be a party in Kathleen's house without Kathleen cooking, too.

People came from everywhere to the concert and filled every seat and every corner of standing room, their hearts in hand, souls in need of washing, hands bent on clapping. I looked up from my seat in the orchestra into the balcony box where Bill Cosby sat; Phylicia Rashad hugged me from the row behind; Jewel Jackson McCabe nodded her head in praise of colored girls everywhere. People held their breath until intermission, some even longer. What glory, what grace. My Lord, what a morning.

Kathleen's gorgeous apartment was all dressed up in scented potpourri, freshly waxed furniture, and southern cooking. Kathleen is a very discriminating collector of china, crystal, and silver from all over the

With Willis McNamee and Jewel Jackson McCabe
at the party after Kathleen Battle's Carnegie Hall recital.

world; and Uncle Joe's fried chicken piled high on the Flora Danica serving platter did him proud. The party was a big success; more than fifty people came, including James Levine, Cornel West, and Toni Morrison. And of course Kathleen's wonderful family from Ohio—her sisters had made beautiful plaid napkins and a matching tablecloth. We wanted the look of a southern picnic buffet in this beautiful formal dining room with its hand-painted silk wallpaper. The table stretched some fourteen feet, neatly styled with flowers and silver candelabra, and laden with chafing dishes filled with corn puddings, mixed greens with hot relishes, macaroni and cheese, sweet potatoes, and lemon sole. Platters of fried chicken, brown sugar–based ham, honey-glazed chicken, and spiced jumbo shrimp with marinated string beans. Crispy chicken livers with a sesame seed crust and a mustard dipping sauce. Cheese boards, bowls of potato salad and cabbage salad, fruit bowls and baskets of sage cornbread, and Kathleen's famous potato and sweet potato yeast rolls. Soft, light, melt in your mouth—to this day I'll walk five miles for those rolls. Dessert was simply a little closer to heaven. Pecan pie, lemon icebox pie, Kathleen's much-in-demand icebox coconut cake, so rich it took the whole party over the edge. But my mom's orange cheese pound cake was the bait that put Toni Morrison and me on common ground. I had the recipe, she wanted more, and that was the start of our wonderful friendship.

All during the party, people were moved to express themselves. We sang hymns, arias, lieder, spirituals. And even after all she'd given, Kathleen sang for us once more. Then, guests all gone and J.J. having skillfully organized the cleanup, he, Kathleen, and I clicked our Champagne glasses one more time. To the past *and* the future.

---⊗---

In case this fact has escaped you—I love to eat, and I love a great party. These offerings leap off the page, beckoning you to drop everything and start cooking. I suggest only that you invite a few friends to join you—you should not do this alone.

---⊗---

STUFFED VEAL CHOPS WITH SAGE SAUSAGE AND CORNBREAD

10 SERVINGS

⊗

10 8-ounce veal chops

1 cup sage sausage, out of casing

1 tablespoon olive oil

1 stick (¼ pound) unsalted butter

1 small onion, minced

2 cloves garlic, minced

2 ribs celery, minced

1 small green pepper, minced

1 tablespoon fresh sage, minced

2 cups cornbread cubes

2 cups chicken stock

juice of 1 large lemon

salt and freshly ground black pepper

2 large eggs, beaten

4 tablespoons vegetable oil

Make an incision 3 inches deep and 3 inches wide in the side of each chop. Set the chops aside.

Sauté sausage in olive oil until browned. Add butter, onion, garlic, celery, and green pepper and cook on medium heat for 10 minutes. Add sage, cornbread, 1 cup chicken stock, lemon juice, 1 teaspoon salt, and 2 teaspoons pepper and cook 3 minutes. Cool to room temperature; mix in beaten eggs. Stuff 2 tablespoons of stuffing into each chop and set aside. Heat a skillet to medium heat and add 4 tablespoons vegetable oil. Season chops with salt and pepper on both sides. Brown on both sides; arrange in a single layer in a roasting pan. Pour in remaining chicken stock and roast in a preheated 400-degree oven for 30 minutes. Serve with orange relish, cranberry sauce, and spicy poached pear garnish.

SPICED JUMBO SHRIMP WITH MARINATED STRING BEANS

✌

3 pounds jumbo shrimp, peeled and deveined

3 tablespoons red pepper flakes

¼ cup honey

¼ cup olive oil

2 tablespoons lemon zest

¼ cup scallions, minced

¼ cup bourbon

STRING BEANS

¼ cup red wine vinegar

2 tablespoons Dijon mustard

1 tablespoon benne (sesame) seeds

2 cloves garlic, minced

2 teaspoons fresh gingerroot, minced

1 cup olive oil

2 pounds string beans, blanched and chilled

Marinate shrimp for 15 minutes with red pepper flakes, honey, olive oil, lemon zest, scallions, and bourbon.

Meanwhile, in a medium-size bowl, whisk red wine vinegar with mustard, benne seeds, garlic, and ginger. Continue whisking and add oil in a thin stream until emulsified. Toss with string beans and chill.

Drain shrimp and cook in preheated skillet for 8 to 10 minutes, turning often.

Serve shrimp on a large platter with marinated string beans.

CRISPY CHICKEN LIVERS WITH MUSTARD DIPPING SAUCE

8 SERVINGS

❧

2 pounds chicken livers, cleaned
1 tablespoon sage, rubbed
¼ cup orange juice
2 cups all-purpose flour
½ cup sesame seeds
1½ teaspoons salt
1½ teaspoons freshly ground black pepper
1 cup oil for deep-frying

MUSTARD SAUCE
½ cup Dijon mustard
¼ cup freshly squeezed orange juice
2 tablespoons soy sauce
¼ cup red wine vinegar
2 tablespoons honey
salt and pepper to taste
¼ cup olive oil
¼ cup scallions, minced

Marinate livers in sage and orange juice for 30 minutes. Mix flour, sesame seeds, and salt and pepper. Heat oil in deep-fryer to 350 degrees. Dredge livers in flour mixture and fry in deep-fryer until crispy, about 5 minutes. Drain on paper towel and keep warm in a 200-degree oven.

Meanwhile, in a blender make the mustard sauce. Combine mustard, orange juice, soy sauce, red wine vinegar, honey, salt, and pepper. With machine running, add oil in a thin stream until emulsified. Pour into a small bowl and mix in scallions.

Arrange livers on a platter and serve with the mustard sauce for dipping.

LEMON SOLE

❧

butter for baking dish
3 pounds sole fillets
1 teaspoon salt
1 teaspoon freshly ground black pepper
¼ cup vegetable oil
10 tablespoons all-purpose flour
1 tablespoon lemon zest
juice of 4 lemons
2 tablespoons chives chopped, for garnish
2 tablespoons parsley chopped, for garnish

Preheat oven to 400 degrees. Butter a baking dish large enough to hold the fillets in a single layer. Season fillets with salt and pepper. Heat oil to medium heat in a large skillet. Dredge fillets in flour, lightly dusting, and brown on both sides. Arrange in buttered baking dish after all fillets are browned. Top fillets with lemon zest and lemon juice and broil four inches from flame under broiler for 10 minutes. Garnish with chopped chives and parsley. Serve at once.

MINIATURE CRAB PIES

12 SERVINGS

❧

BASIC PIECRUST

2 cups all-purpose flour, sifted

1 cup cake flour, sifted

1 teaspoon sugar

2 sticks (1 cup) unsalted butter, cut
into 1-inch cubes

1 cup ice water

FILLING

½ stick (¼ cup) unsalted butter

2 tablespoons olive oil

1 small onion, minced

1 rib celery, minced

½ large red pepper, minced

3 cloves garlic, minced

2 pounds fresh crabmeat

¼ cup parsley, chopped

1½ tablespoons fresh thyme leaves

1 tablespoon Worcestershire sauce

1 tablespoon Tabasco sauce

1½ teaspoons kosher salt

2 teaspoons freshly ground black
pepper

1½ cups plain bread crumbs

2 large eggs, beaten

½ cup mayonnaise

1 cup heavy cream

CRUST

Put flours, sugar, and butter into mixing bowl. With the paddle attachment, turn machine on low and run until mixture resembles coarse meal, then add ice water little by little until mixture forms a ball. Refrigerate until needed.

FILLING

In a medium skillet melt butter and olive oil together. Add onion, celery, red pepper, and garlic. Cook on medium heat 10 minutes. Cool to room temperature. Combine onion mixture with rest of ingredients.

ASSEMBLY

Take dough from refrigerator and roll out ¼ inch thick. Using a 6-cup muffin tin as a guide, cut out circles to fit tin. You will need two 6-cup muffin tins to get 12 pies. Spray tins with cooking spray. Press dough circles into tins and, using a fork, crimp edges. Loosely fill pie shells with filling and bake 35 minutes in a preheated 350-degree oven. Cool 5 minutes. Run a small knife around edges and take shells out of tins and serve.

PUFF PASTRY SHELLS STUFFED WITH SAGE SAUSAGE AND GORGONZOLA

8 SERVINGS

❧

1 pound sage sausage, out of casing
2 tablespoons olive oil
1 small onion, minced
2 cloves garlic, minced
2 pints light cream
1 box (8) puff pastry shells
½ pound gorgonzola, crumbled

In a medium-size skillet brown the sausage in olive oil. Add onion and garlic and cook 5 minutes. Add cream and reduce by half. Cool to room temperature. Lay the eight shells on a large cookie sheet. Divide sausage mixture among eight shells. Top with crumbled cheese and bake in a preheated 325-degree oven until slightly bubbling and pastry is browned, about 18 to 20 minutes. Cool 5 minutes before serving.

SALMON DILL SPREAD
ON SLICED CUCUMBERS

10 SERVINGS

&

12 ounces salmon, poached and chilled
½ cup unsalted butter, softened
½ cup cream cheese, softened
¼ cup fresh dill, chopped
juice of 1 large lemon
1 teaspoon Worcestershire sauce
1 teaspoon Tabasco sauce
1 teaspoon kosher salt
½ teaspoon white pepper

Put all ingredients in the large bowl of a food processor and pulse to combine. Let machine run about 45 seconds until smooth. Put into bowl and chill. Put mixture into pastry bag fitted with the star tip and pipe onto cucumber rounds and serve.

18 ALEXANDER'S RAGTIME BAND

*J*ust about the time I'd had to leave Camp Carmel, David Goodman's elderly parents had moved from their country place, an old rustic gate-keeper's cottage in Tea-Town, New York. The house sat way back from the road on a tiny pond surrounded by unkept lawns and overgrown shrubs and flowers. I moved in, lock, stock, and barrel, and we worked on the house all through the fall and winter of 1990. I say "we" because the price of a weekend visit meant pulling weeds, trimming hedges, cleaning out the pond, and generally joining in to fix up the neglect. This did not discourage a soul.

Terry Beans, one of those guests who never seemed to go home, took on the job of raking and remaking the pond and its shoreline, wading in daily in rubber boots up to his waist, an old bandanna on his head. That's where he was one spring morning when Anne De Ravel, of the *New York Times,* pulled into the driveway in a little beige rented car. Anne had come to see me following a phone call from Donna Gelb, who was married to Peter Gelb, president of Sony Classical. At Kathleen Battle's party Donna had told me that she thought the food was wonderful and would mention it to her friend at the *Times.* That would be great, I'd thought at the time, then thought no more about it. Now here was Anne to see if I existed and if I was in fact newsworthy. Could I invite thirty or forty people for a typical Sunday-afternoon buffet in the country? No problem, I assured her. I had three weeks to beat the place into shape, send out personal invitations, employ a staff, create a menu, rent tables, chairs, and porta-toilet, and calm myself so as to appear natural, at ease, and smartly confident. As you can see, not nearly enough time at all.

My life, it seemed to me, was being guided by an unseen force. Was it my heart that pushed me forward? Certainly I had great ambition; when I truly wanted something I could rock heaven and earth to that end. If I had not yet decided what I was going to be when I grew up, was I putting off the decision, or was I putting off growing up? "No matter," as my mom would say, her way of resting the burden of responsibility on the shoulders of the perpetrator. In this case I stood at center stage in a state of mind that could be expressed as "How did I get here?" and "Now that I'm here, what do I do?" I rally!

For that party I rallied the troops to action. J.J., Terry, Steve Hanagan (the caretaker and an avid gardener), and Barton Campbell, a friend from Connecticut, arrived on Saturday morning to ready the site. Fresh plantings with full blooms were placed in the various gardens along the front terrace and the walkway leading to the drive. Hedges were clipped, volleyball net raised, lawn furniture cleaned, awnings and windows washed down, and water lilies arranged about the recently cleaned pond. We scrubbed and polished the house to a clean even Mr. Clean himself would have noticed—the smell of Pine Sol threatened to overtake the aroma of my chocolate pecan rum pie, coming into its own as it slowly baked in the old but sturdy kitchen oven. I set out my prize silverware, bought at various auctions, a multipatterned collection reflecting style on a budget. I had purchased emerald-green hard glasslike plastic plates and found a brilliant striped cotton and linen bedspread that would make a perfect tablecloth.

I spent much of the afternoon running from supermarket to liquor store to specialty store to one roadside vegetable stand after another; being distracted by yard sales, flea markets, and the occasional neighbor who had too much to say; returning exhausted, as evening approached, with bags and bags of groceries, too many to be put in the kitchen— and much still to be done, especially the cooking.

We worked well into the night. I remember sending out for Chinese food, since we were too busy to stop and cook dinner, and there were no free burners left on the stove. I wanted to have all the prep work done, because it has been my experience that the day of any event brings with it unanticipated issues of its own. The *Times* was arriving around eleven, the party scheduled for two, and games, food, bar, and final touches had to be coordinated. I had a waiter and bartender coming up from the city, as well as friends with last-minute supplies and party favors.

By nine the next morning the house and grounds resembled Santa's workshop. Everybody was doing everything, chopping vegetables, stuffing deviled eggs, peeling shrimp, washing arugula, and preparing crudités. Outside the guys were laying out the horseshoe and croquet courts, and mounting flags from my friend Denise's company all along the driveway and front gate near the road. I was well into Maria Callas's *Prima Donna* tape and did not notice the *New York Times* crew until they were in my face, mouthing instructions and asking questions with the camera clicking, having caught me matching Callas tone for tone while beating the cornbread batter silly with a wooden spoon.

Barbara Johnson, for whom I often catered, grew flowers at her country home, and per agreement arrived with a van of wildflowers, roses, peaches, all kinds of greens, Spanish moss, baskets, ribbons, and string, and in a relatively short time had created beautiful arrangements for the tables and buffet. J.J. kept us all well in line and on schedule. In his classic white shirt and tie, black pants, and spit shine, he greeted guests, both friends and new faces, politely and with restraint; but you knew, when J.J. started laughing out loud and waving his hands high, that the party was on.

They came in cars, taxis, and limos. They ate hors d'oeuvres of pickled shrimp and okra, peppery chicken-liver mousse in puff pastry, sweet potato pecan balls with lemon honey mustard, and spicy catfish and rice croquettes with mint-flavored tartar sauce. Then they ate marinated chicken slow-cooked over charcoal and smothered with barbecue sauce down to the bone, brown-sugar-glazed ham, black-eyed pea and arugula salad, she crab and deviled corn salad, potato salad, and sage-spiced cornbread.

The story, written by Sara Rimer and featured by the *New York Times* in its June 1991 *Entertaining Magazine,* put me out there. Ready or

With Valerie Simpson at one of her famous White Parties.

not, I was to the public at large Alexander Smalls the Caterer. The day the article appeared, I catered a large brunch for a church in Harlem and afterward, with my friend Freddie Clark, attended a birthday party for the fashion diva and socialite Audrey Smaltz. Audrey appeared at the door in one of the largest hats I'd ever seen, ushered us in, and immediately instructed Lionel Hampton and his band to play "Alexander's Ragtime Band." Introducing me to the hundred or so people present, she called me an opera singer, a man about town, the host with the most, and—most of all—caterer extraordinaire! I was touched by this gesture, but more important, it was finally clear to me who I was. Not *all* that I was, but that I was all of that, and it was perfectly okay to be that—and even more if I should choose.

Every summer around the Fourth of July, Nick Ashford and Valerie Simpson throw what they describe as the "white party," at their country home in Connecticut, a mega-gathering of some of the most colorful people anywhere, dressed in white from head to toe. At Nick and Val's one year I spent most of the afternoon talking with Willis McNamee and his wife, Laura Smalls, who own Day-O, a small southern-Caribbean restaurant in Greenwich Village. Willis was doing what I was only giving lip service to. He had created his own party, seven days a week, from floor to ceiling, with food, exotic beverages, and a following of devotees.

Willis and Laura became family. We were often together for dinners and holidays, and on occasional weekends we'd gather at Kathleen's beach house. Whatever we did, I would often cook and try out new recipes. One day Willis offered me Sunday brunches at Day-O. I could create whatever I wanted to. After the wave of flattery passed, fear of the enormous responsibility grabbed hold of me. This was the most important bridge I'd had to cross, the closest I'd come to operating a restaurant.

The menu was challenging. I spent days coming up with what I felt were new, exciting, and innovative southern dishes. I also sought to put new twists on traditional fare and feature signature dishes that were always in demand. My plan was to work the room while a chef prepared and garnished every dish to my specifications. Since this would take teamwork and checked egos, I called Michael Small, whom I'd met back in the days of Le Chanteur. Michael had come to New York as a dancer in the Joffrey Ballet School and somewhere along the line had become full-figured and a professional chef. He agreed to take on the brunches with me (which ultimately led to his becoming chef of the entire restaurant). Nervous and boiling over with excitement, we opened with she crab omelettes, white potato and sweet potato clusters, sherry-spiced catfish and hominy grits, creole steak and eggs, black-eyed peas and arugula salad, and fried chicken and pecan waffles that were standouts on the menu.

The fried chicken was hit-or-miss at first. I had created a very successful spicy grapefruit marinade for oven-baked poultry, and I decided to do this with fried chicken as well. I cook most things and taste them first in my mind, and so it never occurred to me to test a small batch. I put several pounds of chicken in to soak overnight, and the next morning we drained the pieces, floured them, and dropped them into the grease. After spitting and spatting juices everywhere, although it tasted sensational, the chicken looked like hell—at first glance like those pieces that always fall off the barbecue grill into the coals. It was clearly not customer-ready. The lesson for me: never again underestimate the test kitchen. After an emergency call home, I succeeded in putting the southern fried chicken back together again. Thank God for Mom and buttermilk.

I did the brunches at Day-O for about nine months. During that time Small Miracle was booming, my business cards into their fourth printing. I was turning down work in order to remain a small operation, but what the catering company could not do, I the consultant could. I was very comfortable in my new identity. I passed out cards and promoted myself as an authority on southern hospitality and entertainment venues. Gone was—not the desire to sing—but the fear of not singing. One of the hardest things in life, I feel, is building one's identity. Not just the image of it but the brick and mortar of its foundation. I had survived the changing of hats. I felt unique in my new role as Chef Smalls, ambassador of style and grace, food and social comfort. For the first time, there were people in my life who'd never heard me sing, and at times it was as if the singing had never existed or was a part of another, foreign and distant, existence. It felt great to have that pressure gone, since as a singer I'd always felt so exposed—naked, vulnerable, and too closely watched. As a chef I wore more hats and clothes than, as southerners say, "one had ought to." But I was confident, proud, and daring.

During this time my longtime friend Freddie Clark was a great source of inspiration and stability for me. So many others, including Bill Bolton and Laura Torbet, had left New York. Gwendolyn now made West Germany her home, and Jeanie and David showed no signs of coming back East. Every morning, no matter how late we'd stayed out the night before, Freddie and I met in Central Park for a walk around the reservoir. Although she rarely talked about her family, one morning she was on a roll about Aunt this and Aunt that, this and that cousin long gone. Her stories were not that different from mine—everybody, it seemed, had a favorite uncle named Joe; in every church there was a Berta, a Miz Hattie, a Shorty, and a Speedy. We stumbled all over the path in delirious nostalgia, calling up characters from the past. I remember reaching deep down for a name while trying hard to catch my breath. "My mama had a *Beulah* in her family," I shouted, knowing I had delivered the queen of southern names. But Freddie screamed, "My mama had a Beulah in *her* family, too!" Weak from laughing, we began calling out variations on the name Beulah—Beulah Mae, Beulah's house, Miss Beulah's. . . .

"Honey, everybody went to Beulah for everything," Freddie exclaimed.

"What a great name for a restaurant," I said. "Goin' to *Beulah*!"

Freddie said, "Yeah, Beulah, a great restaurant."

And then I said, "*Cafe* Beulah!" And we looked at each other and her eyes got really big and we both said, "We gotta *use* that name."

And so we shook hands and said, "That's our name; we're goin' to Cafe Beulah one of these days."

One morning Jewel Jackson McCabe rang to say that she was working on the opening of the new North General Hospital in Harlem. Would I be willing to cater the opening party—a cocktail reception for six hundred and a sit-down dinner immediately following for two hundred fifty? I held my breath and sank into the sofa, holding back any signs of terror. The last thing you wanted to be with Jewel was uncertain. She is a three-minute girl: either you can do it or you can't, and you have only a few moments to decide before she moves on. That was the hardest "yes" I'd had to say so far.

After we hung up, I sat staring at the ceiling. My kitchen couldn't even begin to address the charge; I had no large catering facility or staff roster, no proven supply directory, and no real knowledge of how to put together this big a shindig from soup to nuts. But I grabbed the phone and got busy. I called J.J. at his paralegal job and assigned him the organizational systems; then I called Dale Isaacs, a friend who worked for every large catering concern in Manhattan, and had her put together a list of waiters, bartenders, porters, and back-of-the-house staff. Dale also contacted rentals, liquor and beverage concerns, and the various support systems needed. This left me free to concentrate on the food. For that there was only one call to be made, to Willis at Day-O. I arranged with him and Michael to prepare and deliver all of the food items. In twenty-four hours we were able to fax off the proposal for the party. After a meeting with all concerned, the contract was mine.

Our plans went forward on a huge wave of momentum that we tried to stay in control of. The event took sheer guts, brute strength, and determination. It was about rising to the call, about being what you say you are, and after its success the phone continued to ring. I began to take on an air of authority—the last word on southern hospitality for the new consumer.

Nevertheless, one afternoon I was lamenting to Freddie that I needed to get on with it, to develop my career to the next level. "You've been talking about doing a place of your own forever, honey," she said, "and the time is not going to get any better than now. What have you got to lose?"

All good advice has to be heard at the right moment, when your mind allows your body to digest it fully. "Don't touch the stove, Bernie, it'll burn you." "Didn't I tell you not to wear your new white pants across that muddy field?" "Why don't you just go after your dreams?" I was listening to Freddie that afternoon with new ears.

"Look, honey, just go out and get a storefront and put together some friends who'll chip in and help pay the rent. I'm good for $500 a month myself!" Her voice rose like a call to arms. I could hear her, though ever so faintly, as she got her second wind, "You're a natural; nobody loves and gives parties like you; you could be big, honey . . . Everybody will come . . . And besides, what's the alternative? . . . You're not going back to Spartanburg . . . You've got to get all this together, darling, and do something definitive!"

I found myself working through the night, putting together the beginnings of my ideas. It was clear that to be taken seriously, I needed something to sell. The next day I borrowed from a friend the first business plan I had ever seen and began to create Cafe Beulah. It became clear to me that it would not happen overnight, but I never lost sight that it would happen.

After fifteen years I had lost my apartment on 80th Street to the landlord. Jordan Lewis, a friend and aspiring opera singer, was also looking to make a move, so we put our resources together and found a huge three-thousand-square-foot two-bedroom two-bath loft in NoHo, with sixteen floor-to-ceiling windows and a very large kitchen. *Party* was the first word that came to mind.

Invading secondhand stores, auctions, and outlets, we whipped the loft into home sweet home. We had two grand pianos and an upright, a Roland synthesizer, and bongos if anyone was inclined. No sooner was the paint dry on the shocking-red kitchen walls than I was elbow-deep in flour, making cakes, frying chicken and fish, and turning out fresh biscuits. Once or twice a week, food covered the massive fourteen-foot table from one end to the other. Never an empty seat when invites went out—only empty plates at the end of the evening. This was the ultimate prelude to Cafe Beulah, my glorious salon in downtown Manhattan, Le Chanteur revisited, 8oth Street enlightened, Camp Carmel citified. Whose life was this, anyway? It was as if I were reading about me in some paperback, and I were just about to get to the best part . . . whoa!!

Freddie hosted our first fund-raiser, a cocktail party at her apartment on Central Park West. I had worked hard on the proposal. My friend Steve Teixeira, an attorney, had offered guidance and legal management, and without his conservative and attentive direction, neither Cafe Beulah nor I would have fared well. The job of putting my handwriting into print and onto computer disk fell to my good buddy Lin McDaniel, a retired I.B.M. executive, whom I'd met in a terrible snowstorm that had left me and all my weekend guests stranded at the Croton Falls train station, unable to get to Camp Carmel. He had delivered us safely home in his four-wheel-drive Jeep, and after that, if ever I needed Lin McDaniel, he was always ready. During this time, all were needed, and so many came to my side.

For the party Freddie pulled out all the stops—wedding crystal, silver trays, linen napkins, and herself dressed in "modest-expense perfection," a walking example for aspiring *Cosmo* girls. I made hors d'oeuvres of salmon and crabmeat mousse, barbecued duck on toasted pepper biscuits, poultry liver pâté, mini corn muffins filled with country ham, and spinach and cheese strudel. Everyone loved the food. I spoke, Freddie spoke, and other friends who were so inspired shared stories. It was a warm, wonderful evening. The most important moment, one I'll always cherish, belonged to Artie Pacheco, president of One To One, the organization for whose benefit I'd sung at Carnegie Hall, who had become over the years a warm, reliable, lovable, and encouraging friend. It was clear that the obvious had become the most awkward. Everyone was there to hear my concept, fully understand it, and take a position. Artie, who either had been to many of these things before or just sensed that it was time to move the venture on, did simply that. "I'm in," he said. "I think it's great; I'm all for Alexander; just tell me how much and when." I almost burst wide open from sheer joy and amazement, the kind you get when you expect a necktie for Christmas but instead get an Armani silk shirt. Artie's proclamation had surprised everyone—I could have run around the room closing mouths and performing the Heimlich maneuver. Freddie exploded with applause. We all did—what else was there to do? We were on our way!

Between the regular parties at the loft, I began to host investor bashes, music soirees, and tastings, with the assistance of Leslie Parks, a

With Wynton Marsalis at Cami Studios.

Gordon Parks, his daughter, Leslie, Monica Lynch (president, Tommy Boy),
and Jenette Kahn (president, D.C. Comics) at one of my loft parties.

chef and daughter of Gordon Parks. Leslie—a bundle of joy and creativity—was enormously helpful in developing the food for Cafe Beulah. She became my constant companion in the kitchen and traveled all
over town with me catering parties.

Southern food has been called the best American cuisine, comfort
food, and stick-to-your-ribs home cooking, but never has it been called
kosher. So one of the most unusual parties at the loft was given for
Jenette Kahn's father, a rabbi. Jenette, president of D.C. Comics, had
asked me to prepare a kosher celebration for fifty people. Once I got
past catfish, dairy, and shellfish, and after a trip to a butcher on the
Lower East Side, we threw a kosher soul food dinner party to beat the
band, which made lasting friends of Jenette and me.

There were never enough hands around to do the work of Small
Miracle. At any given time my friends could be recruited as waiters,
cooks, or bottle washers. The photographer Lorna Simpson, with shows
all over the globe and a waiting list for her work, made the mistake of
stopping by one day a few hours before a party. As I was short-staffed I

immediately got her an apron, and she was soon dicing, peeling, mixing, and tossing with the rest of us. Rony Weissman, who had also wandered by, became bartender, busboy, and coat check. No one—the chic, the trendy, the well-heeled, or the famous—was safe from duty.

Every story has its knights in shining armor, its heroes and angels. Phylicia Rashad, whose Christmas party every year is legendary (I know because after the first one I attended I began catering them), was one of those people. In a brief conversation, I spoke about Cafe Beulah and my determination to create a restaurant we'd all be proud of and be a part of. She displayed that slow-to-rise smile of hers, those eyes that beam like headlights. "You will, Alexander, 'cause you are truly blessed," she said. Two months later Phylicia took me to lunch high above Manhattan overlooking Central Park. We dined for well over three hours, and upon paying the check, she presented me with her generous investment in Cafe Beulah and in me.

The restaurant seemed closer than ever before, and singing seemed the farthest thing from my mind. But I struggled with where I'd been, how I'd gotten here, and where I was going. At times it was as if I'd swum too far from shore. Sometimes I'd scream into my bed pillow, demanding a rematch, a reprieve, a lifeline. But I always had hope. I thought of the line from Monday Smalls to Ned, to Ed, to Alec, to me. I had to have faith now.

For almost two years Freddie and I walked all over town looking. She literally walked the heel off a brand-new shoe one day, but without stopping marched into Bergdorf's, demanded and got another pair free. The search was relentless but somewhat strategic as well. Cafe Beulah was to be a new concept in southern restaurants. I was looking to break the mold, to challenge people's stereotypes of what a southern restaurant or a black-owned restaurant was all about. Every component of the creation of Cafe Beulah had to be significantly weighed.

I eliminated certain sections of the city, settling on the Flatiron district, Union Square area. At this time it was the budding flower in the garden of restaurant communities. Hot but not scorching, it seemed the perfect place to launch a new movement based on an old tradition. Historically, black-owned restaurants, most notably the ones serving southern and soul food, have been located on the Upper West Side, Chelsea, midtown, the Village, and of course Brooklyn and Harlem. I avoided those neighborhoods because of the expectations that would have labeled me. The most common pronouncement was simple: "You're black, your food's southern, it's soul food!" And that was that, as they say in China. But that wasn't it at all.

I had coined the phrase "Southern Revival" in part because of Lisa Cortes, who had offered me the Tony Toni Tone record party. When she'd called, she'd said, "Alexander, these people need some of your revival cooking, child. Lay it on them!" And so it was that my beloved Low Country cooking gave way to Southern Revival cooking. This was also appropriate because, under the ever-present gaze of southern Low Country purists, "revival" allowed me some liberties when it came to adding arugula to my salads, duck sausage to my gumbo, or wild rice to my Hoppin' John cakes. I was committed to bringing a new, refined face to the southern kitchen, reshaping people's impressions of the bounty of southern cuisine, and doing it in style, with elegance, charm, hospitality, and grace.

Slowly but ever so surely, friends were seduced to be a part of the Beulah family. There were many setbacks, some too painful to speak of, even now. But Jordan, my roommate, wrote an amazing check; Artie brought in Brad Zipper, and Brad brought in his boss, Buzzy; Bennett Egeth came onboard, followed by Paul Ostergard. Laura Torbet, who had cashed in her subway tokens and pocketbook Mace spray and now nested in the San Marino valley, was not to be left out. Jeannette Kahn, who held my hand through one disaster after the other, invested with her heart and compassion for the cause, and steadfastly cheered me on.

Determined to have great food at Cafe Beulah, I began having parties weekly. On one particular evening I was hosting one of my best dinners to date. Among the guests were Barbara and Gerald Levin, Percy Sutton, Nat Sutton, Gordon Parks, Toni Morrison, Ornette Coleman, Karen Alpert, Reginald Hudlin, and Monica Lynch. Leslie and I had cooked everything we could think of. Hominy grits cakes with roasted sweet red

With Lorna Simpson (photographer), Thelma Golden (curator), Peter Norton (Norton computers), and David Ross (director of the Whitney Museum) at Cafe Beulah for the Jacob Lawrence party.

peppers, roasted corn and chopped sweet Vidalia onions smothered in my daddy's crabmeat gravy, sherry-mustard-and-brown-sugar-glazed duck soaked overnight in grapefruit juice and sherry marinade. Pan-roasted salmon stuffed with chopped carrots, turnips, and turnip greens in a garlic-and-herb-infused white sauce. I was going for big taste, robust flavor, food that slapped the senses. This was no everyday gathering, and the food needed to be as strong as my guests. So I chose the bold taste of root vegetables, mixing quartered sweet potatoes, white potatoes, chopped leeks, garlic cloves, finely chopped celery, chopped rosemary and thyme, salt, pepper, and a dash of nutmeg, tossing them with olive oil, and roasting them in a hot oven. Only country cornbread with spiced sage and carmelized onions baked inside could stand up to the challenge of flavors.

It was like the Last Supper, kind of, I imagined. Food is a wonderful social aphrodisiac; it can bring out people's senses, leaving them open, vulnerable, and ripe. I pushed the climax further into the evening, so that my guests would not stray from my food seduction, pressing

Life: long awaited at Cafe Beulah.

them onward with chocolate raspberry bread pudding with a light rum sauce, and mint- and orange-spiked tea with brandy. Surely there could be no resistance after that. I had made my point, had my way with them all. Still, the shopping, preparing, and cooking were only as brilliant as the guests who ate the results. How clear it all becomes when you match and balance all of that.

Toni Morrison and Percy Sutton were the surprises in my mission to open Cafe Beulah. Toni had been an icon for me since I'd picked up her first book more than twenty years before. Over the last few years we had grown close, lunching, going to concerts, and amusing ourselves with long, lazy conversations. Still, I honored our relationship so much that it took all that was in me to ask if she might be interested in investing. And she said yes.

Percy, who never misses an opportunity to encourage someone, was more than eager to have breakfast with me early one morning. Nervous, yet confident, I returned his warm greeting with affection, feeling special just because he had come. When I presented him with my proposal, he praised my spirit, my homework, my courage and drive. He also gave me money and his blessing.

Now I had a name, a family, a team. I just had to find the right four walls and ceiling.

Flying by the seat of my pants, I searched from Avenue of the Americas to Gramercy Park and back. Three or four times I came close, and then finally my broker, Ernest Graziano, showed me one last place on 19th and Park. Freddie gave her nod of approval, as did Artie, Jordan, and the lot. The restaurant had just recently been renovated, though this was hard to see. It was green and pink, with a long mahogany bar, a carpet that needed to be thrown away, and the worst lighting for dining anywhere. Day and night I stalked the block, checking the traffic flow, the customer profile, and anything else I could discover. I visited so often the owners started to believe I liked the food. I had to be sure—or be comfortable with not being sure, because it's times like these that "sure" is way overrated. But I felt in my heart that this was the place.

A month later I stood on the corner of 40th and Madison clutching a street sign, a thunderstorm between my ears. I had just bought myself a restaurant. It was by far the most decisive thing I'd ever done.

Ornette Coleman (composer and musician), Toni Morrison (Pulitzer and Nobel winner), and me, having feasted well at my loft apartment.

*With my proud parents at Cafe Beulah. From left,
Aunt Elma (my father's sister-in-law), Karen Alpert,
Donna Berwick, Rony Weissman, and Lorna Simpson.*

There was so much to do that thinking of it all only paralyzed the process. As soon as I got home I made my favorite food, chili cheese dogs and coleslaw, and at two in the afternoon jumped into bed, sipping Champagne and feeding myself silly.

I couldn't help but think about everyone who wouldn't know— what Uncle Joe might have said, Aunt Laura and Grandpa. Aunt Daisy would probably have wanted to cook and hang out at the bar on her days off. I thought of how I'd traded Sparkle City's familiar surroundings and limitations for the latitude the world had offered. I mourned the dreams and lost moments of my music career. And then I took stock of my brilliant good fortune—those who'd found a way to love and support me. I had achieved and been generously given the stuff to go on, and I was taking everyone along. I was going to open the restaurant of my life. And I would grace the table with food I'd taken a lifetime to make.

I think the only thing better than pickled okra is pickled shrimp. A plate of roasted salmon with root vegetables followed by "stick to your fingers" glazed duck (a small salad on the side) can't be beat. And deep-dish chocolate raspberry bread pudding swimming in smooth rum sauce puts the "d" in decadence. Don't forget brandy with this one.

PAN-ROASTED SALMON STUFFED WITH VEGETABLES AND HERB WHITE SAUCE

8 SERVINGS

SALMON AND STUFFING
1 stick (½ cup) unsalted butter
1 small onion, minced
2 ribs celery, minced
4 cloves garlic, minced
½ cup carrots, chopped
1 cup turnips, diced
6 cups turnip greens, chopped
2 tablespoons fresh sage, minced
1 6-pound whole salmon, boned
2 cups chicken stock

SAUCE
2 sticks (½ pound) butter
¼ cup all-purpose flour
4 cloves garlic, minced
1 pint milk
2 pints heavy cream
½ cup chicken stock
2 tablespoons fresh chives, chopped
1 tablespoon fresh tarragon, minced
pinch nutmeg
pinch cayenne pepper
salt and pepper to taste

In a large skillet, melt butter. Add onion, celery, garlic, carrots, and turnips and cook 15 minutes, stirring often. Add turnip greens and sage, season with salt and pepper, and cook 10 minutes more. Cool to room temperature. Open up cavity of salmon and pack stuffing in. Tie crosswise with butcher's string and set in a buttered roasting pan. Pour in 2 cups chicken stock and bake in a preheated 400-degree oven for 25 minutes.

SAUCE

Meanwhile, melt butter in a medium-size saucepan. Add flour and cook 3 minutes. Add garlic and cook 4 minutes. Add milk, heavy cream, and chicken stock and bring to a simmer. Whisk in chives, tarragon, nutmeg, cayenne, and salt and pepper to taste. Simmer for 5 minutes.

Arrange salmon on a large platter and serve sauce separately.

DUCK GLAZED WITH
SHERRY, MUSTARD, AND BROWN SUGAR

4 SERVINGS
✧

2 quarts water
1 3-pound duck
1 quart grapefruit juice
2 cups sherry
2 large oranges, sliced crosswise
8 bay leaves
1 tablespoon whole cloves
1 tablespoon salt

GLAZE
1 cup Dijon mustard
1 pound dark brown sugar
½ cup sherry

In a large stockpot, bring 2 quarts of water to a boil. Plunge duck in for 10 minutes to render fat. In a large bowl, mix grapefruit juice, sherry, oranges, bay leaves, cloves, and salt. Take duck out of liquid; let cool, refrigerated, in grapefruit marinade, turning often, for 24 hours.

Place duck in large roasting pan with marinade. Bake in preheated 375-degree oven for 90 minutes, basting with marinade.

Meanwhile, mix glaze ingredients in a medium bowl. For the last 15 minutes of cooking time, brush duck with glaze, taking care so the glaze does not burn. Carve duck and arrange on serving platter.

PICKLED SHRIMP

10 SERVINGS

❧

2 cups sherry vinegar

1 cup water

1 tablespoon allspice berries

1 tablespoon fennel seed

1 tablespoon coriander seed

1 tablespoon mustard seed

1 tablespoon fresh ginger, minced

2½ pounds large shrimp, peeled and
* deveined*

1 large Vidalia onion, thinly sliced

2 lemons, thinly sliced

3 cloves garlic, peeled and roughly
* chopped*

6 bay leaves

1½ cups extra-virgin olive oil

1½ teaspoons salt

In a medium-size saucepan, combine vinegar, water, allspice, fennel, coriander, mustard seed, and ginger. Bring to a boil and simmer for 5 minutes. Add shrimp and stir. Turn off flame and let shrimp cool in pickling liquid. In a large crock, mix onion, lemon slices, garlic, bay leaves, olive oil, and salt. Add shrimp mixture and combine well. Chill uncovered for 30 minutes. Cover tightly and refrigerate for 1½ days (36 hours). Serve shrimp slightly chilled.

CHOCOLATE RASPBERRY BREAD PUDDING WITH LIGHT RUM SAUCE

8 SERVINGS

❧

3 cups buttermilk

3 cups heavy cream

2 cups sugar

4 large eggs

1 tablespoon cinnamon

1 large loaf bread or 1 dozen buttermilk biscuits

1 cup semisweet chocolate, roughly
chopped

2 pints fresh raspberries (some
reserved for garnish)

mint sprigs for garnish

LIGHT RUM SAUCE

1 pint heavy cream

1 cup sugar

1 tablespoon vanilla extract

4 large egg yolks

¼ cup rum

In a small bowl, whisk together buttermilk, heavy cream, sugar, eggs, and cinnamon.

Thinly layer a baking dish with slices of bread (or biscuits). Sprinkle chocolate on top of bread. Place a second layer of bread on top of chocolate. Layer raspberries on top of second layer of bread. Place a final layer of bread on top of raspberries. Pour milk mixture on top and let stand in refrigerator for 15 minutes, or until all liquid is absorbed.

Cover with foil and bake in water bath in preheated 325-degree oven for 25 to 30 minutes, or until bread pudding solidifies and begins to pull away from the sides of the baking dish.

SAUCE

In a small saucepan, whisk together cream, sugar, and vanilla. Bring to a simmer and add some of the hot mixture to the yolks off the heat, then put the warmed yolks into the saucepan with the rest of the hot mixture. Cook, stirring constantly, until mixture coats the back of a spoon. Remove from heat at once and allow to come to room temperature. When cooled, stir in rum and refrigerate.

To serve, cut pudding into eight pieces. Drizzle with rum sauce and garnish with fresh raspberries and mint sprigs.

INDEX

beef:
    roast loin of, 11
    salad, spicy, 241
    steak au poivre, 133
    stew, country, 219
"*Bella siccome un angelo*" (Donizetti), 173, 236
Berezin, Netty Bourgogne, 123–24, 125
Berwick, Donna, 276
Bildner, Mossa, 158, 159, 166–67, 172, 173,
    175, 176
Bill T. Jones/Arnie Zane Dance Company,
    234
Bisconti, Emma, 167–68, 176
biscuits, oversized (hoecakes), 24
biscuit toast, country ham and spinach paste
    with sliced pears and, 115
Black, Joel, 235
black beans, in spicy beef salad, 241
black currants, couscous with, 164
black-eyed peas:
    in field salad with endive and roasted pep-
        pers, 224
    in shrimp paste with hot pepper, 201
blacks:
    in France, 127
    in South, 74–75
Blackwell, Harolyn, 228
Bob, chicken, 148
Bohème, La (Puccini), 170
Bolton, Bill, 245–46, 265
Bonmartini, Contessa, 167, 168, 170
Bonmartini, Count Sebastiano, 169, 171
Boston lettuce, salad of marinated cucum-
    bers, avocados, and, 203
Bougie, *see* Leavy, Gregory "Bougie"
Bradley, Gwendolyn, 158, 159, 166, 172–73,
    175, 176, 209, 236, 265
brandy-lemon pineapple sauce, roast stuffed
    Cornish hens with, 220–21
Brasserie Flo, 125–26
bread:
    biscuit toast, country ham and spinach
        paste with sliced pears and, 115

cinnamon toast, 70
hoecakes, 24
pudding, chocolate raspberry, with light
    rum sauce, 280
pudding, dark, 204
sage cornbread, 105
sticky buns, 70–71
breakfast:
    buttermilk pancakes, 69
    catfish, onions, and scrambled eggs, 21
    cinnamon toast, 70
    fried rice cakes, 23
    hoecakes, 24
    hot and spicy sage sausage with redeye
        vinegar gravy, 22
    scrambled eggs with sweetbreads, 67
    sticky buns, 70–71
    sweet potato waffles, 68
Bridgewater, Dee Dee, 234
Brie, in cheese and strawberry platter with
    orange-chocolate dip, 120
brown onion gravy, caramelized, 13
brown sugar, duck glazed with sherry, mus-
    tard, and, 278
Bulgari, Gianni, 159
buns, sticky, 70–71
Burden, Wendy, 231, 232, 233–34, 235
Burden, William, 231
Burton, LeVar, 172–73
Burton, S.C., 16
Butlered Watermelon, 247
butter frosting:
    chocolate cake with toasted pecans and,
        205
    yellow cake with, 59
buttermilk pancakes, 69
Buzzy (Zipper's boss), 272

cabbage:
    salad with raspberry vinaigrette and rose-
        mary croutons, 119
    savoy, in spicy beef salad, 241
    slaw, cold, 32

potato(es):
  salad, 46
  seasoned rabbit with country ham and, 55
  sweet, *see* sweet potato
Poularde Landaise, La, 188
poultry:
  barbecued chicken, 239
  chicken and shrimp in Marsala sauce, 179
  chicken Bob, 148
  chicken in spiced tomato sauce, 180
  citrus chicken strips with puree of sweet
    potatoes and roasted garlic, 116
  crispy chicken livers with mustard dipping
    sauce, 255
  duck glazed with sherry, mustard, and
    brown sugar, 278
  roast stuffed Cornish hens with lemon-
    brandy pineapple sauce, 220–21
  roast turkey with sage sausage and veg-
    etable stuffing, 101
  Southern fried chicken, 12
Price, Leontyne, 171
Prima Donna (Callas), 262
Prima Donna (Price), 171
Puccini, Giacomo, 170
pudding:
  chocolate raspberry bread, with light rum
    sauce, 280
  dark bread, 204
puff pastry shells stuffed with sage sausage
  and Gorgonzola, 258
puppies:
  cheese corn, with fresh herbs, 117
  seafood, 240
puree of sweet potatoes and roasted garlic,
  citrus chicken strips with, 116

Quitman, Sylvain, 156

rabbit, with country ham and potatoes, seasoned, 55
race:
  in France, 127

opera and, 109, 235–36
  in Rome, 172
Radio City Music Hall, 227–28
Rashad, Phylicia, 251, 271
raspberry(ies):
  chocolate bread pudding with light rum
    sauce, 280
  vinaigrette, cabbage salad with rosemary
    croutons and, 119
red beans, in mixed bean succotash with
  fresh tomatoes and mozzarella, 182
Red Brigade, 143–44
redeye vinegar gravy, hot and spicy sage
  sausage with, 22
red peppercorns, for spicy lamb loaf with
  currants, 99–100
red peppers:
  chilled tomato soup with roasted corn
    and sweet, 183
  field salad with endive and roasted,
    224
  in grilled vegetable and rice salad, 242
  in Maryland crab cakes, 162
  in spaghetti alla carbonara, 181
  sweet, in spicy lamb loaf with currants,
    99–100
  in sweet and peppery corn cakes, 184
René, Madeline, 209, 211
Reola, Miss (Roosevelt's girlfriend), 79
Revival, 246
ribs, barbecued, 239
Ricci (opera coach), 159
rice:
  cakes, fried, 23
  Carolina, 32
  and grilled vegetable salad, 242
  salad, salmon and spinach, 221–22
  rigatoni, in seared tuna and pasta salad,
    104
Rigoletto (Donizetti), 192
Rimer, Sara, 262
Robeson, Paul, 236
Robison, Joshua, 192, 196, 197, 217

rolls, grilled swordfish, 149

Rome, 166–77, 231

   Jewish quarter of, 171

   race in, 172

Roots, 172

Rosco (restaurant worker), 62

rosemary croutons, cabbage salad with raspberry vinaigrette and, 119

Ross, David, 273

Ross, Diana, 127

Rowlands, Gena, 155

Rule, Janice, 154, 155

rum sauce, light, chocolate raspberry bread pudding with, 280

rutabagas, in lamb in Creole sauce, 134

sage cornbread, 105

sage sausage:

   puff pastry shells stuffed with Gorgonzola and, 258

   with redeye vinegar gravy, hot and spicy, 22

   spaghetti with cream sauce and homemade spicy, 151

   stuffed veal chops with cornbread and, 253

   and vegetable stuffing, roast turkey with, 101

salad:

   of baby lettuce, marinated cucumbers, and avocados, 203

   cabbage, with raspberry vinaigrette and rosemary croutons, 119

   cold cabbage slaw, 32

   field, with endive and roasted peppers, 224

   grilled vegetable and rice, 242

   pasta, seared tuna and, 104

   potato, 46

   salmon and spinach rice, 221–22

   spicy beef, 241

salad dressing, *see* dressing, salad

salmon:

   dill spread on sliced cucumbers, 259

   and spinach rice salad, 221–22

   stuffed with vegetables and herb white sauce, pan-roasted, 277–78

sauce:

   caramelized brown onion gravy, 13

   catfish tartar, with mint, 118

   cream, spaghetti with homemade spicy sage sausage and, 151

   herb white, pan-roasted salmon stuffed with vegetables and, 277–78

   honey mustard, 102

   lemon-brandy pineapple, roast stuffed Cornish hens with, 220–21

   light rum, chocolate raspberry bread pudding with, 280

   Marsala, chicken and shrimp in, 179

   mustard dipping, crispy chicken livers with, 255

   redeye vinegar gravy, hot and spicy sage sausage with, 22

   spiced tomato, chicken in, 180

sauce, Creole:

   pepper-based, onion, veal, and, 57

   petit venison meatballs with, 43–44

sausage, sage:

   puff pastry shells stuffed with Gorgonzola and, 258

   with redeye vinegar gravy, hot and spicy, 22

   spaghetti with cream sauce and homemade spicy, 151

   stuffed veal chops with cornbread and, 253

   and vegetable stuffing, roast turkey with, 101

savoy cabbage, in spicy beef salad, 241

Scotto, Renata, 232

scrambled eggs:

   catfish, onions, and, 21

   with sweetbreads, 67

sea bass wrapped in lettuce leaves, 199

seafood:

   chicken and shrimp in Marsala sauce, 179

   fried calamari, 147